MW01173273

THE CELL BLOCK PRESENTS...

THE MILLIONAIRE PRISONER

MIKE ENEMIGO & JOSHUA KRUGER

Published by: The Cell Block™

The Cell Block
P.O. Box 1025
Rancho Cordova, CA 95741

Website: thecellblock.net
Facebook/thecellblock.net
Instagram: @mikeenemigo
Corrlinks: info@thecellblock.net

Copyright © 2015, by Joshua Kruger

Cover Design: Mike Enemigo

Send comments, reviews, interview and business
inquiries to: info@thecellblock.net

All rights reserved. This book may not be reproduced in
whole or in part without written permission from the
publisher, except by a reviewer who may quote brief passages
in a review; nor may any part of this book be reproduced,
stored in retrieval system, or transmitted in any form or by any
means, electronic, mechanical, photocopying, recording, or
other, without written permission from the publisher.

CONTENTS

WARNING DISCLAIMER

This book is designed to provide helpful and informative material on prosperity, building a better life, and achieving your dreams. It contains the opinions and ideas of its author. It is sold with the understanding that the author and publisher are not engaged in rendering professional services in the book. If the reader requires personal assistance or advice, a competent professional should be consulted.

It is not the purpose of this book to reprint every tip, tactic, and/or strategy that is available to a prisoner for achieving prosperity, but instead to complement, amplify, and supplement other books. You are urged to read all the available information and material, including the books listed throughout this work, learn as much as you can, and then develop your own strategies and work your own plan.

Having true prosperity is not some pie-in-the-sky get-rich-quick scheme. Anyone who wishes to achieve success must decide to invest a lot of time and effort into it. The advice and strategies contained in this book may not be suitable for every situation. The purpose of this book is to educate and entertain. Every effort has been made to make this book as complete, up-to-date, and error free as possible. However, there will probably be errors, both typographical and in content. Because of this, it should be used as a guide, and not the be-all, end-all book on prosperity and success for prisoners.

The fact that a website, business, organization, and/or association is listed or referred to in this book as a citation and or a potential source of further information does not mean the author or publisher endorses the website, business, organization, and/or association, or what those entities may offer. It should also be noted that the Internet websites listed, and other entities referred to, may have, by the time you are reading this warning, changed, disappeared, closed and/or dissolved.

Some terms mentioned in this book are known to be or are suspected of being trademarks of different entities. Use of a term in this book should not be regarded as affecting the validity of any trademark or service mark.

The author and publisher specifically disclaim any responsibility for any liability, loss, or risk, personal or otherwise, which is incurred as a consequence, directly or indirectly, of the use and application of any of the contents of this book.

Invictus
by W.E. Henley

Out of the night that covers me,
Black as the pit from pole to pole,
I thank whatever gods there be
For my unconquerable soul.
In the fell clutch of circumstance
I have not winced or cried aloud;
Under the bludgeoning's of chance
My head is bloody but unbowed.
Beyond this vale of doubt and fear
Looms but the terror of the Shade
And, yet, the passing of the years
Finds, and shall find me, unafraid.
It matters not how straight the gate,
How charged with punishments the scroll
I am the master of my Fate,
I am the Captain of my Soul.

INTRODUCTION

Prison

Sadly, that one word defines my whole existence. It may define yours also? But now you don't have to allow it to continue to do so. There are over 2 million prisoners in the American prison system. The majority of them have dreams to make their mark on this world and get rich. But there are some reasons why most prisoners will never achieve anything significant in their lives.

Few have a legitimate plan or *objective* of where they want to go or be in life;

Few have thoroughly examined themselves to find their weaknesses and/or sticking points that hinder their quest for prosperity;

Few are willing to put forth the effort to find the answers to problems and/or acquire sufficient facts to enable them to complete their *objectives*;

Few have the *attitude* that even though they're in prison, they can still make things happen and achieve their dreams;

Few are willing to go against their prison peers and form the daily *habits* that will deliver success and prosperity.

Even though lots of prisoners will agree that the above reasons are the major stumbling blocks in their way, few will take the steps to overcome them and achieve their dreams. Fortunately, you are not one of them.

This book started with a vision. My vision is that prisoners can rise above the walls that confine us and overcome the chains that bind us. That you'll never make the same fatal mistakes that I've made, and never hear the judge say you'll never walk the street again. That you won't have to continue, year after year, to see your loved ones in a prison visiting room. That you'll run from the self-defeating behavior that caused your incarceration. That you'll grow from a convict into a success, and become a Millionaire Prisoner.

That is why I wrote this book. I care about you. You are my fellow prisoner. My situation is yours... your situation is mine. Unless we come together, learn together, and grow together; we'll stay together. We'll stay in prison, in poverty, in chains, and in an existence that is not our destiny. I don't want that and because you're reading this book shows that you don't want that either. We can begin to change our destiny right now. And we can do it the way psychologist William James said: "immediately and flamboyantly."

Some prisoners said the original edition of *The Millionaire Prisoner* was too long. Others thought the Introduction was too long. I can understand why they would say so. Because Mike Enemigo has the good habit of listening to his customers and friends, he told me to separate *TMP* into two books. Being the good author, I am, I listened to his publishing wisdom and you now have *The Millionaire Prisoner Part 1* in your hands.

What You'll Find in This Book

Unlike other books aimed at prisoners, this book contains practical tips and strategies that you can implement into your life *right now*! My aim was to write a book that you could come back to, time and time again, for inspiration, hope, and sound advice. Each chapter should give you something you can use daily to improve your life.

The Millionaire Prisoner Part 1 is divided into 13 chapters. Briefly, I'd like to tell you about each one.

In the chapter on *Attitude,* you'll learn the Millionaire Prisoner mindset; how to use the power of your subconscious mind to recreate yourself; and what words to use and not use in your speech so that you can form a success mindset.

But you can't have the right mindset unless you get over your past. That's why in the *Baggage* chapter you'll learn how to use the power of forgiveness; overcome the fear of failure; use your past as a lesson; how to clean out the clutter in your life, and make your past dance.

Since this is a book entitled *The Millionaire Prisoner*, I had to have a chapter on money. Therefore, Capital will teach you how to think like the rich; find lost money; prepare a financial mission statement; find your number; and give you the 6 money principles of a Millionaire Prisoner.

Of course, along your journey you will face obstacles. That's why I've included a chapter on *Determination.* In it you'll see that it's your time to shine and how you can easily overcome the hills and mountains in your life. Also, you'll learn the power of putting on blinders and 6 steps to developing an Iron Will.

In the *Education* chapter you'll learn the most basic way of educating yourself; the art of reading nonfiction; how to get FREE money for college; and the ways to turn your cell into a classroom or cell-office.

In the *Favor* chapter you'll learn what favor actually is; how to acquire it through mentorship; 3 steps to getting the most out of every mentor; and the true power of having and being a mentor.

But you cannot experience success by standing still, that's why in the *Growth* chapter you'll learn how to formulate a Millionaire Prisoner Growth Plan, be given a few examples of prison growth, and the way to becoming who you were meant to be.

Habit will teach you about your greatest helper, and the greatest enemy to your success; how to make the most of your time; the secret of Benjamin Franklin and how you can use it; and the easy way to get rid of bad habits.

You must be able to see over and around your prison and that's why you need the power of *Imagination.* In that chapter you'll find a way to capture ideas; a goldmine ready to be seized; how to solve problems; and the Art of Thinking Big and Visualization.

In the *Justice* chapter you'll learn the law of Consequences; the fallacies of illicit prosperity; why it's best to always be fair; and why you should never give up on your case.

In the *Knowledge* chapter you'll find the answer to how you can become more knowledgeable; the self-knowledge 101 test; what the most important selection of your life is; how to become an expert on any topic; and the definition of true power.

None of this will do you any good unless you can have fun along the way. That's why I've included a *Laughter* chapter. Inside it you'll find 5 easy steps to a happy life; the most famous leader in history and e used laughter; and the key to finding your final destination.

Lastly, you can't make money unless people know who you are and what you have to offer. In the *Marketing* chapter you'll learn the basics to effective promotion of yourself; your products, and your services. You'll also learn 12 different types of marketing; how to profit using a blog; and eight tips to building your brand.

Some of you may wonder why there are no numbered chapters in the traditional sense of most books. Instead, each chapter is a letter of the alphabet that makes up these ABCs. This idea came to me from the book, *Don Quixote,* by Miguel de Cervantes. In that book, the Don lists his "ABCs of Love." I liked that idea and decided to try "ABCs of Success and Prosperity." It worked out, and these ABCs form the foundation of the TMP books.

Each chapter has a word that defines what the chapter is about. For instance, *A = Attitude, B = Baggage, C = Capital*, and so on. These are the words that I came up with after careful study of numerous self-help and business books that I read during my research. The order of these ABCs is determined by the alphabet and not their order of importance. But I do believe that *Attitude* is the most important chapter of this book, because without the right attitude about life you'll never have true success or prosperity.

Throughout these ABCs you'll find numerous books mentioned or recommended. This is done to help you, should you like to continue your research. It's also done because I know that I'm not an expert on everything, and I didn't have the space available to elaborate further on each chapter. Plus, I would not be doing my job as a good information provider if I didn't give you additional resources where you can follow up. At the end of each chapter you'll also find a few "*Prosperity Keys*" that summarize the main points of that chapter's principle. They are provided as a quick reminder and reference too! You can use them for many years to come.

As you read through these ABCs you'll come across Millionaire Prisoner Case Studies. These are examples of people who have turned obstacles into opportunities. Men like Don King, Malcolm X, Chef Jeff, Omar Broadway, Nelson Mandela, Danny Trejo, Felix Dennis, Dan Manville, Bernard Hopkins, and Allen Iverson. All of these people are considered successful in what they did or do. But what makes them important for us is that all of them have been in prison. The secret to their success is contained throughout these ABCs. Our country has many famous prisoners and ex-prisoners. The ones that I've used in these ABCs are just a few of the many who have used their ABCs to accomplish great things in life. Use them as a guide and encouragement on your climb up the success ladder. Hopefully after reading about these prisoners you'll no longer use words like *can't, won't, never,* and *impossible* in your vocabulary.

Also, this book is quote heavy. The quotes show that these ideas and principles are timeless, and have already been accepted by the great people who have gone before us. If you would just highlight the quotes, study them, and put them to use in your life, you could be successful. Taken together, all the letters, words, quotes, case studies, ideas, and principles can give you a whole new life.

> *"The individual letters of the alphabet convey little or no meaning, but when they are combined into words, may express any thought one can conceive."*
> —*Napoleon Hill*

How To Get the Most Out of This Book

Read these ABCs carefully. Focus on the tips offered. They have the ability to change your life. Don't just read this book once and forget about it. Come back to it. It's a conversation between us -- two fellow prisoners. You want to become a Millionaire Prisoner and I'm here to help you on that journey. As you read this book, keep a pen or highlighter handy. You'll find a wealth of knowledge that you may want to underline or highlight for emphasis. It is my mission to bring to your cell quality how-to information that you can use in your life. But the only way this knowledge can become wisdom is if you implement it into your life. To help you do this, I came up with a simple formula for reading and studying how-to information that can help you master it. (For more about this, see the "Art of Reading Non-Fiction" in the *Education* chapter.) Here's how you should read this book so that you get the most from it:

1. Read through this book quickly to get the gist of the message, underlining or highlighting the things that really "grab" you. Only stop to look up words you don't know, or write them down to look up later. The first reading allows you to become familiar with the book.

2. As you read this book the second time, keep a notebook of ideas generated by the book that you can personally use. The objective is not to see how quickly you can get out of the book, but what you can get out of the book.

3. In your third reading, invest time and patience in gleaning additional ideas you may be missing in your second reading. Carefully examine each chapter. Go over what you have highlighted or underlined. Put anything you missed in your notebook.

4. The fourth reading will enable the book to become an integral part of you, enhancing your effectiveness. After this reading, you can place the book in your collection, and it will be a treasure trove, ready and willing to supply you with any knowledge you may need.

5. Find other prisoners who have read this book, or share it with them, and then discuss it together to see what you get out of it. You may gain additional insights from their ideas and thoughts you didn't see on your own.

Who I Am and My Role in Your Life

I am, by profession, a writer of "How-To" information. I am, by captivity, a prisoner in Illinois. Think of me as a messenger. I only hope to reveal to you what you already have inside of you, and the principles that you may utilize to achieve success and prosperity.

I have been in prison for more than half my life and know all about the struggles of a prisoner trying to make something of their life. I started my quest with nothing, just an idea and a dream. Along the way I've graduated from Crown Financial Ministries and experienced numerous successes. You'll read about some of these successes and some of my failures also. This book is just another step in a series of steps that lead to my ultimate goal of helping as many of my fellow prisoners as I can achieve their own success.

For the past ten years I have researched and analyzed successful and unsuccessful people. At first, I did this so that I could find the keys to building a better life, and to see what I was doing wrong. But then I realized that by helping my fellow prisoners out of their ruts, I could benefit all mankind and help myself at the same time. As Dr. Mike Murdock says, "Your mess becomes your message."

When I started my research, I began reading books. Lots, and lots of them. Some were great, and others were just saying what the classic self-help and business books had said before them. I'm not knocking their hustle, I just felt they weren't talking to me. They weren't talking to the prisoner. They weren't talking to the convict. They didn't speak our language. They didn't have this experience. I kept asking myself why I couldn't write the book that prisoners needed? So, I took the principles contained in the classics and addressed us prisoners and convicts. We needed a book that we could understand and relate to. One that was spoken in our language. I believe these ABCs do just that.

You may have heard of these ABCs before and be tempted to allow them to go in one ear and out the other. Don't! These ABCs, and the principles they contain, work. I know this to be true because I've put them to use over the last ten years. Using these ABCs, I was able to complete this book. I was able to repair a few broken relationships with family members. I was able to complete a lawsuit acting as my own attorney, even though the highest formal *education* I have is a GED obtained while in juvenile prison. I helped my mother start her own company and

I've sold ideas and received payments directly to my prison trust fund account. I've done all this from a maximum-security prison cell, with no access to a computer or the internet. You can do the same because you now hold in your hand the keys to your success.

Our journey is just beginning. The Buddhist prisoners say that a thousand-mile journey must start with a single footstep. Let's make sure that our first step is in the right direction. Ever mindful of the proverb: He teaches that which he needs to know most himself. I can honestly say that we are making this journey together.

Why you? Why me? Why start now? Because right now you have nothing to lose and everything to gain.

> *"Some men see things as they are, and say 'Why?' I dream of things that never were, and say, 'Why not?"*
> -George Bernard Shaw

Why not indeed?

This book can be your guide in the quest to free yourself from the bondage of prison and unleash your power. If that happens then I will consider it a success. You can start your journey by turning the page.

ATTITUDE

Your world is an outer manifestation of your inner thoughts and attitudes. As within, so without.
— *Greek philosopher Hermes*

It's fitting that this *principle* comes first in our ABCs. Without the right attitude in life you will not have success, let alone become a Millionaire Prisoner. Your attitude is the most important part of who you are in life and who you are trying to become. It includes your state of mind and how you think. It is your beliefs, thoughts, feelings, and judgments about people, objects and ideas. If you would just change your attitude you could change your circumstances. In this chapter, you'll learn how to acquire the Millionaire Prisoner Mindset and develop the right attitude for success.

<u>State of Being</u>

Right now your state of being is prison and some of you have negative attitudes about this. But you must alter the way you think about this captivity. It's a universal law that life will give you the product of your thoughts. All that you accomplish, or all that you fail to accomplish in life, is the direct result of your thoughts. Your state of mind either makes or breaks you because it controls your state of being. What you dwell on in your mind will deliver either prosperity or poverty because thought is the foundation of life. Millionaire Prisoners choose to dwell on thoughts of abundance and health instead of lack and sickness. What kinds of daily thoughts do you have? A simple shift from negative thought to positive thought can open your world to a new beginning.

The Major Barrier to Success

In conducting research for these ABCs I interviewed hundreds of prisoners and asked them what they wanted out of life. Most of them said two things:
1. They wanted to get out of prison and stay out;
2. They wanted to get rich.

The truth is, the majority of these prisoners will get out, but staying out is a different story. When I asked them how they planned on getting rich, they had no concrete idea or plan and were only hoping or wishing to get rich. But the revealing thing about these interviews was the overall negativity about their life and what they could accomplish *right now*. Most of these prisoners didn't understand that it is their own negative attitude keeping them from success and not anything else.

What were some of these negative attitudes that I found to hinder their progress? The most prevalent are those that fall into the category of passing blame. Thoughts like:
"It's the world's fault that I'm poor."
"It's the government's fault I'm in prison."
"It's my parents' fault because I grew up in the projects."
"I had to sell drugs to feed my children."
"I went to public schools."
These thoughts are negative because when you make them, you're passing blame to others for your own bad choices in life. In your mind you think someone else is at fault, but in

2

THE MILLIONAIRE PRISONER: PART 1

reality, it's your own attitude that caused the problem. Because you look elsewhere for the solution, you never stop to realize that the answer to your problems in life can be found in your daily thoughts.

I write from experience because I was a prisoner who passed blame to others. But my life began to change when I stopped looking outward to solve my problems and began to look inward for the answers. This ability, to look at the root of the problem instead of the fruit of the problem, has helped me immensely. In our case, the fruit of the problem is prison. But the root of the problem is the attitude that brought us to prison. Think about your life in this regard.

Another attitude that hinders us is the something-for-nothing fantasy. This mindset is widespread in prison and society. A lot of us thought we had the perfect get-rich-quick scheme. We thought we could beat the odds. That same scheme is why we're in prison. You must get rid of the something-for-nothing attitude because there is no such thing. The universe doesn't allow it. You get what you pay for.

What is "nothing" in the prison complex? Nothing is watching TV all day. Nothing is wishing for something to happen instead of *making* things happen. Nothing is going through the daily prison routine day after day, expecting a different result. A lot of prisoners I spoke to said they wished to get a piece of the "wealth" pie. Well a piece of the nothing pie is *nothing*! *You must do something*! Do the opposite of what every other prisoner is doing. Think different. Read different. Talk different. Act different. Be different. Don't be a prisoner clone, only to walk out of prison and return a short time later. People are recognized for their difference. Acting like, and doing what other prisoners do, will get you the same results that they got— *nothing*. You must eradicate the something-for-nothing attitude if you want to become a Millionaire Prisoner.

The Destructive Power of a Negative Attitude

To illustrate this power, allow me to share the story of J-Roc. Of course, J-Roc is not this prisoner's birth name, but an alias, a moniker. As you will see shortly, it was an alias that he created and became.

J-Roc grew up in a small Midwestern town and in school he was a straight A student. His father was away in the Army, so it was his mother and grandparents who raised him. As he got older, the town school district decided to close the neighborhood schools and bus kids to one major school. It was at this time that the alias J-Roc began to take form in his mind. Introduced to new people from the other side of the tracks, he began to run with the wrong crowd. He changed the music he listened to and began walking and talking different. He started getting into fights at school and eventually got expelled. Because his mother worked long hours to support the family, he would spend days with his grandfather. At this same time, psychologists diagnosed J-Roc with ADD and impulse control, and people started telling him he would never amount to anything in life. Then his grandfather died from cancer and he was left to roam the streets while his mother was at work. He started saying "screw the world, I'm a gangsta." He blamed his mother for them being poor. He blamed his grandfather for dying too soon. He blamed his father for not being around. Every thought that came out of his mouth was preceded by "If only." Every positive statement or thought was followed by a "but." He *believed* that he was destined to fail.

During this time period, J-Roc developed a fascination with prison life and culture. On his bedroom wall he placed a map of Illinois. On that map he put different colored push-pins. Green push-pins were placed next to the minimum-

4

security prisons. Yellow push-pins were placed next to the medium security prisons. Red push-pins were placed next to the maximum-security prisons. He would stare at that map before going to sleep every night and tell himself that he would visit those joints one day. J-Roc watched every prison movie or television show that he could. He even purchased a rap tape from the Lifers at Rahway State prison in New Jersey. He listened to that tape religiously. Because his daily thoughts were centered on prison, he received prison.

At the age of 13 he went to jail. At the age of 15, he went to juvenile prison where he spent the next two years. Four months after his release from juvie, he was back in jail, arrested for Armed Robbery, and because he was 17, he went to adult prison for three years. Six months after being released on parole, he was back in jail, this time charged with murder. Eventually sentenced to spend the rest of his life in prison, J-Roc had lived up to his thoughts and attitude.

I remember the first day I met J-Roc. He told me about his map of prisons on his bedroom wall and how he has visited all the red colored push-pinned maximum-security prisons. He told me about his lifer's rap tape and his buddies from the hood. He told me about his father not being around and his grandfather dying too soon. He told me all this and blamed his miserable existence on factors other than what he controlled. To say I was disgusted was an understatement. There I was, looking at J-Roc in the mirror, and he was telling me what I had become, but I didn't want to believe him. The decisions that I made as a child began a pervasive pattern of "prison" thought that created a detrimental impact in my future. This future I am now living out in a Natural Life sentence. I was dissatisfied with my circumstances, but because *I had the wrong attitude*, I failed. My attitude and thoughts were of prison, and prison is what I received. As we think, so we are.

<u>A New Beginning</u>

After this talk with J-Roc I began reading books to try and find the answers to how and why I became this other self—an alias. I came across thoughts from some of the greatest philosophers in history that said my mind needed work. I remember reading what Plato stated thousands of years ago: "The greatest mistake physicians make is that they attempt to cure the body without attempting to cure the mind. Yet the body and the mind are one and should not be treated separately."

Epictetus expressed the same thought: "The husband man deals with the land; physicians and trainers with the body; the wise man with his own mind."

It was evident that I had to find my own cure, and I couldn't neglect my own mind in finding this cure. I began reading any self-help book I could get my hands on. During this time of study, one name and one book kept coming up as a source. That name was Napoleon Hill and the book was *Think and Grow Rich*. It was only common sense that I needed to investigate who Napoleon Hill was and read *Think and Grow Rich*.

Born in 1883, in a one-room cabin in Virginia, Napoleon Hill was surrounded by poverty. Orphaned at the age of 12, he started writing for small town newspapers for pennies a line. At the age of 25, as a magazine reporter, his first assignment was to interview steel magnate Andrew Carnegie. During the interview he was given the chance to put together a *Law of Success* philosophy, which would consume the next twenty-five years of his life. But Hill's journey to success and prosperity was not an easy one. He lost jobs, several of his businesses went bankrupt, and he was unjustly accused of fraud, and *put in prison*. His personal life was rocky as well, having had several different wives and a son born without ears.

THE MILLIONAIRE PRISONER: PART 1

Think and Grow Rich was Hill's second book and he most likely is the inventor of motivational writing. *Think and Grow Rich* became the number one motivational bestseller of all time, selling over 15 million copies and counting. Hill lent his name to several magazines, seven books, a foundation, and a movie. He died in 1970 a rich man. Not only did Hill *think and grow rich*, but he achieved true prosperity against almost impossible odds. His words have been very influential in the writing of these ABCs. It was during my reading of *Think and Grow Rich* that I had an epiphany. Hill showed me why I came to prison and it was at that moment that everything in my life made sense.

> *"A positive mental attitude is the starting point of all riches, whether they be riches of a material nature or intangible riches."*
>
> —*Napoleon Hill*

The Power of the Subconscious Mind

Most of us understand that our mind controls what we say and do in life. We also understand that there are positive thoughts and negative thoughts. What Hill's book introduced me to, was the fact that there are "vibrations" that our mind releases and picks up on as well. Let's call these vibrations "radio stations." There are negative radio stations (vibrations) and there are positive radio stations (vibrations). Negative vibrations are attracted by the mind that is *tuned* into negativity. My own life is evidence of this fact. My mind was keyed up for prison, and the prison radio station is what I attracted. Be mindful of what vibrations you give off and those vibrations that people give off around you. For more about the energy you give off, read *Frequency: The Power of Personal Vibration* by Penney Peirce.

Now, your subconscious mind doesn't know the difference between a negative thought and a positive thought. It will only dwell on what thoughts you submit to it, or those radio stations that it receives. Just as you cannot listen to two radio stations at the same time, a negative thought and a positive thought *cannot* occupy the mind at the same time. If, while you're sleeping your subconscious mind is dwelling on the negative thoughts and vibrations that you've submitted to it throughout the day; how do you expect to create anything positive in your future? If you want to become a Millionaire Prisoner you must learn to control the thoughts, vibrations, and attitudes that reach your subconscious mind.

How do you begin to control this? Especially after so many years of negativity? The simple way is to reprogram your mind, or to tune into a different radio station. You can do this in several easy steps. First, be aware of the words you speak, and the words you listen to. We all know prisoners who complain about everything and anybody. If the food is bad, they complain. If they raised the price of an item on the commissary, they complain. If the mail is late, they complain. If they see another prisoner get a blessing, they complain about their lack of opportunities. Is it any wonder that these prisoners are broken and have the fewest friends? They're a product of their own thoughts. You can't achieve success with a bad attitude. Don't be like these prisoners. Don't complain and criticize. Most important, don't allow these prisoners to bring you down. Keep your mind tuned into the positive radio stations of the Universe.

Second, be aware of your intake. What you bring inside of you is what will go out of you. It determines what you produce. Think of J-Roc. His intake was crime and prison and he produced a natural life prison sentence. To change your intake, you must read positive books. Watch positive and educational television. Associate with positive people. In essence, you must do the opposite of what you've been doing up to this point in your life. A successful prisoner will do what an unsuccessful prisoner won't do.

Prison is not a positive place. You can gain some positive lessons from prison if you're looking for them. But overall, this environment is filled with negativity. It's one of hatred, contempt, and hardship. Prison destroys families and friendships. It kills hopes, dreams and ideas. You don't have to be in prison to be seduced by prison. Just look at J-Roc.

Throughout these ABCs you'll be given tips and tactics on how to change your life. Put them into practice. You don't have to do them all at once, just work on a few at a time until they become *habit*. But a positive attitude is the most important trait you can acquire.

"Mental attitude plays a far more important role in a person's success or failure than mental capacity."
—*Charles Kemmons Wilson*

That's why attitude comes first. It's the foundation for all of these ABCs. If your foundation is built on negative thinking you can expect negative results. But build your foundation on the positive and you can expect positive results. What kind of results do you want? Because you're reading this book you evidently want positive results. You can have them by getting the right attitude. For a thorough examination on the subconscious, read *The Power of Your Subconscious Mind, Revised* by Joseph Murphy.

Verbal sWord Power

The Oxford English dictionary now has over a million words. But studies have shown that most people only use a few thousand words in their vocabulary. The Bible has 7,200 different words; and Shakespeare used over 24,000 words in his works. Malcolm X said that the only reason why we use curse words is because we don't know the right word to use. Words have power, and I would like to share with you an example of verbal sWord power.

In an interview with Anderson Cooper on *60 Minutes*, Eminem said that he read the dictionary because he wanted all the words to be at his disposal. He also keeps stacks of notes and ideas in boxes that he calls "stacking ammo." Eminem's *zeal* for rhyming is so powerful that he thinks about it every day, all day. As I watched the interview it became apparent and enlightening that he was using these ABCs. The revelation was that *to become master of your craft*, no matter what it is, *you have to lose yourself in it.* It's a 24-hour process. But if you're doing something you love to do it won't be work, but play. And finally, that words have power.

But why are words so important? Because they have the ability to influence your feelings and beliefs about things and others. Using the right word can be the difference between taking action or sitting on your hands. For instance, if I tell myself, "Josh, you suck at writing," then I probably will not *feel* like writing that day. But if I tell myself, "Josh, you're a great writer," then I'll want to continue my craft. Be careful in your choice of words, especially when it comes to what you say about yourself. You don't have to be a word dink and use big words. No, it's much more important to use positive words instead of negative words. Also stay away from absolutes like: *Can't, won't, never, impossible, every* and *all.*

Here is a list of the words that you may hear prisoners say, or you may have used them to describe feelings that you have. Get rid of these words, take them out of your vocabulary.

afraid	hurt	overwhelmed
depressed	hate	sad
disappointed	insecure	scared
disgusted	irritated	sick
dread	jealous	stressed
		stupid

One of the above words is sick. I don't know what being sick is like. I haven't been really sick in a long time. The word is not in my vocabulary. Since I never speak or think about sickness, I don't get sick. Some of you may believe that I don't get sick because I have a good immune system, but I believe that my choice of wordplay influences my immune system. Many other experts believe the same thing as well. So what words should you use?

Here is a list of words that Millionaire Prisoners use:

attractive	brilliant	gifted
energized	extraordinary	invincible
unstoppable	fantastic	empowered
enthusiastic	phenomenal	loved
perfect	confident	awesome
incredible	smart	Blessed

These are just a few. Reread the above list and pay attention to how these words make you feel. Fill in the following sentence with any word from above: I AM _____. Say it over and over. Believe it. Practice using positive words. Cut out words that speak of or mean negative things like lack, poverty, sickness and pain. As you do this, you'll become more energized about yourself and your life. You can transform your life by changing the words you speak.

"The pen is mightier than the sword only if the brain behind it knows how to wield the word."

—*Tony Buzan*

If you would like more on the power behind the words you speak, check out the following books: *What You Say Is What You Get* by Don Gossett and *The Tongue: A Creative Force* by Charles Capps.

Recreating Yourself

It's well known that you begin to believe what you repeat to yourself. Whether you tell yourself something that's false, or something that's true, is irrelevant. My own life is illustrative. When I began telling myself that I was J-Roc, a gangsta and convict, I was only a kid. But because I kept telling myself this, and then acted on it, I became J-Roc the gangsta and convict. The Universe gave me what I asked for.

The process of constantly telling yourself something over and over is called "self-suggestion." When you use self-suggestion, your subconscious mind picks up the words, thoughts, or images that you suggest to it and then will automatically suggest them to your conscious mind. This process is called "autosuggestion." Napoleon Hill's *Think and Grow Rich* has a whole chapter on autosuggestion. Another book, *Money, and The Law of Attraction* by Esther and Jerry Hicks, calls this process "telling yourself the story of your life." No matter what you call it, you can use this process to either change your life, or continue to stay in prison. That's a mental prison just as much as the physical one you now find yourself in. The thoughts that reach your subconscious mind that are given into action are the ones that attract your harvest in life.

I understand that it's common for most of us to be skeptical about anything new. Especially ideas we read or hear for the first time. Knowing this, allow me to remind you of my experience with J-Roc. Using self-suggestion and autosuggestion, I delivered myself to prison. It did not matter that my *knowledge* at the time didn't allow me to understand the process. The principle was utilized by my subconscious mind to attract the desires of my heart and the desires of my thoughts. Unfortunately for me and my family, those desires were of prison.

Also remember that the subconscious mind doesn't care if the thoughts are negative or positive. It only dwells on the thoughts or vibrations it receives. The great thing is that we have the ability to control the thoughts and vibrations that reach our subconscious mind by using self-suggestion. If you can do this with faith and belief in the words that you speak, your subconscious will take those thoughts and words, and auto-suggest them back to you while you're asleep. This is the basic philosophy behind a lot of prosperity books, like *The Secret*. It's the law of attraction in a nutshell: *what you constantly think about, you attract into your life.* Before we get into the steps of using self-suggestion, here is an important fact to remember about the subconscious mind. Seventy-five percent of all your mental activities are performed by your subconscious mind. Think about this when considering the fact that your subconscious mind will work with either negative or positive thought.

> *"Your subconscious mind knew more from the time you were a baby than is in all the books in all the colleges and libraries of the world."*
>
> —*Robert Collier*

Your first step in using self-suggestion is to write out the new story of your life that you want to live. Make it explicit. For an example I've included the one that I use. Yours doesn't have to be as long as mine, but you may borrow any or all of it in your new story. Here it is:

I do not wish for prosperity, but *desire* it. I do not wish for success, but *demand* it. I might not know all the answers, or recognize all the opportunities that are available, but my path will show itself. I realize that the thoughts of my mind will eventually become my reality. I also recognize that I have the right to choose my own thoughts. Therefore, I will concentrate my mind on who I want to become. I will become a great man of wisdom and understanding. Fair dealing, *justice*, and *quality* will be the calling cards of my everyday actions with others. I am choosing for myself thoughts of health, happiness, prosperity, and love. Fear, hate, sickness, and poverty have no place in my thinking. My old bad habits will give way to new, great habits. I will form daily habits that will encourage the development of my positive emotions into some form of useful action. In my habits I will find my success.

I know that I have the ability to achieve my objectives in life. I know that I need sound plans and ideas for the attainment of my objectives. Therefore, I will build definite plans to achieve my goals. I am bigger than this stupid prison cell because my dreams and imagination have no boundaries. I will develop my imagination by calling upon it daily for help in the formation of my plans. Where other prisoners tear down, I will build. I demand continuous action towards reaching my objectives, and promise myself to take such action.

I will take care to submit to my subconscious mind a clear and definite picture of my objective in life, and my plans and steps to achieve this objective. I shall keep this objective before my subconscious mind by repeating it day and night. Any thoughts, ideas, or plans that will not aid me in accomplishing my major objective in life are unimportant. Only those facts that pertain to my major objective in life are important. Once I build a plan I will begin to implement it right away. I will use whatever tools are available to me until better tools are provided or found. Through action I can take a substantial step towards becoming a Millionaire Prisoner.

As a prisoner, my greatest asset is time. While others must worry about daily tasks such as food, shelter, and medical care, I do not. These things are provided to me. Therefore, it's not my mission to spend my time in prison unwisely. Every hour will be a productive one. While others are asleep, I will produce. Every adversity produces a benefit. Every obstacle produces an opportunity. Failure is only failure if I quit. If knocked down, I will get back up. I will not try, but *do*. I am a winner, not a whiner. Mediocrity is not my mission in life. This prison is a stepping-stone. I will turn these bars into stars. My time in prison will be spent preparing myself. I will do the tasks that other prisoners only talk about. I will not end the day on a temporary defeat, but a success. I will not fall asleep angry, disturbed, or confused. I will not take no for an answer. I will market my ideas, products, and services so that I may hear as many "yesses" as possible. I will not look back, but to my future. I will live in the present and not allow my past to be a prison. I will not trust my memory to remember all that I need. Instead, I will write down every thought or idea in my idea folder. This will allow me to use my memory for the most important recollections needed.

Lastly, I will choose my associates well. Only those with positive thoughts will be allowed into my life. Those with negative, ill dispositions will be shunned. I will seek out positive mentors that I can learn from. In this I can stand on the shoulders of giants, thereby leapfrogging others on my way to the top. Fortune favors the prepared and the bold. I am both. My desire and my obsession are prosperity. I have faith and believe in these words. My legacy on this earth will be great. No longer am I a convict. I've become the CEO of my destiny. I am a Millionaire Prisoner, and from this moment on, I am the captain of my ship, and I'm sailing to the stars.

These are the words that I use. I understand that it's long, but I was a mess mentally when I decided to change. I needed a lot of work and a lot of self-suggestion. Change these words if you want, use what you want, but write yourself a new story for your life.

Have you ever wanted to be the star actor or actress in a movie? Well, you already are, except the movie is your life. You are the screenwriter, actor, producer, and director all rolled into one. All you have to do is write out your script and *become* the role that you want to play. *Act out* the life you want.

After you have your words written down, follow the steps below to make sure this principle becomes *habit*:

1. Find a spot where it's quiet and you will not be disturbed. Alone in your cell works best.

2. Read the words you wrote down out loud to yourself.

3. As you do this, try and visualize yourself already in possession of the character traits or state of being you want to acquire. Imagine yourself as a Millionaire Prisoner.

4. Repeat this program every night and every morning until you can see it happening in your life. (I still do it because prison is so negative, and I don't want to slip back into an old frame of mind.)

5. Place a written copy of your words where you can see them every day. Read them anytime you feel yourself slipping into an old mindset.

This process works. I learned it from Napoleon Hill, and it can work for you in anything you want to accomplish in life. You *can* recreate yourself. Your life doesn't have to run on the tracks that others have laid out for you, but the ones that you want to run on. By utilizing the process of self-suggestion described above, you can take a substantial step to becoming a Millionaire Prisoner.

Write out the story you want to live no matter what it is. Because no matter what anyone else had told you, you can live the life you want. As you tell yourself this new story your subconscious mind will deliver to you the keys to achieving your dreams. As you get these ideas from your subconscious, act on them. Act out your script in life.

"By changing the inner attitude of our mind, we can change the outer aspect of our lives."
—Dr. Mike Murdock

Right now, your circumstances are prison, parole, probation, and more prison. It's a never-ending cycle. Your attitude has been one of acceptance. You've been accepting that prison is where you belong. But you don't belong in prison, any more than the tiger belongs in a zoo. The difference between you and the tiger is that you have the power to change your thoughts and free yourself. The tiger can't. He is truly a victim held captive by his keepers and dependent on their mercy.

So why continue to accept prison as the place where you belong? Why not in the corporate boardroom? Why not in the classroom of a major university? Why not on the floor of the New York Stock Exchange? You could plug yourself into any scenario and it would fit your talents and abilities. You only have to *believe*. Right now, your field of vision is being limited by your experience, instead of being led by your *imagination*. First your attitude must change, then everything else will begin to change.

A Proper Outlook and Perspective

Your outlook is a part of your attitude as well. Outlook is how you see the world. Let me share with you a story I once read about outlook.

Two prisoners were sitting at the window staring out into the night. One said, "Look at all that mud on the ground out there. How are we going to play softball tomorrow at yard time?" The other one said, "Yeah, but look at all the stars shining in the sky!"

What do you see when you look outside at night? Are you looking down? Or are you looking up? Do you see mud? Or are you too busy paying attention to the stars? You must turn your bars into stars!

Your attitude also determines your perspective. Perspective is what you see in the world. A Buddhist prisoner once told me a fable about some blind men that expressed the ability to see. These blind men were asked to describe the part of an object they were touching with their hands. The first man stated that he put his arms around what seemed like the trunk of a tree, but it was softer. The second man said that he ran his hand down a rounded, smooth, and very hard object that came to a point at the end. Another man described a long hose-like object, and the last man said that his outstretched arms could not enclose the soft coarse object he was touching. The truth was that they were all touching the same object just different parts, but when taken together made up an elephant.

You must not become blind to the other parts. A proper outlook and perspective take in other points of view. This will allow you to see the big picture. You will see the whole elephant. That is a healthy and successful mind at work. Remember, preconceived notions and bias are a mental prison.

Before I get to the final part of this chapter, I would like to offer you a couple more tips on how you can change your state of being.

The Power to Change

Imagine the type of change you could bring forth if you only focused your mind. Behold the prison you find yourself in. See the bricks in the walls that make up your cell. See the barbed-wire fences and guard towers that loom outside your window. All this came about because someone utilized the power of thought. They had thoughts to hold people captive. But this same power is available to everyone, including you. Take hold of it, become its master, and achieve your destiny. Have thoughts of freedom.

Here's a simple method for developing your power and assisting you on your journey.

Keep a folder or composition notebook with your accomplishments in it.

• Anytime someone gives you a compliment or acknowledgment on paper, put it in your folder or notebook.

• Keep any certificates you obtain, any letters of recognition, and any acceptances or sales receipts of your work.

• Reread through all these past successes when needed. Doing this allows you to keep a positive attitude about your life.

My first success in writing was getting one of my poems published. I entered a poetry contest where the winners would be included in the anthology, *Cellblock Poetry*, by Shot Caller Press. My poem, "*Isolation*," did not win, but was selected to be included in the book as a poem of "honorable mention." The letter from the publisher acknowledging my poem for inclusion in the anthology is still in my success folder. If I ever feel like giving up, I get out my success folder and read all of my past successes. You can do the same. It's a simple tactic, but it works.

Just remember, you are valuable, worthy, and capable of becoming a Millionaire Prisoner.

Music Can Change Your Life

I've already expressed the power of self-suggestion and autosuggestion, but the music that you listen to can severely affect your mental state. When you listen to music as religiously as prisoners do, that power multiplies. I learned this with my experience with J-Roc. It was only later when I began studying Attention Deficit Disorder did I realize how much music played a part in my life and how I could use it to be more productive. Not only does it act as an uplifting source, but it acts as a barrier to all the prison noise.

So what should you listen to? Stephen King listens to hard rock while writing his horror novels. I like listening to songs that uplift and motivate me. Songs like *Hall of Fame* by The Script; *Lose Yourself* by Eminem; and *I Just Want to be Successful* by Drake, all move me. Find out the songs that motivate you. Use them to get energized and tune out the daily prison white noise. With a lot of prisons now allowing prisoners MP3 players, you can put together a nice playlist of music that moves you. Do so!

Shortly after I began putting the final touches on this book, Galina Mindlin, Don DuRousseau, and Joseph Cardillo published their book, *Your Playlist Can Change Your Life*. They go more in-depth into how music can help you than I could here. Check it out if you're still not convinced about the power of music.

No More Excuses

Hopefully by now you are beginning to believe that you can change your life. Maybe you've gained a couple of tips or insights on how to develop a positive attitude? Some of you may still feel that you have legitimate excuses that hold you back from success. Let's review some of the most common excuses that I heard in my research and some people who overcame these so-called excuses.

Excuse #1: The fact that you are or were a drug addict?

In 1999, Josh Hamilton was selected with the number one overall pick in the major league baseball draft by the Tampa Bay Rays. He was called the best prospect ever by some scouts. Then he became addicted to drugs, got kicked out of baseball, and went to rehab. He didn't make any excuses and he didn't give up. He got his life together. Now he's a star outfielder with the Los Angeles Angels, and a past MVP award winner. Hamilton overcame, and his positive attitude allowed him to rebound in a big way.

Excuse #2: The fact that you grew up in the projects?

So did Farrah Gray. He grew up in a notorious housing project on the South Side of Chicago. What has he done? Gray started his own business at the age of 9, selling painted rocks. He moved on to another business and at the age of 14, had sales of $1.5 million. He is also the author of two books, *The Truth Shall Make You Rich* and *Reallionaire.* He didn't allow the projects to stop him because his attitude allowed him to achieve prosperity.

Excuse #3: The fact that you got all the bad breaks in life?

Alan Simpson had trouble with the law when he was a youngster. But if you were to type his name into a search engine you would see that he's a United States' Senator from Wyoming. Another example that people can, and do, change. You can be one of those people with the right attitude.

Excuse #4: The fact that you're too old?

In 1982, Bernard Hopkins entered Graterford State Penitentiary for armed robbery. He spent five years inside where he found the prison boxing ring. After his release, he became a world champion and defended his title—a record 20 times. In 2011, at the age of 46, he became the oldest man to win a championship.

Dewey Bozella served 26 years in prison for a crime he didn't commit. At the age of 52, he became the only person to get approved by the California Athletic Commission to box professionally who had reached the age of 50. He won his fight. Understand, age is just a number for those who choose to put limits on life.

Excuse #5: The fact that you are or have been in a gang?

Maybe you've heard of Bill Bartmann? Or seen his ads for his bestselling books: *Billionaire: Secret To Success* & *Bailout Riches!* Bartmann left home at 14 and lived on the street. Just like so many of us, he panhandled and joined a street gang. Eventually he completed his *education* by getting his GED and law degree. He made his first billion buying debt and collecting on that debt. His company collapsed in scandal, he went bankrupt and was indicted for fraud and money laundering. The jury acquitted him of all charges, and Bartmann recreated himself as a motivational speaker. He's back at it again, this time with a credit card collection agency. Take a cue from him, rebrand yourself, and become a Millionaire Prisoner. Who knows, you could become a Billionaire Prisoner?

Remember, you're reading this book and it was written by an ex-gang member who decided to do something positive.

Another former gang member is Ryan Blair. He grew up with an abusive father, had to sleep in a lice-infested shack, and was put on medication for ADD and depression. He wound up in juvenile prison but that didn't stop him. He reprogrammed his mind and has become a multimillionaire CEO. His book: *Nothing to Lose, Everything to Gain: How I Went From Gang Member to Multimillionaire Entrepreneur (www.nothingtolose.com)* should be on every prisoner's must read list.

Excuse #6: The fact that you're in prison?

Robert Beck, using the pen name, Iceberg Slim, wrote his first book, *Pimp: The Story of My Life*, while in jail.

Sir Walter Raleigh wrote *The History of the World* while in prison.

Casanova was arrested and imprisoned for being a spy. It was in prison where he wrote his memoirs.

Vickie Stringer wrote *Let That Be The Reason* while serving a seven-year stretch in federal prison for drug trafficking. Inside, she read every book in her prison's library. Upon her release, she self-published her book and it sold over 1,000 copies in one week. She is founder and CEO of Triple Crown Publications, which has published over 50 urban novels since 2002.

Charles "Roc" Dutton is also a former prisoner. While he was inside, Roc started a prison drama club and got his GED. Upon leaving prison he went to college. He's now an actor, whose credits include the Fox TV series *Roc*, and movies such as *A Time To Kill* and *Legion*. He's more evidence that prison doesn't have to be the end of your dreams.

Mike Delucia went to prison for a racketeering conviction. But you probably know him from his television show *Car Fellas*, on the Discovery channel. On the show, Mike and his two friends, Mario and Tommy, run the car lot, Broadway Motors. He changed his attitude and changed his circumstances.

Duane "Dog" Chapman joined the Devil's Disciples motorcycle gang. After a drug deal went band and another member of the gang killed a man, Dog went down for accessory to murder. He spent time on a chain gang in Texas. Now he has his own TV show, *Dog The Bounty Hunter*, which is watched by millions of people across the world. He changed his attitude and changed his life.

Another bad boy turned actor is Mark Wahlberg. He spent 45 days in jail and realized that he had to do something else with his life. So, he followed his brother into music and became "Marky Mark" the rapper. Eventually Wahlberg graduated to movies and became a star actor in movies like *Shooter* and *The Departed*, where he was nominated for an Oscar. Now he is executive producer of hit television shows like *Entourage* and *Boardwalk Empire*. He made it and you can too!

Millionaire Prisoner Case Studies

In 1967, a man was sentenced to life in prison. That sentence was later changed on appeal to a shorter term for manslaughter. In 1971, at the age of 39, he was released from prison. Thirty-five years later in 2006, *Forbes* estimated the net worth of this ex-con to be at least $350 million. We've all seen him promoting major boxing fights all over the world. Don King didn't serve time, but made time serve him. While locked up, King educated himself by reading history books and classics by Homer and Shakespeare. No excuses from him, he made things happen and achieved prosperity.

Danny Trejo started using drugs at the age of 8 when his uncle turned him onto marijuana. To support his habit, he started doing armed robberies to get drugs. He wound up in prison and spent his time in Cali prisons like San Quentin, Soledad, and Folsom. He got his high school diploma in the joint and became the welterweight boxing champion of San Quentin.

Released in 1969, he started working in a junkyard. Then he and a friend started a landscaping business doing yard work using the homeowner's tools and mowers. He also went to work with the Narcotic Prevention Project and began speaking at schools to help kids stay away from drugs. He got his start in movies when a director needed a tough looking guy as an extra. Sober 42 years and counting, you have seen Trejo in movies like *Blood In, Blood Out*; *Spy Kids*; and *Machete*. From now on every time you see him on the big screen you can think that he was once where you're at. Get your attitude right, and you could be where he's at.

> *"The greatest discovery of my generation is that a human being can alter his life by altering his attitude."*
> — *William James*

Throughout these ABCs you'll find many more examples of Millionaire Prisoners who changed their attitude and changed their life. These people come from the same backgrounds as you. But they decided to use their mind as a weapon and became successes at the game of life. These are the winners that you need to emulate. It's time for you to become who you were destined to be. No more excuses!

> *"When you get your attitude right, you can handle anything the world throws at you. Even life in prison."*
> — *Bill Dallas*

Anything Is Possible

In 1920, convict #9653, Eugene Debs ran for president of the United States while incarcerated in the U.S, Penitentiary at Atlanta. It was the first time that a federal prisoner had ran for the presidency. In the midst of doing a 10-year bid for opposing

World War I, he ran under the Socialist Party banner and received 919,000 votes on his behalf. Almost one million people voted for him, and *he was in prison*. Before Debs went to prison he gave these encouraging words in a speech:

America is preeminently the land of great possibilities, of great opportunities, and of no less great probabilities. Look around us, no matter what our position may be, we all stand on the great field of renown, with a free and equal chance to go to the supreme height of all that can be desired of earthly grandeur. We all have a fair chance and an open field. Long may it so remain. The time, the occasion is auspicious. Nothing like it was ever known before.

How true these words are, even today. Nothing is impossible. Nothing is improbable. Your attitude will determine what happens to you. Take the above words and make them your own. Positive thoughts and ideas are the keys to opening doors you never thought could be unlocked from inside these walls. If you can learn to open doors from inside prison, imagine what you can accomplish once you're released?

Your attitude determines your altitude. With a positive one, the sky is the limit. It's time for you to soar like the eagle that you are. Do not settle for something that's not your destiny. Believe in yourself and your dreams. Believe that your entitled to a better life. It all starts with your attitude. This attitude determines whether your prison is a tombstone or a stepping stone. Either a barrier or a bridge. It's your choice. Which one is it going to be?

Resources

For more help getting your attitude in order, check out the following books:

Changing Your Game Plan by Randy Kearse

Success Through a Positive Mental Attitude by Napoleon Hill and W. Clement Stone

Attitude Is Everything: 10 Life-Changing Steps to Turning Attitude Into Action by Keith Harrell

As you think, so you are.

Millionaire Prisoner Prosperity Keys

- A negative attitude will never allow you to achieve success.
- By using the power of the subconscious mind you can recreate yourself.
- Write out the story you want to live, and then make it come true by using self-suggestion and autosuggestion.
- Develop a healthy outlook and a proper perspective.
- Keep your past successes handy in case you need a mental boost.
- Do not make excuses for yourself, make things happen!
- Always remember that nothing is impossible; you can achieve anything that you desire.

BAGGAGE

We ought not to look back, unless it is to derive useful lessons from past errors and for the purpose of profiting by dear bought experience.

—George Washington

Now that you know how to begin acquiring the right *attitude* you must clear one more mental hurdle stopping you from success. This mental hurdle is your past.

Are you allowing your past to hold your future hostage? Does your past control you? Is your past a crutch? You must live in the present and look forward to the future if you want to become a Millionaire Prisoner.

The Past is a Ball and Chain

While researching these ABCs, I read about how elephants were once captured and treated by circus trainers. When the wild elephants were first captured, their handler's would attach an iron ball and chain to the elephant's hind legs. If the elephant tried to run away, it found it impossible because of the huge iron ball and chain. Slowly, the elephant would become docile and stop trying to run away. Their handler's would then lower the weight of the ball and chain. If the elephant tried to run, he still felt the weight of the ball and chain tugging at its hind leg. The ball and chain would get smaller and smaller as the elephant got tamer and tamer. Eventually, there wouldn't be any ball and chain on the elephant. Would the elephant try and run away? No. Why not? Because it was allowing the past ball and chain experience to control the present. The elephant had been trained to believe it was still attached to a heavy burden—the iron ball and chain.

Are you allowing prison to be your ball and chain? Are you allowing childhood experiences to be your ball and chain? Are you allowing your past to limit your future? You'll never soar to the heavens like the eagle that you are if you allow past to hold you down. The difference between you and the elephant is that you have the ability to choose your thoughts and *attitude*, thereby changing your future. If you continue to say you "won't" or "can't" because of the X on your back, you never will. Do not allow the past to hold you in second place. Become a first-place person and prosperity will find you.

> *"Once you settle for second, that's what happens to you*
> *in life."*
> —John F. Kennedy

One question that prisoners like to ask is: "If you could go back in time and change one thing or do something different, what would it be?" Many of us have thousands of things we would change or do differently if we had the chance. But we don't get a do-over. The only thing that matters is the here and now. How you deal with today determines what you'll be tomorrow. Don't worry about the past.

Some of you had drug addictions before you came to prison. Some of you had strained relationships before you came to prison. Some of you experienced poverty. Some of you were orphaned at a young age. Others were abused by parents and family members. Guess what all this means? Nothing! It means nothing because it's in the past. Don't let it define you. Don't let it control you. It can't hurt you against your *will*. It can only hurt you if you allow it to. You must sever the ties to the past pain if you want success in your future.

The Power of Forgiveness

Your inner game is more important than anything in the outer world. One of the best ways to tighten up your inner game is to use the power of forgiveness. There are people in your life who've hurt you in the past. Because of this hurt you may put up a wall to keep people out. You do this so you won't be hurt again. But pain and bitterness can be harmful to your future. Let me give you an example.

My father left when I was 2 years old. I never had a dad growing up and was raised by a single mother. As a kid I hated seeing other kids with their dads. It was painful and I began to resent my father. I became angry and bitter. As I got older, I started to blame him for everything that went wrong in my life. People around me saw my anger and began to stay away from me. I eventually realized that I was a grown-up and I was not going to allow my past to rob me of my future. So, I made a decision that I had to forgive my father. I wrote him a letter telling him how I really felt. Then I told him that I forgave him. That's when I began to experience peace in my life. I felt a weight lift off my shoulders. From that point on I began to see improvements in my life. The decision to forgive my father was one of the most powerful lessons I've learned.

Now I'm not trying to say that I know what it's like to be sexually assaulted by a family member or some other heinous act. I did experience mental and physical abuse as a kid, but I know there are a lot of you who have experienced much more pain than I have. I wish I could take the pain away from you, but

I can't. What I am saying is that if you want to become a Millionaire Prisoner you have to forgive those who hurt you and let go of the past. Until you can do that, you may never know your full potential. As long as you hold grudges and are angry at someone, they have power over you. When you forgive them you get your power back. It may be hard to do, but it will be rewarding. Learn to use forgiveness as a weapon on your journey.

Clean Out the Clutter

Some of you were raised by single mothers and or grandmothers. Those of you who were, will appreciate and understand this analogy because you have seen it first-hand. Women clean out their purses and handbags periodically. This allows them to sort out what's in their bag, and get rid of all the junk that has built up. We've seen them doing this and wonder how all that junk got in there? Where did it come from? But they get rid of all the junk, their purse is much lighter and they feel better. They got rid of the *excess baggage*.

Some of you are carrying around imaginary duffel bags filled with past excess baggage. These mental bags contain bad memories from the past and are a burden. It's time to get rid of these imaginary bags and throw away all the excess baggage cluttering up your life. It's the same as spring cleaning. Most people clean out their houses after the winter. This brightens up the house and gets rid of that gloomy winter feeling. Why not conduct a spring cleaning on your mind? Your mind is your mental estate. Go through your estate and get rid of all the junk you're holding onto. Don't stay in a mental winter. Any baggage that is holding you back is held in your mind and you have to clean it out.

"He who wants to keep his garden tidy doesn't reserve a plot for weeds."
—Dan Hammarskjold

Unfortunately, too many of you reserve plots for weeds in your mind. Don't lose your passion for today by constantly reliving yesterday's problems over and over again. If you dwell too much on what you did in the past, you will lose focus on what you're going to do in your future. Get rid of the weeds that have crept up.

A simple way of doing this is to get a blank sheet of paper and write down every thing that bothers you. Write down every problem, past pain and worry that you have. Then wad it up and flush it down the toilet. Or burn it. This symbolic act can be freeing. After you do this, focus your thoughts on the positive things about yourself. Focus on your future. Be done with the past. This is why I refer to J-Roc as another person. I'm no longer him, he's dead to me. Make your past dead to you.

How To Clean Out Your Mind

This simple technique will help you clean out your mind so that you can devote all your mental capacities to creating your future. Most of you have heard of meditation and the reasons for doing it. Some of you have been turned off by certain religious gurus who preach the power of meditation? I'm certainly not a religious guru, but I know that Millionaire Prisoners practice positive steps that help them improve. Without clearing out your mind of all the negative emotions and bad memories, you won't be able to focus and concentrate on the task at hand. Here are some simple meditation steps that will increase your ability to create and prosper:

1.Select a soothing piece of music that calms you. Classical or instrumental music works best. This allows your brain to focus on something while all the small noise of the prison is negated.

2.Place a "Do not disturb" sign on your cell door, and sit comfortably in a chair or on your bunk. You don't have to sit cross-legged. Just find a position that is comfortable and relaxing for you. You can lie down if you want.

3.Close your eyes and imagine yourself surrounded by nothingness. Allow yourself to calm down. Slow your breathing and relax.

4.Once you are calm, imagine yourself standing at a bottomless pit. As you stand there, drop all your worries, problems, and wants into the pit. Then imagine yourself turning around and walking away.

5.Remain in your meditative state as long as you like. To come back to reality, just become aware of your body and open your eyes.

Practice this process daily. If you have an alarm, set it to go off 15 minutes after you start. Discipline yourself to stick to your daily meditations. Once you become adept at this process you'll be able to use it anytime you want to get away from the problems of the world. It's simple, but powerful.

Overcome Fear of Failure

Because some of you are constantly looking back, you're scared you're going to fail in the future. But why suffer now? Why cause yourself so much pain when it's not even necessary? Everyone fails. If we haven't failed it's because we haven't tried. Only look back to learn, not to relive failure and pain.

"A man who suffers necessary before it is necessary,
suffers more than is necessary."

—*Seneca*

Some of you don't try harder because you don't want to experience any more failures. So you lower your expectations for your life and practice defeatism. Prison is the breeding ground for this *attitude*. It's easy to accept a life of failure when everyone else around you is failing also. You become just like your prisoner peers and failure becomes normal. At all cost, you must get rid of this mindset.

Failure is only failure if you quit. Thomas Edison tried over 10,000 times before he got the light bulb right. His *attitude* was not one of failure, but of finding what didn't work so that he could eventually find what did work. He never quit and is recognized for his many inventions.

"I failed my way to success."

—*Thomas Edison*

Babe Ruth is one of the greatest baseball players in history. He hit 714 home runs, but he also struck out 1,330 times. We don't remember him for his strike outs, but for his home runs.

Cy Young is the all-time leader for most pitching victories in Major League Baseball story. But he is also the leader for most losses as well. With that being said, every year the best pitcher in baseball gets an award named after Cy Young. He is remembered for his wins and not his losses.

Brett Favre holds National Football League record for many quarterback statistics including games played consecutively and most touchdown passes. He has also thrown the most interceptions by a quarterback. We remember him for his magic on the gridiron and not the interceptions. These people are not failures, but success stories. They chose to keep trying. They chose to learn from their mistakes. They found what didn't work so they could find what did work. They weren't perfect, but nobody is. Failure is only failure if you quit. Past mistakes do not have to be a burden. Keep stepping up to the plate, eventually you're going to hit your home run.

"I just keep goin' up there and swingin' at 'em"
—*Babe Ruth*

Use Your Past As a Lesson

Learn how to use your past as a learning tool. It can be good to look back and evaluate past performances, mistakes, and calamities. You can ask yourself questions like:

How did I err?

Why did I err?

Could I have done better?

Could I have made a better impression?

What did I miss?

Were my calculations correct or wrong?

What can I use from this experience in the future?

You don't ask yourself these questions to relive past mistakes, but to learn from them. Since your *objective* is to achieve success and prosperity you need to know what not to do. If you keep making the same mistakes over and over again, you'll have a hard time achieving your goals. Learn from the past then cut it loose. Let others worry about your past while you live in the present. Your scars are only a reminder of what not to do. Don't dwell on them.

While looking back you must be careful not to blame others for your mistakes. It's easy to do, but detrimental to your *growth*. Remember that you're building a positive *attitude*

35

now. Blaming others for your mistakes is unhealthy. Also, unhealthy, is blaming yourself so much that you start to relish it and believe it. We've all made mistakes in our past, and we'll make mistakes in our future. But only a quitter really fails. You're just learning what not to do. Don't believe that because of past mistakes you're a failure. Don't allow your past to hold your future hostage.

It's time for you to take the garbage out once and for all. It's time for you to get rid of all the baggage holding you back. Carefully avoid past errors, and stop living in reverse. Don't rehash your mistakes over and over again in your mind.

Cut Away the Dead Weight

Many ex-cons have cut away their prison baggage on their way to success. Some examples have already been given in the chapter on attitude. Another prisoner who dropped his baggage at the prison gates is Dan Manville. He is a legend in prison lore and must be included here.

Manville did a stint inside the Michigan prison system, but chose to develop good *habits* that would be beneficial to him and many other prisoners. One of these habits was to get an *education*. He received a Bachelor's Degree in Science from Central Michigan University in 1976. Manville also received a General Studies Bachelorette from Wayne State University that same year. He enrolled in Antioch School of Law in Washington, D.C., and received his Juris Doctorate in 1981. After graduating from Antioch, Manville interned with the ACLU's Prison Project. Eventually he made his way back to Michigan, where he passed the bar exam and started practicing law.

In 1985, Manville received a Master's Degree in Criminal Justice from Michigan State University. From 2003-2007, he was Clinical Staff attorney for Wayne State's Civil Rights Litigation

Clinic. At Wayne State, Manville taught students about prisoner rights and how to run a legal clinic. He's best known in prisoner circles as the co-author of the *Prisoners' Self -Help Litigation Manual*. The *PSHLM* has been called "the bible" for prisoners who need to litigate lawsuits by themselves. Manville is also author of the *Disciplinary Self-Help Litigation Manual*, which deals with prison disciplinary hearings.

Manville is a shining light providing hope in the bleak prison industrial complex of America. The fact that his father was a prison guard, and he's an ex-con, makes his accomplishments even more remarkable. Remember his story as you have thoughts that your past could hold you back. It will only do so if you allow it to.

Drop your prison baggage in the trash and start living for your future. It's been said that the reason the rearview mirror in a car is so small and the windshield is so large is because things that are in front of you are a lot more important than the things that are behind you. Make a pact with yourself right now that you're going to forget those things that are behind you. Only look to those things ahead of you.

> *"Success is how high you bounce when you hit bottom."*
> — *General George Patton*

How To Make Your Past Dance

Pierre Julitte was a member of General de Gaulle's staff and involved in the French Resistance during World War Two. He was captured by the Gestapo in March 1943, and spent 25 months in prison and concentration camps, including the infamous Buchenwald. He was awarded the *Croix de la Liberation* for his service. After his release, Juliette wrote the bestselling novel, *Block 26: Sabotage At Buchenwald*, based on his experiences in the concentration camps.

Another French prisoner wrote one of the all-time classics. Henry Charriere penned *Papillion*, a novel about a prisoner on Devil's Island, based on his own personal experience from prison.

Ben Steele was taken captive by the Japanese during World War Two. He created art based on the atrocities he saw while being held as a prisoner of war. His 11 oil paintings and 80 drawings now reside in the Montana Museum of Art and Culture. His past has become a historical legacy.

Your personal experiences are a goldmine waiting to be tapped into. You must drill the holes, blast away the rock, and extract the golden nuggets of wisdom and lore that can be found. You can make the past dance if it's used properly. Just like the miner who gets rid of the excess rock and waste, but keeps the gold, so must you. Extract the gold first, then throw away the baggage.

Millionaire Prisoner Case Study

On January 1982, at the age of sixteen, Marina Nemat was arrested and taken to Evin, a prison in Iran for political prisoners. Evin has been used as a torture chamber for many years. Marina was taken there to be questioned about articles she wrote for her school newspaper that were critical of the government, and her role in leading a strike by the students. Because she wouldn't give up the names of her friends from school, she was handcuffed and tied to a bed. She was tortured using a small black cable cord that whipped across the soles of her feet. Still, she refused to give up any names. Taken outside to be executed with other prisoners, she was given a last-minute reprieve and her sentence was commuted to life in prison. As she was being led away from the firing squad she saw the other prisoners being executed.

Inside Evin, her room was given warm water once every two or three weeks, for only two to three hours at a time. Each prisoner would be given 10 minutes to shower. Close family members were allowed to visit once a month. The visiting room consisted of a room separated by a glass partition. There were no openings in the glass, and no phones to communicate with. Prisoners used sign language, slow pronunciation, and lip reading to talk with family. Marina was forced to marry one of her torturers or her parents would be arrested. She was also forced to renounce her religious beliefs and convert to Islam. She was kept in an isolation cell and raped by her husband. Eventually, her husband moved her out of the prison and into house arrest. He was assassinated in front of her and she lost the baby that was in her womb. She went back to Evin, and was eventually released after two years of captivity. Once released, she married her boyfriend and in 1991, they emigrated to Toronto, Canada. They now have two sons together.

In writing her memoir, *Prisoner of Tehran*, Marina faced her fears and courageously wrote about her past ordeal as a political prisoner in one of the world's most dangerous prisons. It takes courage to write about painful memories and then offer them to the world as a gift to be read. But she dealt with her past in a way that is profitable to all who read her memoir.

Learn to mine the gold from your past and move on. Don't allow your past to hold your future hostage. You can make it dance, just like all of the above prisoners have done. Don't waste time on things you can't change. We only have one life and we don't get a do-over. Only use your past as a tool. It can teach you what not to do. Bury your past and move on, so will the world.

Remember, you are not your past. You are whatever you choose to be. It's your choice.

Resource

If you would like to read more about getting rid of the mental baggage clogging up your mind and how to get rid of it, you should check out:

Head Trash: Cleaning Out the Junk that Stands Between You and Success by Tish Squillard and Timothy L. Thomas.

Millionaire Prisoner Prosperity Keys

- Your past is a ball and chain that you must free yourself from.
- Get rid of the clutter in your life and do some weeding in your mental estate.
- You do not fail, because failure is only final if you quit.
- Your mistakes are opportunities to see what doesn't work so you can find what does work.
- Learn to make your past dance on the path to prosperity.

CAPITAL

*Money doesn't make you different. It makes your
circumstances different*
— *Malcolm Forbes.*

There is a belief held by many that you need money to
make money. That belief is false. To make money all you need is
a brain, the ability to read, and your *imagination*. The power of
your brain is not subject to any economic law like inflation and
or a recession. The principles contained in this chapter are
timeless. They will point you in the right direction so that you
don't lose money. The rest of these ABCs will give you
everything you desire if you put them to use. But first you need
to acquire the Millionaire Prisoner money mindset.

The Root of All Evil

The only reason I did crime was because I had no money.
Plain and simple. For me, *the lack of money* was the root to my
evil. My mother slaved away all day at a day-care center making
chump change. She did the best she could trying to support 3
kids as a single mother, but it wasn't enough.

Not having money as a kid hurt because I went to a middle
school with all the rich kids from my hometown. They had all
the new clothes and latest gadgets. I had hand-me-downs from

Goodwill. I was told the answer was to get a job. So I did. I worked as a dishwasher. I had paper routes. I detassled corn. I stocked shelves and loaded semi-trailers. I worked at a chemical factory. I've had lots of jobs. But getting minimum wage and a check every other week didn't help me. Why? Because no one taught me what to do with the money. I thought it was something to spend. This led me to want more money, and I wanted it faster. So, I started robbing people. Of course, I wound up in prison. It was only after I began my study on money and business that I realized my *education* had been wrong. Getting a job was not the answer for me. I found it in these ABCs.

"The lack of money is the root of all evil."
—*Mark Twain*

Getting A Ph.D.

Most of us prisoners didn't have money growing up. Just like me, you lived off Public Aid, numerous state/federal welfare systems, and food stamps. A lot of us ate generic food. A hunger for riches burned inside of us, but we were ignorant to the legitimate avenues that could provide wealth. To obtain wealth we became illegal entrepreneurs. We sold drugs, robbed, stole, and committed other crimes. The streets gave us Ph.D.'s: we are poor, hungry, and driven. Now it's time for us to break that cycle. It's time for you to break the back of poverty so that your children, and your children's children, don't have to suffer a world of lack as you did. Instead, they can live in legitimate prosperity with no fear of losing it.

"A criminal is a person with predatory instincts who has not sufficient capital to form a corporation."
—*Howard Scott*

Let's look at some wealth principles that will help you obtain sufficient capital, so that you may achieve your dreams and leave your future sons and daughters the wealth they deserve.

Think Like The Rich

As you think, so you are. In 2008, Robert Kiyosaki, the author of *Rich Dad, Poor Dad*, stated on the financial show *The Millionaire Inside* that, "Money gives you freedom. The middle class want security, but that's a wrong way to think, because the people with the most security are in prison. That's why they call it a maximum-security prison." It was a great line, and it hit me like a ton of bricks. There I was, in a maximum-security prison, with no money, but complete security.

What Mr. Kiyosaki does best is show us that the rich think differently than we do. But the rich have given us their secrets. They have given us the keys to wealth in their examples and the books they've wrote. All we have to do is look at the examples of their lives and implement those keys and strategies into our own lives. By using these wealth tips and tactics you can change your life and your family's financial future.

Let's go back to Napoleon Hill's *Think and Grow Rich*, previously mentioned in the chapter on *Attitude*. Notice the title: *Think and Grow Rich*. "Think" comes first. It's your state of mind that matters most. *You will not grow rich by watching others. You will not grow rich by wishing for riches. You have to think different to get different results. It's a rich person's state of mind that you need to develop. Because if you have a Millionaire Prisoner mindset, you can become a Millionaire Prisoner in your trust fund account.*

So how do you acquire this state of mind? Read any books that you can on money, investing, and business that you come across. Begin with *Think and Grow Rich*. Read magazines like *Money, Inc., Forbes,* and newspapers like *The Wall Street Journal, Barron's,* and *Investor's Business Daily.* Watch financial TV shows. Educate yourself about wealth. Learn how to acquire it, create it, save it, invest it, and then give it away. Read about people like Warren Buffett, Conrad Hilton, Sam Walton, and other billionaires from the past and present. It was Buffett who said, "Rule number 1: Never lose money. Rule number 2: Never forget rule number 1." It's simple principles like this that have made Buffett one of the richest men in the world. It's simple principles like this that you need to master if you're going to become a Millionaire Prisoner. As a prisoner your resources are limited and you have to stop the leaks. Leaks are areas where you lose money. Playing prison parlay tickets can be a leak. Buying every new pair of shoes on the commissary can be a leak. Pornographic books can be a leak. You're losing money because it's not being reinvested. Think about the ways that you are currently losing money and stop the leaks. Our first money principle is borrowed from the great Warren Buffett. You should: *NEVER LOSE MONEY!*

How To Find Lost Money

You may have already lost money and not even known about it. There are millions of dollars of unclaimed property in the U.S. This money stems from life insurance policies, refunds from utility companies, and proceeds from the estate of relatives who died without a will. The money is just sitting there waiting to be claimed. You may have some in your name that you don't know about. Here is how to find out.

Have someone in your *network* conduct a search using your last and first name on the free websites: *www.unclaimedproperty.com* and *www.missingmoney.com*. If you find some in your name, file a claim with your state's unclaimed property office. Even if you don't find anything, you should still conduct a search every year because of how slow things are when it comes to bureaucrats processing paperwork. If you don't have someone in your *network* to assist you with this search, I'll show you how to find someone in the chapter on *Network*.

Pay Yourself First and Keep It

You are probably thinking that you already do this, but do you? When you get a money order from a loved one, what do you do with it? Let's use a $100 money order as a base. The typical prisoner gets a $100 money order and immediately starts spending it in their head. He gets out his commissary price list and decides he will spend $50 on a new pair of shoes. Then he decides to spend $10 on hygiene items, leaving him $40 from his original $100. Next, he decided to spend $20 on food so he can make some burritos. Don't forget that prison staple: coffee. There is $5 more gone. He has $15 left and it's burning a hole in his pocket, so he buys some pornographic books and now he has none of the $100 left. Where did he pay himself first, let alone keep it? He didn't. He thinks he did, but in reality, he paid the commissary and pornographic book publishers. He never paid himself. He didn't follow the principle to pay yourself *first*. That means before you pay someone else.

> *"A part of all you earn is yours to keep."*
> —*George S. Clason*

Let's use the same $100 money order, but this time we shall examine what Millionaire Prisoners do with it. When our Millionaire Prisoner gets his $100 money order he immediately makes a mental note that he is paying himself $10 and keeping it. He can't spend that $10 because he is *keeping it*. As you will understand in a few minutes, this step is crucial in your quest to acquire sufficient capital. Then our Millionaire Prisoner spends $40 on ordering some *business* books. The leftover $50 is what he'll use at the commissary. Notice the difference between these two examples? Their *habits* are different. One has a poor prisoner's mentality, the other has a Millionaire Prisoner mindset. Which one do you think will be more profitable? So principle number two is *pay yourself first and keep it!*

The Power of Compounding Interest

Some prisons offer classes on finances, money, and staying out of debt. If your prison offers these types of classes, then sign up for them. I had the opportunity to attend a class presented by Crown Financial Ministries. The class was based on the foundation of using Bible-based ethics to get out of debt, invest, and so forth. The prisoners who participated in this class came from all kinds of different backgrounds and religious beliefs and we learned a lot. But one of the best lessons was about compound interest and I want to share that with you.

Some bankers call compounding interest the eighth wonder of the world. What is compound interest? Simply put, it's the art of growing money. In our class this power was illustrated by giving two examples. We called these two examples Prisoner A and Prisoner B. Prisoner A had a sentence that required him to serve 36 years in prison. He got locked up when he was 18 and would be released when he was 54. Knowing this, Prisoner A invested $100 every year into an investment strategy that received an annual interest of 10%. (10% was used because it's an easy number to calculate percentages with). But every year, Prisoner A deposited $100 into this account. His total investment amounted to $3,700, counting his first deposit in the beginning to open the account, and his last deposit on year 36, a total of 37 deposits. What happened to his money? This is where the power of compounding interest becomes evident.

After one year, Prisoner A had $110 in his account. He had his original $100 plus $10 interest gained on that original sum. After his second deposit of $100 and second year of gaining interest he had $231. His $110 plus $100 is $210, times 10% is $21, which equals $231. For the sake of brevity, let's skip ahead to his release year, and keep in mind that he deposited only $100 a year into his account. At the age of 54, Prisoner A walked into his bank manager's office and told him he was cleaning out his account. After some formalities, the bank manager cut him a check for $36,304 minus fees. He grew his $100 a month, or $3,700 total investment, into $36,304. That's the power of compound interest. That is why you have to pay yourself first and keep it. That way you'll have money to put into an investment strategy where you can use the power of compounding interest.

Now we can look at Prisoner B. When Prisoner B came to prison, he was 21. He had the same 36 years to do as Prisoner A. But Prisoner B had a wealthy girlfriend who gave him $2,000 every year to use for his wants and needs while he was in prison. But our Prisoner B was no dummy, he knew that his girlfriend wasn't going to wait around for 36 years for him. So, he took $1,000 out of every $2,000 she gave him and paid himself first. He put these $1,000 deposits into an account getting the same 10% interest as Prisoner A. Sure enough, as Prisoner B foresaw, his girlfriend left him after 8 years. Altogether, he had deposited $8,000 and never deposited anymore after that. Prisoner B got a job in the prison kitchen that paid him $45 a month and he learned to survive off that income alone. That way, he would never have to touch his interest-bearing account. At the age of

57, after 36 years in prison, Prisoner B walked into his bank manager's office and asked to clear his account. Just like Prisoner A, the bank manager cut him a check. But his check was for $199,542, minus fees. Almost $200,000 on an investment of $8,000. That is the power of compounding interest.

Of course, this is the short version. I took the liberty not to include a calculation of every years' increase. But I wanted you to see the ability for *growth* by using compound interest. Robert Allen, author of *Multiple Streams of Income*, notes that in a span of one's life, an investment of $1 a day, or $30 a month, could grow into $1 million by using compounding interest. So, there is principle number three: *Use the power of compounding interest!*

When interest is working for you, you're on the right track to acquiring sufficient capital. If it's working against you, you're in deep trouble. Be mindful that most bank accounts don't give you anything close to 10% interest. If you must use a regular bank savings account, then use one where the interest is compounded daily, not quarterly. That way you'll make more money.

> *"Money is in some respects like fire—it is a very excellent servant but a terrible master. When you have it mastering you, when interest is constantly piling up against you, it will keep you down in the worst kind of slavery. But let money work for you and you have the most devoted servant in the world."*
>
> —P.T. Barnum

Never Buy On Credit

Both of the prisoner examples from above paid themselves first and kept it. They made interest their servant. It became their slave. They put their keep to work for them. But there is always two sides to every coin. The other side of interest as servant is interest as master. Here is another example. We'll call this Prisoner—Mark.

Mark gets a $50 money order and orders $40 in food and coffee from the commissary. He saves $10 on his trust fund account in the case of an emergency. Mark then eats all his food and drinks his last cup of coffee the day before he is scheduled to go back to the commissary. The next morning during breakfast, there is a riot in the chow hall, and the prison goes on lockdown. Now Mark is friending for some candy bars and a shot of coffee. He figures that since he still has $10 in his trust fund account, he can go to the box, i.e., the prison black market, and borrow one candy bar and a bag of coffee. He can cover the interest on that. So, Mark sends a kite down the gallery and requests these items from the box. When the kite comes back, it has the candy bar and bag of coffee in it. But there is a note saying that because of the lockdown the normal interest rate of 50¢ on the dollar has been suspended. The new rate is $2 for every dollar. So, Mark will have to give two candy bars and two bags of coffee back to the box. Against his better judgment, Mark agrees to the terms. He figures he can pay for it, and he really wants a cup of coffee.

But Mark forgot something. He forgot that at his prison, you can only buy two bags of coffee a week at the commissary. How will he drink coffee next week when the two bags he buys have to go to the box? Eventually the prison comes off lockdown and Mark goes to the commissary. He gets the items to pay back the box and doesn't owe anyone. But there is still the problem of his coffee drinking *habit*. So, Mark goes back to the box and gets another bag of coffee. He repeats this process over a few months until it becomes routine. He doesn't think anything of it because he always pays his debts and has good credit. But the interest has mastered him by working against him. He loses $5.58 a

49

week. That adds up to $22.32 a month, and $287.84 a year. If he doesn't break the cycle, sooner or later, Mark will have nothing.

This prison coffee example is just one example of debt and how it masters people. In the free world, the biggest example of debt and interest becoming master is credit card debt. The interest rates charged by credit card companies are outrageous. You need your money to invest. So principle number four for acquiring sufficient capital is to: *Never buy on credit!*

Forbes magazine polled the richest 400 people for their annual *Forbes 400* issue and 75% of them said that the number one key to making money is to get out of debt and stay out of debt. Never buying on credit will allow you to stay out of debt. By staying out of debt you can use your money to invest. If anything, *become the man who runs the store*, or box. Companies like Check Into Cash and Advance America have gotten rich off legalized loan sharking. Why not you? Use your "store" to free up your trust fund account to build your brand, business and investments!

How To Stop Harassing Debt Collectors

Because of poor financial decisions before you came to prison, some of you have outstanding debts from unpaid bills and you're being harassed by debt collectors. Not only do they bother you, but now they are harassing your family members as well. This is illegal. The Fair Debt Collection Practices Act, known as the FDCPA (15 U.S.C. Sec. 1692), was enacted to eliminate illegal and abusive debt collection practices. The FDCPA provides up to $1,000 per case for a violation of the Act, plus requires that the party violating the Act to pay all of your attorney's fees and costs. Here are some of the most common ways a debt collector can violate the Act:

1. You, your family, and your acquaintances are flooded with letters and phone calls from debt collectors or law firms.

2. The debt collector agency calls and leaves a message which fails to give the name of the agency, fails to give the name of the debt collector, and or fails to state that they are a debt collector.

3. Pre-recorded or automated calls to phone numbers that are not listed in your, or your family and friend's name may be a violation of the Act.

Under the Act, intent doesn't always have to be shown, so even if a debt collector isn't intentionally trying to harass you or your family, they are still violating the law and you're entitled to compensation. There is a 1-year statute of limitations on violations of the FDCPA, so you are limited to collecting on violations that occurred in the last year.

If you believe that you or your family are being harassed by illegal debt collectors and their bogus practices, contact attorney Allison Polesky. She runs the website: *www.prisonersdebthelp.com*. and her firm specializes in protecting consumer's rights under the FDCPA. Mrs. Polesky's full information is provided in the appendix. Stop being harassed by illegal debt collectors now.

Live Well Below Your Means

In their book, *The Millionaire Next Door*, Thomas Stanley and William Danko discuss comprehensive research into some of the millionaires next door. In researching over 500 millionaires they found that the number one theme from these millionaires is that they live well below their means. Stanley and Danko stated that the average millionaire invests 20 percent of their income every year, while non-millionaires spend everything that comes in. The non-millionaire sounds like Mark from our coffee *habit*, doesn't it? Take a cue from these millionaires and learn to live well below your means.

Why buy a new pair of shoes at the commissary when you have three new pairs in your cell? Why not invest that money in something that will produce more income or interest on your money? Most times, you're just buying things trying to keep up with your prisoner peers. Think of what you would buy if it didn't matter if anyone saw you or cared about what you had materially? Change your attitude about money. People who are poor think of money as something to spend. Wealthy people see money as something to invest. Imitate the wealthy way of investing, not the poor way of spending.

> *"The difference between rich people and poor people is where they sign their checks. Poor people sign the front. Rich people sign the back."*
> —Ric Edelman

As long as you're paying yourself first and keeping it, you will always live well below your means. But to truly live *well below* your means is to go even further than 10%. Go for 20 to 30% of what you bring in as to what you're going to invest. The more you allocate for investing, the more you can get in return. So principle number five for acquiring sufficient capital is: *Live Well below your means!*

Guns and Butter

Investing has been mentioned throughout this chapter, and a few moments must be spent on this topic. To understand investing you must learn about the Guns and Butter Theory. You may have heard rapper Jay-Z say "guns and butter" and not know what he actually meant. This theory comes from the common sense approach that if you have a pound of butter, and I have a gun, then I can easily relieve you of your pound of butter. He who has the guns has the power. This theory has evolved over time, but its application is even more needed today. In the present sense, guns are items that appreciate in value, such as stocks, gold, real estate and land. Guns are assets. Butter being items that depreciate in value like cars, TVs, stereo systems, and cell phones. Butter are liabilities. If you invest your money in guns, you'll see your net worth grow. But if you spend your money on butter, you will not see any return on your investment. Learn to spend your money on guns, thereby investing in your future and experiencing *growth* in your net worth.

Divide Your Investments

If you had all of your money in the stock market in 2008, you probably lost considerable amounts of money due to the market crashing. Many people did lose all of their savings because they didn't follow the simple principle of diversification.

> *"Divide your portion to seven, or even to eight, for you do not know what misfortune may occur on the earth."*
> —*King Solomon*

There are numerous things you can invest in, whether you're in prison or out of prison. In the prison complex, you can invest in artwork, crafts, commissary products, pen-pals, sports betting, and numerous other prison hustles. I will not deal with those in this chapter. Instead, I will briefly discuss real world investment strategies that a prisoner can *utilize* from inside prison to build wealth. If you're interested in any of these areas past what will be said, then by all means conduct your own research. Get more information. Your prison library should have some adequate books on money and investing. If not, utilize the Books to Prisoner Projects listed in the appendix. Begin your training now while you're in prison. In short, here are a few different types of investments:

CDs

A CD is a certificate of deposit. Most banks sell them. You can purchase them for a term of 1 month or up to 10 years. The longer your term, the higher the rate of return. Most major newspapers, *USA Today* included, list the major CD rates every week. Some people like to stagger their CD purchases, or roll them over. They will get one 1-year CD, one 2-year CD, one 3-year CD, and so forth. That way every year they have a CD reach maturity and they can reinvest it in another CD, or use the money if need be. If you purchase a CD do not expect a lot of money because interest rates are low. CDs are a low-risk investment vehicle.

I-Bonds

I-Bonds are U.S. government savings bonds issued at face value. A $500 bond would cost you $500. I-Bonds pay two types of interest: a fixed rate, plus an inflation interest adjustment every six months, based on the federal governments' Consumer Price Index. Interest on federal I-Bonds is exempt from state and local tax, and you can defer federal tax on the interest until final maturity of the bond. I-Bonds are safe, easy to purchase, don't require monitoring, excellent investment tools for kids, can be used for *education*, and are logical alternatives to CDs. I-Bonds are a long-term investment with penalties for selling before maturity.

Real Estate

The housing market of today's America doesn't allow young people to buy homes right away. Renting is their only option. We've all heard the mantra in real estate that "location, location, location" is everything. If you find a piece of property that you can buy, then rent out, you may have a lucrative investment. You must be careful. Be fair to the renter and yourself. Make sure you have enough funds to cover needed maintenance and improvements, without having to borrow. If you don't want to be a landlord, don't buy rental property. For a prisoner, this type of investment will require outside help. Make sure it's someone trustworthy before you venture down this road. Rental properties will be the hardest for a prisoner to maintain, but there are professional companies who manage properties for a fee. This might be something you could look into if you have the seed money.

But you might want to check out investing in a Real Estate Investment Trust (REIT), also known as real estate stocks. REITs are companies that own income-producing real estate, and were created by Congress in 1960 to give everyone the ability to invest in large-scale commercial properties. REITs offer a possible venue for prisoners to own a piece of real estate with a little investment, but like any investment there is risk involved so do your research first.

Stocks

Stocks are shares in publicly held companies. They allow private individuals such as you or me, to be part owners of a company like Wal-Mart, Coca-Cola, or G.E. Stocks can be very profitable, but they are risky. A few years ago, there was an article in *USA Today* about a prisoner who taught himself how to pick stocks. He started with a $1,000 birthday gift from his father and turned that into a mansion, a Lamborghini, and a job at Merrill Lynch upon his release. He said he watched CNBC all day and read financial magazines and newspapers. He would phone his father and tell him what stocks to buy and sell. So, it's certainly possible for a prisoner to become a Millionaire Prisoner by picking stocks. There are a few advantages to owning stock. Some of them are:

- stocks grow in value;
- stocks can generate value and income;
- stocks are a hedge against inflation;
- stocks offer tax advantages.

For more information on investing in stocks, some great books to read are Phillip Fisher's *Common Stocks and Uncommon Profits*; and Peter Lynch's *Beating the Street*.

With the advent of internet stock trading companies like E-Trade, you may wonder how to get started. Personally, I would suggest buying stocks on your own without a broker. This will save you money. If you want to learn how to do this then check out *Buying Stocks Without a Broker* by Charles Carlson. Jeff Reeves, editor of *InvestorPlace.com* and author of *The Frugal Investor's Guide to Finding Great Stocks*, offers some simple tips beginners need to know when buying stocks:

1. Don't chase the herd, i.e., don't make investment decisions based on what's popular. Buy low, sell high is still the way to go!

2. Don't fall in love with your investment. Know when to get out is the other part of "sell high."

3.Don't try to wait out a bad stock and cost yourself more money. A loser is a loser and it may be better to try a different stock or investment.

4.Don't get greedy and put all your eggs in one basket, or one stock. Remember to diversify.

5.Stick to long-term investments and don't try to "time the market."

I add the following that you need to remember:

Investing in stocks is not a get-rich-quick scheme. It takes patience and income that you can afford to use as an investment. So think long and hard before you start buying stocks.

Mutual Funds

A mutual fund is basically a big pool of money from different investors, managed by a full-time professional, who invests according to specific guidelines. Before you invest in a fund, do research on it. There are many different ones, and they invest in different things. Mutual funds require less money than other investments. Check the fund's goals, whether long-term or short? Check their long-term history using fund indexes. For instance, *Money* magazine has an annual review of mutual funds. If the management of the fund has a history of *growth* and consistency, it *might* be a good investment. Like any investment, there is risk involved. Mutual funds are a good investment for prisoners because most of us don't have the requisite tools to evaluate stocks.

For more information on investing in general, I recommend the following books: *The Only Investment Guide You'll Ever Need* by Andrew Tobias; *The Richest Man Who Ever Lived* by Stephen S. Scott; and *The Intelligent Investor: A Book of Practical Counsel* by Benjamin Graham. There are many more great books about wealth and investing out there, but these are just a few to get you started. Principle number six for acquiring sufficient capital is to: *Divide Your Investments!*

If you can master these six principles, then you can easily become a Millionaire Prisoner. Use these principles as the foundation for acquiring sufficient capital.

Turning Your Stamp Trash Into Ca$h

You've probably seen the advertisements in prison magazines offering to buy your new postage stamps. But did you know that the used stamps on your incoming mail are worth money also? Stamp collecting is big business all across the world, and there are over 10,000 stamp dealers in the U.S. alone. Anytime you have that many dealerships you have a substantial market and potential profit source. There are 3 ways you can profit from your used stamps:

1. Sell them to stamp dealers.
2. Sell them "retail" to stamp collectors.
3. Become a stamp dealer yourself.

It might be hard for a prisoner to become a stamp dealer without free-world help, but you could certainly do the first two. You're not going to get rich off your used stamps, but you could make some extra dollars. I recently saw an ad where a dealer was selling 120 "big and unusual stamps" for $5. So the market is still there. Some jails and prisons tear the stamps off the envelopes because they're worried about the stamps being laced with acid and other drugs. If your prison doesn't do so, then save any overseas stamps that you get. And all the big, unusual and/or special commemorative U.S. stamps that come in on your mail. These will be worth the most. Have your friends save theirs for you also, but don't tell them why.

If you are interested in collecting stamps or selling them, then you should get a copy of *The Official Blackbook Price Guide to*

U.S. Postage Stamps. Also subscribe to *Linn's Stamp News, The Stamp Wholesaler,* and *Scott Stamp Monthly.* You'll find dealers and possible buyers in them. As e-mail and the internet continue to take over daily communication, letter writing will become rare. That should mean that stamp collecting will be even more profitable in the future. It's definitely something worth looking into, but as with anything, do your own research and decide if it's an avenue you want to pursue.

How Much Money is Enough?

As a prisoner, your number is much different than someone in the free-world. My number is $240,000. I am 35 and can expect to live at least until I'm 75, a difference of 40 years. So $240,000 divided by 40 years is $6,000. This averages out to $500 a month. I just want to be able to order books or magazines when I want; go to the commissary and spend what I want and not worry about a budget; and to be able to send my kids *quality* gifts. Basically, I want the financial freedom to do what I want and not have to worry about money. This is all I could want or need in prison. Ten million dollars does me no good because I'm a lifer. Should I get out, my number will change. Of course, I will never stop helping my family and friends make money. Some prisoners say $100 or $200 a month is all they need and that's fine. Find your own number, then go get it.

Financial Mission Statement

You must form a clear financial statement that you write down on paper. This will be your mission statement. Do this before you start researching about wealth. Whatever you put in your mission statement is your purpose and your plan. Only after formulating your own plan can you seek advice without compromising your mission. If you started reading first, then your mission statement would be based on someone else's thoughts and ideas and not your own. First, formulate your own thoughts about what you want and need your financial wealth to be, then seek advice from books and other sources that will help you execute your mission. You will keep your integrity and stay true to yourself in the process.

To aid you in coming up with your mission statement I have included one here that you may use as a format to perfect yours:

I, (your name here), hereby acknowledge that I have formally adopted the following financial goals:

On the _____ day of _____, 20___, my net worth will be at least (your number). I have renounced my old poor mentality and will devote time to do the things which I need to acquire wealth. I understand that wishing will not bring riches, but with the right *attitude*, and a definitive *objective*, I can become rich.

I will sacrifice excess material possessions that I don't need to acquire this net worth, and spend my time writing and creating. I will utilize the following six principles to acquire this net worth: I will never lose money; I will pay myself first and keep it; I will use the power of compounding interest; I will never buy on credit; I will live well below my means; and I will divide my investments. These principles shall become my daily *habits*.

In order to achieve this goal I will give my best possible *quality* of service as a (your occupation here) and investor. I will learn all that I can about money and wealth. I will also seek out wealthy role models and mentors, who will guide me and aid me in my quest for financial freedom.

Signed this day of _____, 20___

After you write down your financial statement, follow the instructions in the chapter on *Attitude* to make it part of your new story of your life. By using self-suggestion, you can develop the proper way of thinking about wealth. This will enable you to utilize capital to take care of yourself, your family, and everyone else that you choose to take care of.

Turning Ideas Into Money

As a prisoner your capital is your time, your ideas, and your artwork. It's your poetry, your manuscript, and any product that you can offer others. Turning these things into money is the way to prosperity. Many prisoners have been included throughout this book that illustrate that you can easily turn ideas into money. Here is one more example.

Joseph Robinson was sentenced to 25-to-life in prison for a 1992 murder conviction. This charge stemmed from his drug dealing lifestyle. Leaving a fiancé and a 2-year old kid behind in the free-world made him rethink his values, and he decided to change. He started reading every business book and magazine he could find. Then in 1995, he started teaching prisoners about business and money matters. He is now a certified instructor of Inmates Teaching Entrepreneurship & Mentoring (ITEM). ITEM trains prison inmates to teach their children and fellow incarcerated individuals the basics of business ownership. From prison, Robinson wrote the fantastic book: *Think Outside the Cell: An Entrepreneur's Guide For the Incarcerated and Formerly Incarcerated. Think Outside The Cell* is a must read for any prisoner who has business aspirations, or who wants to know more about money matters. Just remember, the best capital is a great idea that is implemented or sold. Robinson's ability to "think outside the cell" has delivered him prosperity. As you think, so you are.

My first profitable venture was an idea to sell a mailing list of wealthy women. It cost me nothing but a few hours time to compile the list. I then sold the idea to my mail-order mentor. That idea is still profitable to this day. Your ideas can make you money. For more information on turning ideas into money, read: *How To Make Millions With Your Ideas: An Entrepreneur's Guide* by Dan S. Kennedy; and *How to License Your Million Dollar Idea: Everything You Need to Know to Make Money From Your New Product Idea* by Harvey Reese.

Why Rob A Bank When You Can Own One?

Michael Benanti went to prison for 20 years for bank robbery. Upon his release, Mr. Benanti started Prisoner Assistant, Inc. which offers banking services to prisoners. He certainly learned from his mistakes, and found a legal way to make money. The other day I asked my counselor about setting up a bank account and he gave me the brochure for Mr. Benanti's company. He has become a millionaire ex-prisoner.

Another former prisoner who became rich is Felix Dennis. He was sent to prison over censorship of one of his magazines. He went from being, in his own words "a hippie drop out on welfare, living in a room without money to pay rent, to being rich." How rich? Billionaire rich. Rich enough to be listed in the Top 100 of Britain's wealthy. He did it without a college degree or any capital. He vowed to never go back to prison and set out to get a piece of the wealth pie. His company, Dennis Publishing, owns magazines such as *Stuff* and *Computer Shopper*. He is also founder of *Maxim* magazine. His book, *How To Get Rich*, is a must read for anyone desiring to get rich.

Ownership Is Everything

One of the best principles that I learned from Felix Dennis is that the owner is the one that gets rich. Years ago when I first came to prison I played parlay tickets. I would put up a sum of money, pick 3 or 4 football teams and win as much as 10 or 12 times my money. Most prisoners know what a parlay ticket is. Well, I became quite good at handicapping sports and I'm at work on another book, *The Millionaire Prisoner's Guide To Sports Handicapping*, in which I will reveal all the secrets I've learned over the years. But I digress. I learned that the person who makes the most money is the man who runs the parlay ticket business. So I became a partner with the man, learned how he did it, then started my own parlay business. I learned a valuable lesson in those days that was only strengthened by every other business book I've read: *only the owner gets rich!* (FYI: I've since quit running the parlay because it's illegal in Illinois.)

So here are some tips to remember along the way:

1. Try and keep ownership of anything you create, especially a business. Your goal is to cut out the middle men and become *the man*.

2. Never sell stock in something unless you absolutely have to. If you hold, you can get money for the rest of your life. If you sell, you get money once. With that being said, if you get offered something that will allow you to live good for the rest of your life, then maybe you should sell out.

3. Even if you can't own it all, own a percentage of it. Remember my wealthy women list? I owned 50% off each sale. Have enough percentage deals and you'll be rich.

> *"To become rich you must be an owner. And You must try to own it all."*
>
> —*Felix Dennis*

The rich use businesses and corporations as vehicles to wealth. You should explore these options as well. For more detailed information on starting your own biz, read *Start Your Own Corporation* by Garrett Sutton; and *Start Your Own Business: The Only Start-Up Book You'll Ever Need, 4th Edition*, by Rieva Lesonsky, et al.

I constantly hear prisoners say that they want to own a corporation, but you already own one— *You, Inc.!* That's what these ABCs are really about: getting you to be the best you can be. If you can do that then you can be successful.

> *"Never be a minion, always be an owner."*
> —*Cornelius Vanderbilt*

How To Get Start-Up Capital

Maybe you have a business idea? But you don't have the funds to start it yet? How do you get this money? It depends on how much you need? My mother started her publishing company on the cheap. She registered it, opened a P.O. Box, and placed an advertisement all for under a couple hundred dollars. She used money from sales to build her business and spread out her *marketing* efforts. Do some research and find out how much you need. Once you have your number, then go get the money you need.

Some of you may already have some personal savings in your prison trust fund account and/or free-world bank account? If you do, you're a step ahead of everyone else. Use this money to start your business, or invest it in a more profitable investment vehicle. For those of you who have no savings, you have to beg, plead, and persuade others to give you capital. Because I'm against getting credit or taking out loans, I will not discuss

THE MILLIONAIRE PRISONER: PART 1

obtaining a loan. Some people believe otherwise, but your reading *The Millionaire Prisoner* and not their book.

In his book, *How To Get Rich*, Felix Dennis has a chapter called "Obtaining Capital." He talks about people who you can borrow money from and calls these people either, "Dolphins, Sharks, or Fishes." We will examine those 3 types, plus one more that I've added myself. A shark, or loan shark, is to be avoided at all cost. There are different types of sharks. The prisoner who runs the "2 for 1 store" is a shark. Stay away from him. There are places that will hold your checks and give you a loan off that check. They charge you crazy interest rates like 30-40%. These businesses are sharks, stay away from them. Credit card companies are sharks, stay away from them. You get my drift. Stay away from the sharks. You can study them and learn from them, but don't get money from them. A great TV show to watch by the way is *Shark Tank*. Here's a small disclosure: I have a shark tattoo on my arm with the words: "A shark never sleeps" underneath it. So maybe you should stay away from me?

Felix Dennis calls venture capitalists "dolphins." And I agree with him that you should stay away from these people in your start-up days. They only care about growing the business as fast as they can so they can get the most money back on their investment. All the while taking a substantial piece of your business with them. I don't blame them either, because if I was a venture capitalist, I would do the same thing. But I'm not a dolphin, I'm a Millionaire Prisoner and I'm advising you to stay away from them.

Before we discuss the "fishes," I want to discuss another creature of the sea. Felix Dennis didn't discuss this creature but I think we should. I'm speaking about the "whale." In the world of gambling, the whale is the player who isn't a professional, but is loaded from a business. But this individual like to gamble, and because they aren't professional, they lose large sums of money at it. Because they are loaded from another business, they can withstand to lose money and it won't affect their bankroll. If you can find a real-life whale and befriend him, by all means do so. You could be very close to your start-up capital. Or better yet, tell the whale to write me and I'll give you a finder's fee. Always be on the lookout for whales because they can change your life.

If you don't know any whales, then you're left with the fishes. It was through the fishes that we started O'Barnett Publishing. All of your pen-pals, family members, acquaintances, friends, and everyone else you know are most likely fishes. Ask for their help. Beg them. Plead them. Persuade them. Do what you have to and get your capital. Here is a tip for dealing with the fishes. Have them pay for your business supplies themselves. Most people won't be quick to send a prisoner money. But they might be open to paying for your business cards, stationary, P.O. Box, and so on. Start small and work your way up. Grow your business slowly. You can start a business and claim tax deductions for up to 2 years so there is no rush. The money is out there, you just have to go out and get it.

Do not take a partner into your business unless it's a silent partner that you trust 100%. But that person is rare, so retain full control and ownership of your business. If you get money from family members and friends, and it's a loan and not a gift, then put everything in writing. Make the terms of the loan specific, and pay back the money as soon as you can. You may need them in the future. Your parents can give you a gift of $11,000 each year and deduct it from their taxes. So, if they give you a $3,000 gift to start your business, make sure they deduct it from their taxes.

There are many places that give away free money so that you can start a business. These gifts are called grants and they don't need to be paid back. The government has over $30 billion worth of free grants available. Other places, such as foundations, must give away free money to keep their tax-exempt status. Most of these places require you to fill out an application and write an essay as to why you should be awarded the money. Keep in mind that I never went through this process because I got my capital from the fishes. But the free money is out there, you just have to find it.

Resources

Here are some books that will help you in the process.

Free Dollars From The Federal Government by Blum;

Starting On A Shoestring: Building A Business Without A Bankroll by Arnold Goldstein;

Guerilla Financing: Alternative Techniques to Finance Any Small Business by Bruce Blechman and Jay Conrad Levinson.

If you have someone in your *network* that is internet savvy, have them check out *www.fastweb.com*. Fastweb is a database of more than 180,000 private sector grants and loans and will let you match yourself to the grants that fit your project for free. Also check out crowdfunding sites like *Kickstarter.com*, *PeopleFundit.com*, *Rockethub.com*, *Indiegogo.com* and *Smallknot.com*.

Boston Tea Party

Since the colonial days, Americans have been rebelling against paying taxes. Just like our founding fathers who organized the Boston Tea Party, the rich believe in their right to avoid taxes. But they don't have to start a revolution to do so because the law is on their side. You can make it be on your side also.

Becoming a Millionaire Prisoner is not only about how much money you make, but how much you *keep!* Your money belongs to you. You worked long hours. You put blood, sweat, and tears into your product or service. Do you want to give 40% of that money to someone else? I think not. The rich don't *evade* paying taxes, they *avoid* it by using the law in their favor. Poor people call these laws *loopholes*. The rich call them *tax advantages*. I like having an advantage and I bet you do too. Part of your financial *education* should be learning about tax breaks and legal deductions. One of the best things you can do is start your own business or corporation. That way you get to deduct all your expenses before you pay taxes.

Never cheat on your taxes, but do everything you can to lower your tax bill. As soon as you're able to do so, hire a good tax lawyer and accountant. A good one will make you money.

"The avoidance of taxes is the only intellectual pursuit that carries any reward."
—*John Maynard Keynes*

Resources

Further reading on this subject should start with the following books:

Doing Business Tax Free: Perfectly Legal Techniques for Reducing or Eliminating Your Federal Business Taxes by Robert Cooke;

Tax Deductions For Professionals, 4th Edition by Stephen Fishman.

Final Thoughts on Acquiring Capital

This chapter is brief in comparison to what is needed to be known to acquire capital. It's certainly not intended to be exclusive. Only an ignorant fool claims to know everything on a subject. The principles contained in this chapter can be your foundation. They can be expounded on . . . and they work in prison as well as in the free-world. The only difference to being out instead of in would be the availability and access that you personally have to your investments and business.

You are not a slave and nothing should control you, least of all wealth. In prison, time is your luxury. Do not waste it. Begin to learn about wealth and learn to make it your slave. Become a Millionaire Prisoner.

Millionaire Prisoner Prosperity Keys

- Begin to think like the rich and stop thinking like the poor.
- Never lose money.
- Pay yourself first and keep it.
- Use the power of compounding interest to build wealth.
- Never buy on credit and live well below your means.
- Invest in assets and not liabilities, and divide those investments.
- Write out your financial mission statement and commit it to memory.
- Learn to turn ideas into money.
- Own your life. Own everything.
- Use existing laws to lower your tax bill.

DETERMINATION

A diamond is a piece of coal that stuck to the job.
—*Michael Larsen*

Your Time to Shine

The prison hierarchy considers most of us prisoners heaps of coal that will only be consumed in the fire. It's your duty to stick to it, and become the diamond that destiny demands of you. It's your time to shine. You can do it by having determination.

Determination is the engine that keeps you moving in the direction of your *objectives*. It will keep you moving forward when everyone else is telling you that you can't, or won't achieve your goals. Without determination, you will have a hard time accomplishing anything worthwhile in your life.

In 1977, at the age of 18, Dewey Bozella was arrested for a New York murder. But the grand jury returned a no bill because there was no evidence linking Bozella to the murder. Six years later, Bozella was in college when he was rearrested after two convicted felons implicated him. They were released from prison after their testimony helped convict Bozella and he was sentenced to life in prison.

While in prison, Dewey joined the prison boxing program and became the undefeated champ. In 1990 his conviction was overturned because prosecutors excused every juror who wasn't white. He was offered a plea deal for manslaughter where he would be released if he signed a paper saying what happened, but Bozella refused because he was innocent. The case went to the jury and they found him guilty. Back he went to Sing Sing where Bozella worked on getting his *education* and got his Master's Degree. He met Trena Boone in the visiting room when she was visiting her brother and they married in 1996. He was denied parole four times because he wouldn't confess to a crime he didn't commit. Eventually his conviction was overturned when lawyers found new testimony that his original lawyers never saw, and the State declined to retry him because he was innocent.

After his release, Bozella started The Dewey Bozella Foundation which aims to help at-risk kids find a place to box and train. In 2011 he was given the Arthur Ashe Award for Courage at the ESPY's. His dream was to have one fight professionally and Oscar De La Hoya and Golden Boy Productions stepped up to give him that fight. But first he had to pass the examination to get a license to box in California and no one had ever gotten approval at the age of 52 like Dewey was. He was denied the first time but given 30 days to train and try again. Bozella trained at Benard Hopkin's gym in Philadelphia and passed the examination. On October 25, 2011 he won his first and only professional fight. ESPN Films produced a movie, *26 Years: The Dewey Bozella Story*, about his life. In that film you can see Dewey's determination to achieve his dream to have one fight professionally. Bozella's motto is one we can all use: "Never give up!"

That's what it's all about: *never giving up*. Go after your dreams. Don't let anyone tell you that you can't. No matter what may seem like a losing situation, no matter what insurmountable odds are placed before you: Don't ever give up. That is how you'll become the diamond that you are. Only by sticking to it, and never giving up, can you accomplish all that you desire.

Another great example is that of Michael Jordan. Jordan is arguably the greatest professional basketball player ever. But in a story we've all heard many times, he was cut from his high school team. MJ didn't give up. He was determined to be the best. He practiced, and practiced, until he made the team. Eventually, he would hit the game winning shot for North Carolina in the NCAA championship game, and go on to a much-celebrated career in the NBA. Jordan was determined not to let his high school experience define him. He never gave up, and became a diamond, after one coach saw a piece of coal.

These are only two examples from history, but there are a million more for you to read about and find. Every Millionaire Prisoner in these ABCs has used the characteristic of determination and persistence along their journey. When you face your own mountains and obstacles, it's your ability to never give up that will enable you to overcome them.

"When going through hell, keep going. Never, never give in."

—*Winston Churchill*

Overcoming Hills and Mountains

You must keep telling yourself, "I think I can, I think I can." Just like the story from the children's book, *The Little Train That Could*. If you're determined to get up the hill, you'll get up the hill. Don't allow the critics to steer you off track. Don't allow the naysayers to force you to quit. Be determined.

Your hill is the prison you find yourself in. But this is only a temporary setback. There is an African proverb that speaks on the ability to get over obstacles: *The Best way to eat the elephant standing in your path is to cut it up into little pieces.* Prison is the elephant standing in your path. Cut it up into little pieces and overcome it. Then your path will be clear. Only with determination can you get through these times of lockdown and succeed. Adversity, obstacles, hard times, handicaps, and setbacks happen to all of us. They are inevitable. Millionaire Prisoners persevere through trying times. Fire is used to test the strength of gold. Nature uses adversity to test the strength of humans. Do not be found to be lacking in strength or determination.

> *"Adversity causes some to break, while others break records."*
> —*Harvey Mackay*

It's not fate that decides things, but you who determines your own destiny. You set your life's path. Become determined to do what others won't do. An unsuccessful person never begins, or gives up halfway. But you must go the full twelve rounds. You must continue until the bell sounds. In your battles and darkest days, that's when you must continue on. That's when you must persist. Determination will prove to the world that you're great, and worth your weight in gold.

> *"Always bear in mind that your own resolution to succeed is more important than any other thing."*
> —*Abraham Lincoln*

Triumph Over Censorship in Prison

In 1987, Paul Wright entered the Washington State prison system to begin serving a 304-month sentence. In 1988 he met Ed Mead, a prisoner who had been locked down since 1976. They decided to start a newsletter about prison related legal news. On a $50 budget, they launched their first issue in 1990. They each typed 5 pages in their cell and sent it to a friend on the outside who copied it, and published it. Wright and Mead sent that first 10-page edition of *Prison Legal News* to 75 potential subscribers and they were off and running. Ed Mead was released on parole in 1993 and left *PLN* to do his own thing in California. He is now on the board of directors at *California Prison Focus*. Paul Wright continued to put out *Prison Legal News*.

Did Wright encounter obstacles? Sure he did. Prison officials tried to stop *PLN* by shipping Wright around to different prisons, banning bulk mail, and even banning the magazine itself. The first three issues were banned in Washington, and the first 18 in Texas. In 1999, Washington prison officials banned correspondence between prisoners which severely limited Wright's ability to coordinate *PLN*. But that didn't stop him from publishing *PLN* because he was determined to get this information out to subscribers.

Paul Wright was released from prison in 2003 after 16 years. He continues to publish *Prison legal News*, now a 55-page monthly magazine with over 7,000 subscribers in all 50 states and other countries. Did the battles with prison authorities stop once he was released? Hardly so. Prison officials are still trying to keep *PLN* from prisoners, even as *PLN* wins court battle after battle over the censorship of *PLN*. Wright had a vision for *PLN* and used a lot of persistence to see that dream accomplished. If you would like more information on the history of *Prison Legal News* and its numerous court battles, see the May 2010 issue of *PLN*.

Determination has the power to break down walls and barriers. It has the power to turn those walls into weapons and barriers into bridges. In Wright's case, it's breaking down the walls that prison officials try and put up. He's sticking to it and we are grateful. There will be tough roads ahead. In prison there are a multitude of critics. We have the bottom rung of the ladder of life contained behind these walls. Some of these people want you to stay down on the bottom rung with them. They criticize you because they can't. They whine because they won't. They procrastinate because they can't demonstrate. They don't have any determination. Because you're reading this book shows that you don't want to be stuck on the bottom rung of the ladder anymore. One step at a time up the ladder is the easy way to achieving your dreams. Begin your journey right where you are.

Cultivate Determination

Is it possible to do so? Yes. Every one of these ABCs can be learned, cultivated and acquired. The way to cultivate determination is to move forward. Stay away from idle days in prison. All day watching TV will not cultivate determination. All day "kicking the bobos" with the homies will not cultivate determination. There will be days when your body tells you to stay in bed. There will be days your mind tells you to put the book down. When you feel like this, keep going. Your reward is just around the corner. Stick to it and never give up. Move forward one step at a time until it becomes *habit*. In later chapters I will show you how to make these steps easy to accomplish. Just keep moving forward.

> *"Life is like riding a bicycle; you don't fall off unless you stop pedaling."*
>
> —*Claude Pepper*

Diamonds In The Ruff

English author Jeffrey Archer lost his father when 14-years old. At the age of 29 he was a member in the Parliament. By then, Archer was rich and owned an art gallery. He then lost all that in a bad investment deal. At the age of 34 he started writing. He paid off his debts, returned to politics, and became a British Lord. But that isn't the half of it. At the age of 61, Archer was sent to prison for lying about being with a prostitute. He did two years in prison where he wrote a three-volume nonfiction trilogy called, *A Prison Diary*. He finished his 14th novel in 2008.

"You're stuck with what you've got, so get on with it."
— *Jeffrey Archer*

Use determination to get on with it. Stick to your guns and prosper. While others wait on things to happen, you're to make things happen. Allow me to share with you another story about a remarkable prisoner. This political prisoner has mastered these ABCs even though he's never read them. He certainly makes things happen, and is truly an inspiration to me.

Maybe Mumia Abu-Jamal's story should begin at the age of 14 when he became a member of the Black Panther Party? Or maybe when he got his degree from Goddard College, or his Master's from California State University at Dominguez Hills? Still, we could begin his story in his free-world journalistic days, in 1981 when he was elected president of the Philadelphia chapter of the Association of Black Journalists? But it's probably best to begin in December 1981 when he was arrested for killing a police officer, who shot him as he ran to help his brother. Bleeding, Abu-Jamal was left lying in a police wagon for almost a half hour. Once he got to the emergency room he was punched and kicked by police officers. His subsequent trial in 1982 was a gross injustice, where racism in the jury selection process and prosecutorial misconduct ran rampart. The trial judge was overheard saying that he was going to "help fry that nigger." Amnesty International dedicated an entire report to the injustices at his trial. Mumia was sentenced to die and that is where our story of determination begins.

From a cell on Pennsylvania's Death Row, Mumia Abu-Jamal has published many articles, and completed six successful books, including *All Things Censored*, *Live From Death Row*, and *Jailhouse Lawyers: Prisoners Defending Prisoners V. the U.S.A.* He has been interviewed by National Public Radio, and phones weekly commentaries to the Prison Radio Project. Because of his own work as a jailhouse lawyer, Mumia was appointed vice-president representing jailhouse lawyers of the National Lawyers Guild. The people of Paris, France named a street after him, and a movie, *In Prison My Whole Life*, tells the story of his case. Considering that he has been on death row for over a quarter of a century makes these accomplishments remarkable. Taken into account what is about to be revealed, makes these accomplishments legendary.

Abu-Jamal's cell is the size of a small bathroom. He has a typewriter, but the prison commissary jacks the prices of ribbons so high, he must reuse his over and over. This causes the words to be faintly legible on the page for the editor to read. The prison system only allows him to keep seven books in his cell at one time. He has no access to a computer or the internet. Even after prison officials punished him for publishing his work, he refused to stop writing. The censorship of his work went before the 3rd Circuit Court of Appeals who decided the case in his favor. The Court told prison officials that he had a right to publish his work and that they couldn't punish him for doing so. Where others give up, Abu-Jamal sticks to it.

The difference between Abu-Jamal and other prisoners is their *attitude,* daily *habits, knowledge, education,* and *determination.* While others in prison may have more physical tools, such as books, computers, and e-mail, Abu-Jamal does more with less. He has become a bright and shiny key in this dark prison world. As he says, you can become a "legend or a lizard." Certainly, Abu-Jamal is a legend, his story should be an inspiration. From behind prison walls and despite the persecution, he is a success. Abu-Jamal's example is proof that you may achieve success and prosperity if you desire it. Just keep moving forward.

> *"The difference between the impossible and the possible lies in a man's determination."*
> —*Tommy Lasorda*

Don't ever give up, and never, never give in. Be determined that you will achieve your goals, and that you will have a successful life. Defy the odds, the critics, and the statistics. Defy everyone. Become one of the chosen few who produce something great. March to your own beat. You are closer to success than you think. Never, ever give up.

> *"Many of life's failures are people who did not realize how close they were to success when they gave up."*
> —*Thomas Edison*

You're a success, not a failure. You're strong, not weak. Always remember that. The easiest way to never quit is to take it day by day. You only have to carry your burdens one day at a time. You only have to work for one day at a time. Day by day is how you can cut up your prison elephant into little pieces. Be determined. Don't take "no" for an answer. Stick to the job, and become the diamond that you are. *Never give up.*

Energetic Determination

Will power has been called the "supreme court of the mind." Someone called it "energetic determination." But it's so much more than that. If determination keeps you going, then will gives you *the edge*.

This edge controls your *habits*. It can over-ride any pain the body feels. By using *self-control*, you can use the power of the will to accomplish anything you want. It controls who and what you are. I *willed* myself to prison and became a convict with a natural life sentence. That decision was made by my will. It controlled my habits and hand delivered me a one-way ticket for a bus ride to prison.

Where is your will leading you? Is it leading you towards becoming a champ or a chump? Without exercising your will you'll never become the champion that you are.

*"The difference between a successful person and others
is not a lack of strength, not a lack of knowledge, but rather
a lack of will."*

—*Vince Lombardi*

Willpower Embodied

We shall now meet a former prisoner who exercised his will and became a champion in the game of life.

Albert Race Sample, or "Racehoss" as he was known, was born to a prostitute mother. His father was one of her tricks. Growing up he would stand "lookout" for police while his mother serviced her clients and ran a gambling house. He ended up running away from home, using freight trains to crisscross the country. Sample ended up getting into trouble with the law, and to escape *justice*, he went into the military. Once there, he was sent to the stockade for going AWOL.

Two years after Sample went to the military he was sent to prison. He was forced to work in the fields picking cotton. He became the fastest cotton picker, and his bags always weighed the most. That's how he got the nickname "Racehoss." After 8 years inside, he was paroled, but violated his parole for aggravated assault with a deadly weapon. Back in prison, Sample had what he called a "life changing moment" while confined in the hole. He ended up getting an *education* by completing his GED, and teaching himself to type. Because of that he got a job working in the warden's house as the clerk. He was eventually paroled again, with his total sentence being 17 years served.

Sample went to a halfway house for ex-offenders. He began living a law-abiding life and became the first ex-con in Texas to work for the governor by running a program to help ex-offenders stay out of prison. He then became a probation officer, and in 1976 he received a full pardon and restoration of all his civil rights. Read his book, *Racehoss: Big Emma's Boy*, and tell me that you can't succeed. If he can, then all of us can. Racehoss didn't allow himself to give in. His will gave him the power to change and succeed.

How To Develop An Iron Will

Here are six steps that will give you an iron will.

1.Decide on the *objective* that you want to achieve in your life. Then determine what steps are needed to accomplish your goal. Once you find them, take them.

Using the steps in the chapter on *Attitude*, recreate your life into what you want it to be. By using *self-control*, direct the thoughts that reach your subconscious mind. Watch out for any negative influences that keep you from accomplishing your goals. Stop reading irrelevant books or magazines that do not pertain to your major purpose in life.

Be ruthless with your time and those you associate with. If possible, surround yourself with people who encourage and inspire you.

Prepare when others are playing so that you'll have more time to play in the future.

Do not stop until you reach your goal. If you fall down, get back up and try again. If your plan doesn't work, make a new one. Keep doing that until you find one that works.

Finally, develop necessity in your life. Put your back against the wall and succeed at all costs.

By utilizing the above steps, along with the principles contained in the chapters of *attitude* and *self-control*, you can achieve your dreams. These chapters go hand-in-hand with each other. They are intertwined, and when combined with *habit*, give one true power.

It was through his will that Malcolm X read and studied by the dim light coming under his solitary cell door. Because of that will, the world was blessed with the *growth* of a felon into a deliverer.

Felix Dennis was put in prison because the powers-that-be disagreed with one of the magazines he was a partner in. He walked out of prison and vowed never to return. In an act of will he became one of the world's richest men. Not bad for a hippie dropout ex-con.

You can find willpower embodied in every example in these ABCs. If you carefully examine the history books, you'll find that those who have success in life are those with an iron will. They had purpose, put blinders on, and went after their dreams with determination. They never took no for an answer and they succeeded. You can do the same.

If you want to read more about the power of the will, then check out *The Willpower Instinct* by Kelly McGonigal; and *Willpower* by Roy Baumeister and John Tiery.

When it seems like there are no doors or pathways to where you want to go, make them. When it seems like you can't take another step, continue on. Turn your will on and allow it to take over. Allow your heart to lead your will, don't stop until your have the life you want. Awaken the supreme power that you have inside of you.

A Word of Caution

If you choose to start making legitimate moves while in prison you must have the *preparation* for any fallback. Most correctional departments frown on prisoners writing books, starting businesses, and organizing. A lot of these prisons have draconian rules and regulations against this. Some courts have thrown out these archaic rules, but it's best to know your prison's rules beforehand.

I went through a rough period when the final draft of this book was seized by the prison gestapo and I was thrown in segregation. The prison administration felt I was running a business form my cell even though O'Barnett Publishing was my mother's entity. But I was determined to continue on. I took strength from my *knowledge* of the other prisoners who've paved the way for me. You've met some of them already in the likes of Paul Wright and Mumia Abu-Jamal. You'll meet lots more in later chapters. If we've done it you can do it. Make up your mind right now that you'll use all your willpower to stay on the path you've chosen no matter what may come. You can and you will!

Be determined.

Millionaire Prisoner Prosperity Keys

- It's your time to shine. Don't ever give up.
- You can overcome any mountain in your path if you cut it up into little pieces.
- You're in this fight for the long haul and it's not over 'til the bell rings.
- Cultivate determination by moving forward one day at a time, one step at a time.
- Make a decision about what you want out of life and then go get it.
- Be ruthless with your time and those you associate with.
- Have a will to prepare when others are playing so that you can win.
- Combine all of these ABCs with an iron will and you have a recipe for success.

EDUCATION

*One could get a first-class education from a shelf of books five
feet long.*
—Charles Eliot, Former President of Harvard

What actually is education? The dictionary defines it as:
"The action or process of educating or of being educated." To
break it down even further, you must determine what educate
means. Educate has several meanings, but two are perfect for our
ABCs: "To learn by formal instruction and supervised practice,
especially in a skill, trade, or profession"; and "to develop
mentally, morally, or aesthetically, especially by instruction."

*"Education is the most powerful weapon which you can use to
change the world."*
—Nelson Mandela

For the Millionaire Prisoner, there are two kinds of
education. One is formal. You can get a formal education by
going to school, college, university, and/or career school. This is
what most people think of when they come across the word
education. But the second form of education is informal
schooling. You don't have to be in college to get a powerful
education or learn. In this chapter I will briefly deal with both

forms of learning and then you can make a decision about what you need. The one thing that I can say about learning, whether by formal classroom studies, or by informal instruction, is that it has the power to free you from enslavement by ignorance. You'll be surprised at how many doors will be opened for you once you begin educating yourself. This chapter will help you on journey.

"Only the educated are free."

—*Epictetus*

Your Personal Style of Learning

There are four main ways of learning. They are as follows:
1. By reading (books, magazines, newspapers, reports, etc.).
2. By hearing (listening to others, audiobooks, TV, and radio)
3. By watching (television, internet, video, demonstrations, etc.)
4. By doing it or through experience.

It's imperative that you find your optimum learning mode. I can learn through all four modes, but my best is by reading. I prefer to learn by reading because it allows me to experience *growth* faster, and work at my own pace, which is normally quicker than others. I can read all day if I want. One of the strengths of having ADD is that I can over-concentrate on something for a long period of time at the exclusion of everything else. This allows me to read nonstop on a subject I'm interested in and learn in a way that is easiest for me. You need to find your own optimal mode of learning so that you can begin reaching your potential.

One word about the last mode of learning above—*doing it* or *experience*. This option is great if you have a mentor helping you. (More about *The Power of Mentors* in the next chapter) But it's not good if you're trying things on your own without doing any research to see what the *right* way is first. I'll have more to say about this in later chapters, but just remember that you need to put yourself in situations where you learn the fastest, gain the most *knowledge*, and comprehend what you learn so that you can use it in your life.

The Most Basic Way of Education

As listed above there are several ways to educate yourself. In prison, the easiest and most important way is by reading. Most prisoners read. The most *popular* reading material being urban novels, and hip-hop and pornographic magazines. But those are not the most *profitable* periodicals to read. You have to read books and magazines that will help you become a Millionaire Prisoner. Let's look at a couple of prisoners who used reading to become great.

Nelson Mandela became a voracious reader while in prison. He read everything he could get his hands on. He didn't have a television in his cell to pacify him. Mandela also completed his Bachelor's degree through a correspondence course. Once he was released from prison he became president of South Africa. It was by reading in his cell that he educated himself in *preparation* for his future.

It was in a dark, solitary cell, using the light coming under the cell door to read by, that Malcolm Little recreated himself and went from "Detroit Red"—the pimp, to Malcolm X—the revolutionary.

These two examples, Mandela and Malcolm, are arguably two of the most famous, and greatest ex-cons that we can learn from. If they spent time in their cell reading books, why aren't you?

"People don't realize how a man's whole life can be changed by one book."

—Malcolm X

English essayist, historian, biographer, and philosopher Thomas Carlyle explained it best: "If we think about it, all that a university or final highest school can do for us, is still but what the first school began doing—teach us to read. We learn to read in various languages, in various sciences; we learn the alphabet and letters of all manner of books. But the place where we are to get knowledge, even theoretic knowledge is the books themselves. It depends on what we read, after all manners of professors have done their best for us. The true university of these days is a collection of books!"

What to Read?

You can't just read *anything*. Sometimes you might not have a choice in what you read or what you have available. For instance, if you go to segregation, you'll most likely be limited in the books you have access to. But if you're able to choose what you can read, then you should choose non-fiction books. *Not fiction.* Fiction is the lazy way of reading. One of the saddest things I overheard a prisoner say was that he needed a set of Harry Potter books to pass the time. He said that he could occupy his time for a week that way. That will be a wasted week.

When you read only fiction books, you allow someone else to think for you. They become your pacifier. You're looking for an escape from prison, so you use fiction books. If you want success and prosperity, you can't waste time reading Harry

Potter books. Only read them after you become a Millionaire Prisoner.

Instead of the urban novel, read history books. That way you won't repeat it. Learn from the mistakes of others by reading about them. You should read about business if you want to start your own business. Read about how to deal with people because you've only been dealing with thugs, criminals and convicts. Dealing with people will be one of your greatest obstacles upon your release. Any books that will help you better your lot in life are more profitable to you than any fiction book could ever be.

"Biographies of great, but especially of good men, are nevertheless most instructive and useful, as helps, guides and incentives to others."
—Samuel Smiles

Reading should occupy your time more than watching television. TV is mostly negative. It's what the old heads call the pacifier or the stupid box. You must turn off the TV and get into books if you want to achieve your *objectives* in life. You don't have to quit watching TV altogether. But you should abstain from daytime TV, and spend your time watching positive television like history shows, documentaries, and educational programs. Especially if these shows will help you succeed in life.

Read a good newspaper and watch the news. Keep up on what's going on in the world. That way you have a way into every conversation. Plus you'll be able to see problems. If you can solve a few of those problems you'll be on your way to becoming a Millionaire Prisoner.

"No matter how busy you may think you are, you must find time for reading, or surrender yourself to self-chosen ignorance."

— Confucius

An Investment that Pays the Best Interest

Some of you may think that you don't have the money to buy books? That is only an excuse, and excuses are the bricks that make the house a failure. There are numerous books to prisoner projects in the United States, and I've included some of them in the Appendix. They offer free books to prisoners upon request. Write them and request books on the topics you're interested in.

But we've all heard the saying "sacrifices have got to be made." When it comes to money, your education will only be expensive until you consider the cost of ignorance. My ignorance, (yes I was a world-class ignoramus), got me life in prison. The cost was immeasurable. You must get the most out of your money. Why pay $10 for an urban novel that will bring you only temporary satisfaction? Instead, you could use that same $10 and buy a business book that will help you make thousands of dollars. My whole financial future changed because I answered a small classified ad that said *How To Get Rich In Mail Order*. In response to my inquiry I was given the opportunity to purchase a book for $26 that would tell me how to make money in mail order . . . that $26 invested has already produced way more in return because of one idea I got out of that book. I will gladly pay $26 for a book that will help me make thousands of dollars. A lot of the books listed throughout these ABCs will help you do just that. Begin investing in them.

MIKE ENEMIGO & JOSHUA KRUGER

"If a man empties his purse into his head, no man can take it away from him. An investment in knowledge always pays the best interest."

—*Benjamin Franklin*

In *Jailhouse Lawyers: Prisoners Defending Prisoners v. the U.S.A.*, Mumia Abu-Jamal tells the story of Warren Henderson. Henderson came to prison barely able to read. But he learned by teaching himself, and became a book lover. After being released and rearrested, he ended up being charged in a jailhouse murder where the state used a plethora of snitch testimony. Henderson made a decision to represent himself at his trial. The jury was out six hours before they returned a verdict of not guilty. How could Henderson, a prisoner with no GED, no college education, and no law degree, successfully represent himself in a murder trial? He did it because the interest on his book reading paid off. As Abu-Jamal reports, Henderson has gone on to write his own books, including *City of Nightmares: BQ477S*. Proof that the best education is not a college or university, but a shelf of books.

There are other prisoners whose educational investment has paid off. Judge Greg Mathis served nine months in jail for carrying a gun. Once released, he got his GED and went to college and became a lawyer. After five years of no arrests he got his record expunged and then became a judge. He now runs the PEER program in Detroit, Michigan. PEER stands for Prisoners Educated for Empowerment and Respect. The PEER program gives ex-cons an opportunity to make something of their lives upon release. Judge Mathis continues to go back to prisons across America and speak. He advised that prisoners take incremental steps towards success. Anyone wishing to learn more about PEER should go to Judge Mathis' website *AskJudgeMathis.com*. In an interview with Larry King, Mathis said that education saved him. It can save you too.

In the last chapter you read about Dewey Bozella. He finished his education in prison by getting his Master's Degree.

In the *Baggage* chapter, you read about Dan Manville, co-author of the *Prisoners' Self-Help Litigation Manual*. He holds four degrees and is a successful lawyer. More proof that education is the key.

Jamal Joseph was a 15-year old straight-A student who joined the Black Panthers. He eventually went to prison for aiding an FBI fugitive. While inside at Leavenworth Federal Prison, Joseph earned his college degree, and began writing and directing plays for other prisoners. Today he is a film professor at Columbia University and author of *Panther Baby: A Life of Rebellion & Reinvention*.

Another ex-convict turned Columbia University professor was author and scholar, Frank Tannenbaum. Education is the key that opens the doors of Ivy League universities. It could open doors for you also.

Where Do You Start?

Any prisoner trying to advance their education should own a good dictionary. You want a dictionary that:
breaks down the word by pronunciation;
tells you the origin of the word;
tells you the root word;
uses the word in a sentence as an example.
Recommended are *Merriam-Webster's Collegiate Dictionary*, or the *American Heritage Dictionary*.

In your reading, as you come across words you don't know, write them down so that you can look them up later. Or look them up immediately, whatever is best for you. This will enable you to experience *growth* in your vocabulary and understanding. Malcolm X studied the dictionary page by page and many other prisoners have done the same. A good dictionary is the foundation to a great education.

A World Almanac, and a thesaurus are great reference tools as well. If you're reading and come across a country or city that you've never heard of, you can look it up in the almanac and get all the vital information. Sometimes in your writing, the word you used just doesn't sound right. With a thesaurus, you can look up the word to find similar words that might sound better. *Roget's Thesaurus, 3rd Edition* is a great thesaurus.

Most of these books can be obtained from bargain bookstores and catalogs for pretty cheap prices. They can also be obtained from the Books to Prisoners projects listed in the Appendix.

How To Get the Lowest Price For Any Book

You'll need to enlist someone from your *network*, but you can find used books online with *Amazon.com* and *Half.com*. My favorite website is *www.BookFinder4U.com*. Book Finder allows you to search over 100 bookstores and 60,000 individual booksellers in a single search. They also have over 90 million used and out-of-print books in their database. All you have to do is have them type the book and author name into Book Finder, then click on "Compare Prices." They will give the best price online.

Also have them check out *AbeBooks.com*. Abe Books has over 100 million books being sold by over 13,000 booksellers around the world. You can use it to find rare books.

Some companies tout Amazon as the best bookseller in the world. But always check elsewhere. Sometimes the biggest isn't always the best when it comes to price. I found books for $1 plus shipping, and even a penny plus shipping. Utilize the web to get the lowest price available. If you don't have anyone in your *network* to assist you, then utilize *Inmate Book Service*. They'll search for the best price of up to eight books at a time and don't charge astronomical fees for orders. But make sure you do the math, it still could be cheaper to order the book from Edward R. Hamilton once you add up all the fees.

Your mind is the only weapon that you're born with. Use it, shape it, hone it, and strengthen it. Don't be caught unarmed. You should learn whenever and wherever lessons are being taught. But the key isn't to just read non-fiction books. You have to read them in a way that allows you to get the most from them.

The Art of Reading Non-Fiction

A sign of ignorance is to take credit for ideas that aren't of our own creation. I've participated in this folly every once in a while. But in this book, I've tried to give credit where credit is due. I first learned about this system of reading from Zig Ziglar and his book *Secrets of Closing the Sale*. I had the opportunity to ask Zig about his system, and he further clarified it for me. His thoughts have been incorporated into mine. Because it has been most profitable to me, and I've yet to find a better system, I include it here for your benefit. Try it out for yourself with these five steps:

1.Read through the book quickly to get the gist of the message, underlining or highlighting the things that really "grab" you. Only stop to look up words you don't know, or write them down to look up later. This first reading allows you to become familiar with the book. For those prisoners who don't have access to highlighters, I advise you to use a ruler or a bookmark with a straight edge when underlining, as this will keep your book from being sloppily marked up.

2.As you read the book the second time, keep a notebook of ideas generated by the book that you can personally use. The *objective* is not to see how quickly you can *get out* of the book, but what *you can get out* of the book.

3. In your third reading, invest time and patience in gleaning additional ideas you may have missed in your second reading. A careful examination of each chapter is warranted. Go over what you have highlighted or underlined. Determine if you have captured the essence of the author's words, and if you can apply it to your life. Put anything you missed in your notebook.

4. The fourth reading enables the book to become an integral part of you, enhancing your effectiveness. After this reading, you can place the book in your collection, and it will be a treasure trove, ready and willing to supply you with any knowledge you may need.

5. Find people who have read the book, or share it with them, and then discuss the book together to see what you got out of it. You may gain additional insights from their ideas and thoughts that you didn't see on your own.

"Some books are to be tasted, others to be swallowed, and some few to be chewed and digested."
— *Francis Bacon*

A word of caution. If you are reading someone else's book, or one on loan from the library, do not dog-ear the pages, or write or highlight in the book. Nothing is more irritating than to loan a book out, only to have it come back with dog-eared pages and someone else's notes and highlighting in it. That may cause someone to stop loaning you books. There goes your investment. Respect books and their owners, and you'll get a great education from them. By using the above system, you can make the most of your time in reading so that its
most profitable to you.

"A reading program should be as carefully planned as a daily diet, for knowledge, too, is food, without which we cannot grow mentally.

— Andrew Carnegie

Read the Relevant

You should study everything you can on the particular field or business you plan on entering. What do you want out of life? What do you want to be? What are your *objectives*? Some of you want to be music producers and/or own a record label. Then you should read anything you can get your hands on about the music business. Two good books to start with are *Start & Run Your Own Record Label, Expanded Edition* by Daylle Deanna Schwartz; and *How To Build A Small Budget Recording Studio From Scratch, Fourth Edition,* by M. Shea and F.A. Everest.

Some of you want to be writers. Then you should read anything you can on or about the craft of writing. For more on writing see the *Ways & Means* chapter later in this book. But what I'm saying is that you should only read the subjects relevant to your goals in life. Do not waste time reading irrelevant books and magazines. Select the books and magazines that can pay the best interest on your investment of time.

Prisoners love magazines, I certainly do. Here are the top 10 magazines for the success minded prisoner:

1. *Success!*
2. *Entrepreneur*
3. *Inc.*
4. *Black Enterprise*
5. *Home Business*
6. *Forbes*
7. *Business Week*

8. *Hispanic Business*
9. *The Economist*
10. *Smart Money*

Have your family and friends check for the lowest price for any magazine you want at *MagazinePriceSearch.com*. Also, write the magazine vendors listed in Appendix A and get their price quotes so you can compare prices. My favorite mag vendor is Inmate Magazine Service. I can get *Inc., Entrepreneur, Black Enterprise, Wired,* and *Fast Company* all for $20. Yes, that's yearly subscriptions to all five mags at once for $20. Check them out.

How to Read Magazines and Newspapers Faster and Better

Like most of the prisoners I spoke to, most of the time I only learn a few things from each magazine issue. Over the years I've seen many different theories and tactics about how to conquer a newspaper or magazine and get the most out of it in the least amount of time. Here is one of them that I've found to be most profitable and productive.

1. Go through the whole newspaper or magazine quickly. Just scan the headlines. As you do this, make a note of the articles you want to read. Pay attention to where the articles are located and to where they are continued at.

2. Have a goal about what you're trying to get out of the material. Stick to that goal. Don't just read to read.

3. Read the articles you noticed or marked when you did your previous scanning.

4. Cut out any articles, photographs, and or comics that may be of use to you later on. Save these items. In the chapters on *Imagination* and *Network* you will see how these items can be of use to you. (If you share your magazines and newspapers with

other prisoners then you will have to wait to perform this step until they're done with them.)

5. Throw out the rest of the newspaper or magazine as soon as possible. Extract the gold from the mine, but get rid of the waste.

If you follow the above steps you will conquer more magazines and newspapers in a shorter period of time. You also won't be filling your mind or cell with useless junk. One prisoner that I taught this trick to went so far as to make Saturday his "magazine day." Throughout the week, he just scanned every magazine or newspaper he got using the above steps. Except he didn't read the articles, he put them in a folder. On Saturday, he reads all the articles that he has saved up over the week. That way, his week is free and he can pursue more important studies.

No matter what you choose to do, do not spend all day reading a newspaper or magazine. Use the steps above and knock them out. These steps have also been proven to increase your comprehension levels as well. You'll retain much more *knowledge* than before.

Last, but not least, unless you're a copywriter or an adman, don't worry about the ads. They are filler fodder and can't help you become a Millionaire Prisoner. Plus you're in prison, what good is a new car or special at Burger King to you? Save your time for meaty reading, mass market mags and newspapers are just the dessert.

How To Enroll In College

Up to this point I've mostly dealt with getting an informal education through non-fiction books and magazines. But some of you may need a formal degree for your chosen profession? A lawyer needs a law degree. A doctor needs a medical degree. A personal trainer needs certification. A paralegal needs a certificate or Associate's Degree. How do you begin this while in prison?

Start by taking any classes that your prison has to offer. If you don't have your GED or high school diploma, get it. If you have your GED, then enroll in college classes. Some prisons still offer them. Others have special college programs that you can enroll in.

The Education Justice Project (EJP) provides higher-level college courses at the Danville Correctional Center in Illinois. The project was co-founded in 2006 by University of Illinois landscape architecture professor Rebecca Ginsburg. She had previous experience working with prisoners at San Quentin while a graduate student in California. The ultimate goal of EJP is to make the case for providing higher education to prisoners. EJP is funded by grants and private donations and is a worthy cause that you may want to consider donating to. For more about EJP, check out their website: *www.educationjustice.net/home* or email Professor Ginsburg at *rginsbur@illinois.edu*.

If your prison offers a program like the one above, enroll in it. If you don't have college classes at your prison then you should enroll in correspondence courses. Remember that Mandela did it. If you must go the correspondence course route, then I highly recommend Dr. Jon Marc Taylor's masterpiece, *Prisoners' Guerilla Handbook to Correspondence Programs in the U.S. and Canada (3rd Edition)* (available from PLN). Taylor is a prisoner who got his B.S., M.A., and Ph.D. all through correspondence while in prison. He is definitely an expert on getting an education by mail. His book gives you the schools that offer correspondence courses for prisoners, ones that you don't need internet access for, and plenty of tips about getting a college degree through snail mail all based on his experience.

Two other books that you might want to read are: *College In Prison* by Bruce Michaels; and *Bears' Guide to Earning Degrees by Distance Learning.* Some of you will not be able to obtain these books right away and may want to start right now. Here are the steps you should take:

1. Get your GED or high school diploma. If you already have it you'll need copies of your transcripts to show the school you plan on enrolling in.

2. Define what level of college you're interested in. This should be based on what you want to do with your life. For instance, "paralegal," "small business," "religious," etc. Some schools even offer classes in "Hip-Hop." So pick something you're interested in.

3. The U.S. Department of Education provides a helpful 60-page booklet *Take Charge of Your Future: Get the Education and Training You Need.* Write them and request a copy of it. (See Appendix for address)

4. Write the schools and contacts listed in the Appendix under *Education Resources* for further information. Request their brochures, course catalogs, and enrollment guidelines.

5. Read all the relevant information that you get from the schools and educational offices.

6. Pick a school and curriculum that fits the *objective* for your life. Don't go to school just to go to school. *Have a plan and a purpose!*

7. Make sure that the school is accredited by the DETC and regional accreditor. All the schools listed in the Appendix are legit. But there are many who aren't. Check them out first.

8. Set up a program with your prison's education department for approval if need be. If your prison doesn't offer college courses your biggest hurdle will be the end-of-course proctored exams that most correspondence courses require. See if the GED teacher

or chaplain at your prison will allow you to take the tests in front of them.

9. Get funding and enroll (more about funding in a minute).
10. Complete all your course work on time and always be respectful to your teachers. Remember, they are there to help you.
11. Keep repeating steps 6 through 10 until you have the degree or certificate you want.

Once you complete your first few courses you can begin to develop your own system of study. Be sure to save all your correspondence with your school, teacher, and examiner. Save all transcripts and diplomas/certificates that you obtain. You may want to transfer your credits, show a foundation of your schoolwork, or need it for a future employer.

Since a legitimate degree by mail will cost you thousands of dollars, funding your education may be the hardest part to obtaining a formal education while in prison. It's not impossible to get, and as proof, allow me to share with you the story of Troy Evans.

How To Get Free Money For College

Troy Evans spent seven years locked up in a federal gulag. He wanted to get a college education so that his time behind bars wouldn't be wasted. Unfortunately for him, around that time, Congress cut Federal Pell grants for prisoners. Did Troy let that stop him? No, he set out to obtain scholarships, grants, and foundation assistance. It took him six months of filling out applications, writing essays, begging, pleading, and selling, before he landed a scholarship for one class. That was his start, and he walked out of prison with not one, but two degrees, and a 4.0 GPA, and designation on both the Dean's and President's list. Troy is now a professional speaker and author, and took time to share some ways to obtain free money for school with me, and I present them to you.

Your first attempts should be through the school or university you have chosen to attend via correspondence. Most institutions will offer some type of scholarship program and/or package through an alumni association, a foundation or a scholarship group.

Next, apply for federal and state aid. Even though prisoners do not qualify for either, most scholarships require that you exhaust those possibilities first before seeking their help. If you sent off for the *Take Charge of Your Future: Get the Education and Training You Need* booklet you'll get additional resources to try. (You did send for this booklet right?)

Get a list from your state's Department of Commerce of all the civic and service clubs in the area. For example, Kiwanis, Rotary Club, Lions, Elks, etc. Also try and get one from the state your school is located in. Contact each group individually. Sometimes they offer money for "hard luck" cases such as prisoners.

Write any nonprofit, social work, and any association involved with helping others in your area. Contact churches and religious organizations within your area. Ask them to help you in your quest for an education.

Look into private scholarships. Troy says these will be your bread and butter in the future. There are scholarships based on every criterion you can think of, and there are several great books on scholarships out there. Three are: Peterson's *Scholarships, Grants, and Prizes*; Daniel Jo Cassidy's *Scholarships, Grants, and Loans*; and *The Ultimate Scholarship Book 2013: Billions of Dollars in Scholarships, Grants and Prizes* by Gen & Kelly Tanabe.

Lastly, you'll need to research public and private foundations, and trusts. These places must give away money for all kinds of things in order to keep their tax-exempt status. For more information on these resources, see: *Foundation Grants to Individuals*, published by the Foundation Center. It will give you the complete contact information, and the criteria for applying for a foundation grant. (Because I was curious, I reviewed the book to see how many foundations and trust I could possibly apply to if I wanted to go to school. I found over 50 of them. These places are out there if you know where to look!)

You must learn how to write essays correctly. Most scholarships are going to require that you write them showing why you deserve the scholarship. Also, in any classes that you're able to get into, do your best. You must be able to show people that their money is going to a worthy investment.

That is the basic outline that was gleaned from Troy. For more information about Troy and his life, have someone check out his website: *www.TroyEvans.com*, or read his book, *From Desperation to Dedication: An Ex-Con's Lessons on Turning Failure Into Success*.

"There is absolutely no reason why you cannot secure funding for your education while incarcerated. It is only a matter of beating the bushes. The money is there, but the effort has to be there to make it happen. If you're serious about obtaining an education via correspondence while incarcerated, I'm living proof it can happen; you only need to want it bad enough."

—*Troy Evans*

Do you want it bad enough? You should, because it's your key to a better life.

Millionaire Prisoner Case Study

In 1987, at the age of 23, Michael Santos was arrested for distributing cocaine under the "Kingpin" statute. Sentenced to

45 years in federal prison, he made the choice to accept responsibility for his actions and to use his time as a stepping-stone. Taking a lesson from Malcolm X, he used flash cards to learn new words and increase his vocabulary. Through correspondence courses he received a Bachelor's degree from Mercer University and a Master's from Hofstra. He began corresponding with professors and wrote two books, *About Prison*, and *Profiles From Prison*, which are used as supplemental textbooks for students in colleges across America. He also made over $100,000 on the stock market from behind bars, buying internet stocks like yahoo and AOL.

Santos built a free-world support group and started a *network* portfolio. In his portfolio, he set clearly defined goals and detailed his progress by sending out quarterly reports every 90 days. He did this not to manipulate his people but for accountability purposes. He started his own website and would send his handwritten pages home to his wife who would type it up and post it online. That was the same process he used for his books, and one of his books, *Inside: Life Behind Bars in America*, was published by a major publishing house. Before his release in 2012, Santos started a non-profit organization: The Michael G. Santos Foundation, to help at-risk youth and prisoners. His latest book, *Earning Freedom: Conquering A 45-Year Prison Term* is a must-read for all Beginning Millionaire Prisoners (BMPs). It illustrates what is possible once a prisoner sets his mind to something. Have your family and friends check out his website at: *www.MichaelSantos.com*.

Informal Education

Some of you don't need a formal education like a degree to be successful in your chosen profession. That doesn't mean you should stop seeking to educate yourself about life, business, and the art of living. Learn to use what you learn in everyday life, and apply it to make your situation better. You can get a great education from books, even if it's an informal one.

"The main part of intellectual education is not the acquisition of facts but learning how to make facts live."
—*Oliver Wendell Holmes*

Education is the key to all success. In October 2009, Northeastern University released a report detailing the effects of dropping out of high school. That report, *The Consequences of Dropping Out of High School*, listed some important facts that prisoners should consider. Northeastern reported that 54% of all dropouts were unemployed in 2008. That dropouts were 63 times higher to be in prison than a four-year college graduate. In 2007, the average annual earnings for a dropout was $8,358. This report shows the importance of education, because you can't do much on eight grand a year.

Get your GED while you're inside. Learn a trade. Enroll in correspondence courses. Read non-fiction books. Educate yourself so that you can free yourself from the bondage of prison.

"I think education is the key to anything you wanna do."
—*Danny Trejo*

Those of us who would have educated ourselves before we came to prison most likely would not have had to experience the pain of prison. The mind is truly a terrible thing to waste. There are only two places you can read all day. One is in school, the other is in prison. Make your prison your school. To get something you've never had, you've got to do something you've never done. For most of us that means getting an education, whether formal or informal.

Audio Books

One of the most underused weapons are audiobooks. Music by Mail offers a whole section of books on CD. If your prison allows you to have CD's you should invest in that opportunity. Audiobooks offer advantages over traditional books. You can listen to an audiobook while working out, watching a game, or cleaning your cell. You can push play as you go to sleep and allow your subconscious mind to pick up your education for you. Learning another language is easier using an audiobook. Remember that non-fiction books offer the best return on your investment. Utilize this tool and watch your profit margin soar. An audiobook can be one more avenue to assist you in turning your cell into an university.

How To Turn Your Cell Into a Classroom or Cell-Office

Prison is not an ideal place to study. The typical prison cell is the size of a small bathroom and must be shared by two prisoners in most cases. But to become a Millionaire Prisoner you must commit yourself to *daily* study. Here are some tips that will aid you in creating the best learning environment out of your cell.

1.*Light*. Prison can be a dreary place, but the best light to study by is daylight. So place your desk or chair by the window if you can. If that's not possible, the light should come over the shoulder opposite of your writing hand. As most prisoner artists already know, this takes away shadow. Do not beam your desk lamp directly on your book or magazine. That creates a contrast in the cell and can be distracting. You want the light to seem as natural as possible.

2. *Preparation.* Make sure that you have all of your study materials and tools within reach before you start. You don't want to interrupt yourself by having to get up to search for something after you've already started.

3. *Posture.* Don't get *too* comfortable, and don't lie down to read. Your desk or table should be set up so that your thighs are parallel with the floor. Keep your feet flat on the floor, back upright. If you want, you may find it more comfortable to hold your reading material in your hands.

4. *Space.* Keep your material spread out so that you have room to work. I turn the bottom bunk in my cell into a desk. Some experts say the material you're working on should be kept approximately 20 inches away from your eyes. A lot of prisoners get strained eyes or headaches after reading for long periods of time. Keeping your material at this distance should help with that problem.

5. *Time.* Try to pick a time when you will not be interrupted by outside influences. In prison, this sometimes means staying up at night when the prison is quiet, or skipping yard so you can study and be alone. I have ADD and I've found that working with headphones on helps me. The music tunes out all the jailhouse jibber-jabber. Keeps out all distractions. One more thing on time: whatever time you pick, stick to it. That's your study time every day. Make it a *habit*.

Learning doesn't have to be hard or difficult. By turning your cell into a classroom you can rise to a level of study never thought possible. Even if you aren't going to school the above tips are useful. I follow them when I set up my cell-office. Do the same. Millionaire Prisoners learn, and learners become earners!

"You are subject to your environment. Therefore, select the environment that will best develop you toward your desired objective."

—W. Clement Stone

You must arm yourself. Do it by reading and educating yourself. Your wealth, your freedom, and other material possessions can all be taken from you. What is in your mind can never by taken. Only the educated are free. Never stop learning. Turn your cell into your school.

"In this world, where the game is played with loaded dice, a man must have a temper of iron, with armor proof to the blows of fate, and weapons to make his way against men."

—Arthur Schopenhauer

Millionaire Prisoner Prosperity Keys

• The most basic way to get an education is to read non-fiction books.
• If you spend your money on good books you'll get the best return on your investment.
• The easiest place to start is a good dictionary.
• Read only the books and magazines that are relevant to what you want to do in life.
• Turn your prison into a university by utilizing books, audiobooks, and correspondence courses.
• Learn to create a productive environment out of your cell.
• Never stop learning.

FAVOR

One day of favor is worth a thousand days of labor.
— Dr. Mike Murdock

Someone once told me: "If the king likes you, it doesn't matter who dislikes you." It sounded cool, so I wrote it down. Later, it dawned on me that he was talking about favor.

Definition of Favor

Favor has been defined as being friendly to another; especially in regards to a superior towards some of lesser standing. Without favor from others it will be impossible for you to become a Millionaire Prisoner.

You receive favor in small things as well as large ones. When you're hired to do a job, someone is showing you favor. When someone gives you a gift, they are showing you favor. When your collect call is accepted, the person on the other end of the line is showing you favor. Anytime someone does something that helps you, they are showing you favor. But this favor is not "favors," as in the exchange of gifts. With *favor*, there is no debt. In this chapter I'll show you some examples of prisoners receiving favor, and how you can cultivate favor in your own life. Right now, let's look at a few examples of favor so that you can understand its power.

Millionaire Prisoner Case Study

Allen Iverson is a well-known professional basketball player among prisoners. He has an *attitude* that prisoners relate to because he came from the street. A lot of prisoners don't know that Iverson was once a product of the system himself. He went to prison as a teenager for a bowling alley brawl in his hometown in Virginia. While in prison, the governor pardoned him after an outcry of community support. Because of his ability to play basketball, he was given a scholarship by Coach John Thompson to play ball at Georgetown University. Later, he would be selected by the Philadelphia 76ers in the NBA draft and see himself winning the NBA's Most Valuable Player award. If you look at Iverson's life you can see three huge doses of favor evident. The first was the governor's pardon. The second was the scholarship to play basketball at Georgetown. The third was the 76ers selecting him with their first pick in the draft. These are the steps that propelled him to become a multi-millionaire. All because of favor.

When Dewey Bozella needed a trainer to help him get ready to pass the boxing license examination, he was shown favor by Bernard Hopkins and trained at Hopkins' gym in Philadelphia. That little act of favor helped get Bozella his license and go on to win his first professional fight at the age of 52. But it was Bob Jackson, a correctional officer at Sing Sing, who showed all the prisoners favor in 1985 when he started the prison boxing program that Bozella got his start in. It's the little things that count.

In 1949, the *Presidio*, a now defunct Fort Madison, Iowa prison newspaper, profiled lifer Ole Lindquist. Once his story hit mainstream news media, he received hundreds of Christmas cards and letters from people from all across the country. These new supporters asked the governor to release him on parole. That request was eventually granted 3 years later. Lindquist went from prison lifer to having an outside life again, all because of favor.

A Little Act of Favor

During the writing of this book, I was confined to the segregation cellblock of my prison. Because of my seg status, I was not permitted access to my television, typewriter, books, or most of my property. Without my typewriter, I was forced to write chapters of this book using 4-inch security flex pens. It became a problem because I was only allowed to buy two pens from the commissary each month, and of course, those two pens never lasted me the whole month.

One morning, I was discussing this problem with my neighbor, Slick, a Mexican prisoner who was interested in my work and changing his life for the better. After hearing my problem, Slick reached his hand out between the bars that separated us, and gave me two new pens so I could work on these ABCs. I tried to reimburse him for the pens, but he refused. He only wanted to show me favor. He was in a position to help and did so.

Why did Slick do this? My belief is that I cultivated favor by a few things I did. Previously, I had shared parts of these ABCs with him, and discussed topics and ideas with him. He was receptive, and wanted me to finish the book, just as much as I did. The seed was planted in Slick's mind that this book was for prisoners, which he is, so it was beneficial for him to help me. This is one of the keys to favor. If someone sees you working on a worthy cause, or something they believe in, they will assist you on your journey.

This incident of favor was minor. It was just two pens. But those two pens helped me finish two chapters. Slick saved me time because I didn't have to wait another month until I could buy pens from the commissary. Always remember that the little things in life have the ability to become big things.

Old Time Favor

In the 1930s, prisoner William 'Ole Wooden Ear" Sadler began a newsletter called *The Angola Argus* based on the daily happenings at the Louisiana State Prison at Angola. He would be released from prison and write a series of articles for the *New Orleans Item* called "Hell on Angola." His articles shed light on the brutal conditions of the prison and helped bring some reforms. While he was away form prison, *The Angola Argus* was neglected and died. Sadler returned to prison in the 1950s and was established as the first editor of *The Angolite*, the prison newspaper that had been started by Director of Institutions, Dr. Edward Grant, and Angola Warden, Maurice Sigler. Because of his work as editor of *The Angolite*, Director Grant requested that then governor, Robert F. Kennon, pardon Ole Wooden Ear. That request was granted and Sadler was paroled in 1958.

In 1918, Huddie "Leadbelly" Ledbetter was sent to the Texas State Penitentiary for murder. He used a guitar and sang the blues to earn a pardon from then governor Pat Neff in 1925. He ended up in Angola in the 1930s as well. Back in prison for assault with intent to murder, Leadbelly once again used his musical talents to be pardoned by then governor, O.K. Allen. Ledbetter wrote the song "Goodnight Irene," which was performed by The Weavers and sold two million copies.

Notice that these two old cons used talents they had to put themselves in a position to receive favor. Yes, it was a different climate regarding pardons back then, but that doesn't mean you should quit trying to put your talents to work, or put yourself in a position to be recognized. One thing is for sure, you can't get the type of favor these cons got by being in seg or the hole.

Finding Favorable Mentorship

In 2007, I began a writing campaign in which I wrote to all the authors of whose books I read in researching these ABCs. I wrote them telling them how their book had helped me, and that I was writing my own book for prisoners. Notice that I was telling the truth. This was not some form of jailhouse game. Their books had in fact, changed my life, and the way I thought, and I wanted to share this with them.

Did I expect responses? Not really. But I was hoping that someone I admired would validate my journey by giving me a reply. We all need a pat on the back every once in a while. A few authors did write me back. I'll share a couple of responses here because they demonstrate favor.

Harvey Mackay is the CEO of Mackay Mitchell Envelope Company in Minnesota. Harvey has written numerous books, authors a syndicated column in many newspapers and on the internet. My first encounter with one of Harvey's books was after my mother picked it up for me at a garage sale. That book, *Swim With The Sharks Without Being Eaten Alive*, was my first real look at another way of thinking about life. *Sharks* is a business book, but it contains principles for succeeding in life in general. Harvey did a wonderful job on *Sharks*, and you must read it if you can.

After finishing his book for the second time, I wrote Harvey and explained how his book had affected my life. What happened? Not only did Harvey write back, but he sent me two other books that he wrote, free of charge. One of these books, *Dig*

Your Well Before Your Thirsty, greatly influenced the thinking behind the chapter on *Network* in these ABCs. Harvey showed me favor, and through his books has mentored me about life and becoming successful.

Another author who showed me favor was a motivational speaker, Zig Ziglar. Zig wrote me back and sent me a copy of his autobiography: *Zig*. He is an inspiration to me, and his books *Top Performance* and *Secrets of Closing the Sale* have helped me on my journey. His autobiography was a great read, and showed me that by helping others get what they want out of life, my prosperity would be given to me. Zig showed me favor, and through his books has mentored me about helping others. It's with deep sadness that I must tell you that Zig passed away at the end of 2012. But his family is continuing on the Ziglar mission and I will also try to hold the standard that he taught me.

Harvey Mackay and Zig Ziglar didn't have to send me anything. But both of them understood that when you're on top, helping someone else up the ladder of success is the right thing to do.

> *"Favor must become your seed, before it can become your harvest."*
>
> —Dr. Mike Murdock

The Power of Mentors

Real estate and *marketing* guru, Robert Allen, says that your income is the average income of your 10 best friends. That's certainly not good if you're only hanging around and talking to your prisoner friends. You need to seek out free-world mentors who are already successful doing what you want to do. This way you can gain a higher perspective and *attitude* than what your prisoner peers offer.

And a mentor is someone who is more experienced than you, someone that could provide insight and guidance. They can help you make connections. I have already explained how Harvey Mackay and Zig Ziglar have mentored me. Before I even wrote them letters they were my coaches in the game of life through their books. When you have a mentor they are bestowing on you their *knowledge*, experience, and wisdom. They are showing you favor.

Dan Manville was mentored by the ACLU's Prison Project during his internship there. Allen Iverson was mentored by Coach John Thompson during his time at Georgetown University. Michael Santos was mentored by Dr. R. Bruce McPherson, Dr. George Cole, and other Professors while in prison. Seek out positive mentors. Do it by letter, email, phone, or in person.

If you're writing them you can say: "I've read great things about you and admire you. I am trying to learn more about (whatever it is you're trying to learn), and would love for you to be my mentor. I would like to know what you've learned, and I'm not out to get what you've earned." (See Appendix C for a complete sample letter.)

How to Get the Most Out of a Mentorship

Here are a few things that you can do to make it a profitable relationship:

1. Choose the right mentor. If you want to be a writer, you don't seek out someone who builds motorcycles for a living. You want someone that's successful in your chosen vocation.

2. Be honest with yourself and your mentor about what is happening. Seek to understand what your mentor has to offer, and what you hope to gain. Discuss this with your mentor, if possible.

3. Be open-minded and humble. Don't allow what you think you know to stop you from learning what you need to know. Don't brag about who's mentoring you to other prisoners either.

4. Have a hunger for learning. Always ask questions. Your mentor will not get mad or upset if they see that you're honestly trying to learn. Become a protégé, not a parasite. You want what's in their head, not anything they could hand out. If you ask the right questions, you'll get the right answers.

Having a mentor will save you time and money. They should show you the errors in your ways and help you excel. One day you'll be able to show them how much their help aided you on your journey. That will be the ultimate compliment.

Cultivating Favor

But favor is not just limited to your mentors. Because you can receive favor from anyone you need to follow a few steps in your everyday life to assist you.

First, always be respectful to those who have the power to bless you. Especially those in higher positions than you.

Second, be ready to accept the responsibilities that others ask of you. If someone asks for help, help them. Do this without expecting any form of payment from them. The Universe will pay you in kind for all that you do for others.

Third, you must always prepare yourself when your time comes. Make your first impression a great impression.

Let me share with you a few more examples of how prisoners cultivated favor. I found this story on the front page of the *USA Today* newspaper. James Church spent 10 years in prison for armed robbery in Michigan. Lt. Ralph Mason told him that if he could stay out of trouble, he would help him find a job. Churchill did just that and Mason helped him get a job at an industrial plumbing company making $21 an hour upon his release.

In the same *USA Today* article, it was reported that Andres Idarraga spent six years in prison for cocaine and weapons charges. He approached A.T. Wall, the Director of Corrections in Rhode Island, for a letter of recommendation to Yale Law School. Idarraga had earned high grades at the University of Rhode Island and Brown upon release from prison. After a series of breakfast meetings, Mr. Wall, who is a graduate of Yale, decided to write the letter. That letter opened the door for Idarraga, and as I write this, he's in law school at Yale.

Both of the above former prisoners experienced the power of favor. Churchill received his from a police officer, and Idarraga got his from the director of the prison system. Sometimes in life you need help from unexpected sources. If you put yourself in the right position, you may get the letter of recommendation that you need.

Brian Hamilton knows firsthand the plight of a prisoner having had a cousin who died inside. Once the owner of his own landscaping business, Hamilton is now CEO of Sageworks, Inc., a computer company that develops software for financial professionals and small businesses. In 2008, Hamilton founded *Inmates to Entrepreneurs*, a community outreach program that teaches prisoners how to start productive, low *capital* service businesses upon release. The key to the program is the goal of connecting released prisoners with mentors who can assist them.

Former prisoner Lawrence Carpenter did time for dealing drugs and armed robbery. Now he runs his own janitor service company that has 53 employees and provides services for businesses in several states. In 2010, Carpenter and Brian Hamilton went to the Eastern Correctional Institution in North Carolina to give a two-hour course on starting a business. They may be coming to a prison near you in the future. If they do, sign up. But you don't have to wait for someone to show up at your prison to get a mentor. Seek them out by letter, email, and through the books you read.

> *"Successful People rely heavily on their mentors.*
> *Ordinary people don't."*
> —*Robert G. Allen*

Resource

For more on mentors, check out:

Who's In Your Top Five? Your Guide to Finding Your Success Mentors by Bertrand Gervais.

Prepare yourself to receive favor. But don't forget to show favor to those you're able to help out. Do this without expecting anything in return. This will increase the favor that is given to you. Always remember, "If the king likes you, it doesn't matter who dislikes you."

Learn to cultivate favor.

Millionaire Prisoner Prosperity Keys

- You must learn to recognize and cultivate favor in your life.
- If someone sees you working on a worthy cause or something they believe in, they will assist you.
- Seek out and utilize positive role models and mentors.
- Prepare yourself to receive favor. Always try to make the best first impression that you can.
- Don't forget to bestow favor on those you can assist, thereby increasing your own favor.

GROWTH

Let others build a cave with their clay.
I will build a castle with mine.

—*Og Mandino*

It's a Universal Law of Life that what doesn't grow becomes stagnant and dies. Life is about movement. Everything grows. As it grows older it grows slower. A baby doubles its weight in about six months. Eventually the human body stops growing altogether. But there is one part of the human that never stops growing and that part is the mind. You can't become a Millionaire Prisoner unless you're growing. You can't stay in the same frame of mind that brought you to prison and expect different results.

"The significant problems we face cannot be solved at
the same level of thinking we were at when we created
them."

—*Albert Einstein*

Right now your problem is prison. How will you solve the prison problem if you continue to think in the same manner that brought you to prison? You can't. If you want success in all areas of your life then you need to put away the childish way of thinking that led you to prison.

Don't Defeat Yourself

You defeat yourself when you don't allow yourself to grow. Your body ages but your mind doesn't. Some of you are still chasing after the lusts of your youth. This is what one Rabbi called the "sexual phase." Think about all the prisoners that you know who only think about sex. They collect pornographic books and every woman they see on TV or in person is a piece of meat that they want to devour. They wonder why they can't achieve their dreams. If you want to get a step ahead of these prisoners just change your thoughts from sex to success. If you can learn to use *Self-Control* against these "urges" and devote your passion towards other profitable areas in your life, you will begin to lead the race.

As a 17-year old convict on my first bid I was in this sexual phase. I too had g-shot books, and my cellmate and I placed naked pictures all over the walls in our cell. I was released on parole after a couple of years and my goal was to have sex every day with as many women as I could. Not only did I come back to prison, but I lost contact with the mother of my kids because I slept around. It was an unhealthy *attitude* that caused pain in my life and others. Because I didn't want to experience that kind of pain anymore I decided to do things different this time. While others in prison read *Black Tail* and *Penthouse,* and stayed up all night to catch *Girls Gone Wild,* I worked on myself. Always remember that a successful person will do what an unsuccessful person won't do. Other prisoners won't use these ABCs. But you will.

It may seem that what I've put together in these ABCs advises you to do the opposite of what everyone else is doing. There is some truth to that. The masses are asses. If they knew how to become a Millionaire Prisoner don't you think they would've done it already? Some of you may feel that if you take the road less traveled in prison that you'll be lonely? The truth is, you won't be. Once you achieve success, everyone will want to know your secrets. Plus, everyone wants to be friends with the person on top. Follow these ABCs and you can grow from prison to prosperity. Your first step is to put away childish thinking in matter of sex.

Another phase that some prisoners stay in is the Warrior phase. To them, every person, place, or thing is a battle. But some things are just not worth your time. Prosperity comes from growth and maturity. It won't come to those who are fighting every day. Learn to pick the right battles. Save your energy for your *objectives*. This will come easier when you learn what your "why?" is for living.

Work on Yourself

Aristotle said many years ago that the hardest victory is the victory over self. What he meant is that it's a constant battle. If you can conquer those things that hinder you, then you can win this battle. This battle is worth fighting because anything that has the opportunity to help you become wiser is worth it. You'll learn more about the battle of Self in the chapters on *Knowledge* and *Self-Control*, but right now learn to build castles instead of caves.

> *"By working on ourselves instead of worrying about conditions, we were able to influence the conditions."*
> —*Stephen Covey*

Because prison is such a negative place, it's useful to read stories of success and inspiration. One of my favorite magazines to read is *Success*. It helps me keep the Millionaire Prisoner *attitude*. It also supplies a lot of "aha" moments. I had one of these moments while reading John C. Maxwell's column on leadership. He wrote that we should stop working on our weaknesses because that's where we're weak at, and that we should grow our strengths to maximum potential with a "growth plan." That was my "aha" moment. I had a growth chapter in these ABCs, but I had no growth plan. So I went through all the books in my personal library and put together a Millionaire Prisoner Growth Plan, and found that it works. You can do the same using the below steps. Make sure you write your plan down on paper, and keep it handy so you can review it. Here's how:

Millionaire Prisoner Growth Plan

1. Identify 3 areas of your life that you want to experience growth in. For example: relationships, health, and business.

2. Study what, and how, successful people in those areas got there. Extract tips and strategies from their life that you can apply to yours.

3. Learn it yourself by actually doing these things in your own life. Once again, act out your script.

4. Set *objectives* that you want to reach, and time deadlines for achieving them. Keep enlarging those goals as you meet them.

5. Reach out to the people that you find in your research, and ask them to mentor you. If one person says no, keep asking until you find someone who will. Don't take "no" for an answer.

6. Never stop learning and growing your potential. Constantly read self-help books and always look to gain at least one tip to use in your life.

Growth doesn't have to be a long drawn out process. If you work on your strengths, talents, and passion, you'll reach new heights in no time. And you'll be so busy living a life at maximum potential that you'll forget about your weaknesses. Successful people never stop seeking new ways to experience growth. They understand that life is a never-ending journey, and you always have room to grow on every level. But I've found that the most rewarding growth is on a personal level. That's when you find out who you really are and why you were born. That's when you become a Millionaire Prisoner.

"Success has to incorporate the personal as well as the professional. And it must be about character rather than property and possessions."
—*Rabbi Shmuley Boteach*

The Easy Road

As prisoners, when you choose this path of growth, you'll be going against the grain. Other prisoners don't choose this road because it's not the easy one. They've been on the easy one all their life. But the easy road doesn't allow you to grow and mature. The easy road is the one where you only care about yourself. Where you wish for a better future, and go through life like nothing matters. Where you pass blame onto others for your mistakes and actions. That road leads to destruction. It leads to pain. That road led us right into prison. Only maturity will pave the way for you to break the cycle of prison for good.

I would like to share a poem with you that I found in an old newspaper. The title of the poem is "Growth" and its author is unknown. Allow the poet's words to speak to you as you read:

For every hill I've to climb,
For every stone that bruised my feet,
For all the blood and sweat and grime,
For blinding storms and burning heat,

My heart sings but a grateful song—
These were the things that made me strong!
For all the heartaches and the tears,
For all the anguish and the pain,
For gloomy days and fruitless years,
And for the hopes that lived in vain,
I do give thanks, for now I know,
These were the things that helped me grow!
Tis not the softer things of life,
Which stimulate mans will to strive;
But bleak adversity and strife,
Do most to keep man's will alive.
O'er rose-strewn paths the weaklings creep,
But brave hearts dare to climb the steep.

It's so easy to stay where you're at mentally and physically. There is no risk involved. You can't get hurt or lose anything by staying there. But this *attitude* is really one of fear. It's a fear of failure and a fear of the unknown. These fears hinder you. By standing still you stay in a mental prison. Thoughts about your fears don't help either, only action does. Move forward and overcome your fears.

"One can choose to go back toward safety or forward toward growth. Growth must be chosen again and again; fear must be overcome again and again."

—*Dr. Abraham Maslow*

A Lesson From The Weight Pit

What would happen to the prisoner who lifts weights if they stopped working out? Their muscles would get smaller and weaker. So, it is in life as well. Growth comes from use. What you don't use becomes atrophied and dies. Muscles need to be broken down to grow. Just like the muscle-bound prisoner, you're going to have to strain through the soreness to get the results you want. By pushing through a barrier or obstacle you experience growth.

Do Not Waste Time

It's a fact of life that everything grows. It either grows for good or bad, positive or negative. Are you growing towards a good, positive mature? Or are you growing towards a bad, negative nature? Even if you are unconscious of which way you are moving, you are still moving. And anything that you allow to continue will increase. Everything increases after its kind. Fruit bears more fruit. Chickens produce more chickens. Humans create more humans. What is increasing in your life?

Think of your first curse word. Or your first cigarette. Or your first drink. Unless you worked on yourself, these things increased in your life. All of them started with a first time, and then increased. You allowed them to grow. You either go forward or back, it's your choice. If you're going back, then that is valuable time you'll waste trying to get back to where you were before. The great general and emperor, Napoleon Bonaparte, said that he would trade space for time. He knew he could trade space because he could make that up, but he could never recover time. How much time have you wasted?

Now is the time to act. Now is the time to grow. Now is the time to build your castle. You allow others to control your life when you fail to act now. Is your life a waste? Is mine? Is your cellmate's? Only each of us has the answer to that question, but if we're continuing to stay in a prison mentality, we'll have to be truthful with ourselves and admit that our lives have been up to this point, a waste.

"Do not act like you had a thousand years to live."
— *Marcus Aurelias*

Millionaire Prisoner Case Study

One of the most profitable aspects of writing this book was being able to read all of the books about other prisoners and their success in prison and after prison. There was a lesson in each prisoners' story. That is why there are so many examples in these ABCs. One of those prisoners is Billy Wayne Sinclair.

Billy Wayne began his journey in the prison system in the 1960s. He started out with a short sentence for stealing a car and driving it across state lines. Introduced to other criminals, he received an education in the life of crime. Five months after his release from prison he was involved in another crime spree. In Louisiana, he tried to rob a store and things went bad when the store clerk was killed. His victim happened to be politically connected and he was found guilty and sentenced to die.

Sinclair was placed on death row at Angola, one of the worst prisons in America. Whether, because of years of mental and physical abuse at the hands of his father, or the fate of his upcoming execution, he started popping pills and doing drugs to escape reality. While on the Row, he watched his fellow convicts go insane, and his friend was murdered over a stick of butter. Sinclair also lost his younger brother in Vietnam. All of these tragedies took their toll, and he decided it was time for a change. He swore off pills and drugs, and began to read books and reflect on his life. He educated himself about the law and filed a civil rights suit against prison officials about conditions on the Row. That case was a success and it gave prisoners on the Row at Angola the right to outdoor exercise.

In 1972, the United States Supreme Court decided *Furman V. Georgia*, which said that it was unconstitutional to use the death penalty in America as punishment. Eventually, Sinclair was given a life sentence and moved off the Row. Because of his previous success as a jailhouse lawyer, he was sought out for advice in general population. He became Vice President of the Angola Jaycees, Secretary of Narcotics Anonymous, and President of the Dale Carnegie Club. Sinclair would later become secretary of the Prison Grievance Committee, and through the Committee would give Angola such privileges as televisions in maximum security lockdown, a better law library, and uncensored mail. The Committee also helped integrate the prison peacefully.

But all was not rosy at Angola. At the time, in the early 1970s, Angola was considered one of the nation's most violent prisons. Sinclair watched a young biker get murdered. Another prisoner was stabbed 39 times, 13 times in the heart, all while the guards watched. One missing prisoner was found buried underneath a dormitory. Because of his jailhouse lawyer work he was set up by prison authorities for drugs and sent back to max lockdown. While in max seg, he watched his friend kill himself by slicing his wrists with a razor.

After a year he was released from seg and his change began to come full circle. With a new *attitude* about life, Sinclair became a staff writer on *The Angolite*, the prison newspaper. In 1980, he won the George Polk Award for the article, "The Other Side of, Murder." He would win another award in 1980, the ABA's Silver Gavel Award. After these awards, he became co-editor of *The Angolite* with Wilbert Rideau. (See *Justice* chapter for more on Rideau).

Because of his work on the prison newspaper he was allowed to travel the state speaking about the criminal justice system. Sinclair would speak to kids at schools and universities, telling them to stay out of prison. Because of his previous time spent on the Row, and his editorial work on *The Angolite*, he was interviewed by a reporter from a local television station. Sinclair and the reporter, Jodie Bell, hit it off. They eventually married by proxy, and would go on to write a book, *A Life In The Balance: The Billy Wayne Sinclair Story.*

Sinclair's story is a remarkable one. It's one of change, redemption, and love. It's also one of growth and maturity. He went from an abused childhood to a life of petty crime. Then grew from a petty criminal into a convicted murderer on death row. From death row prisoner to a winning jailhouse lawyer. From a jailhouse lawyer into an activist and award-winning author. All of it happened because *he chose* the road of growth. He was released in 2006 and wrote another book, *Capital Punishment*, which shows why the death penalty does not work. You can have success in your life if you choose it. Follow the steps in this chapter and throughout these ABCs and become who you are supposed to be.

Learning From the Old Heads

If you would like to read more about growth from the perspective of a prisoner, I recommend *The Autobiography of Malcolm X*, and *Soul On Ice*, by Eldridge Cleaver.

In *Soul On Ice*, Cleaver wrote: "I realized that no one could save me but myself. The prison authorities were both uninterested and unable to help me. I had to seek out the truth and unravel the snarled web of my motivations. I had to find out who I am and what I want to be, what type of man I should be, and what I could do to become the best of which I was capable . . . I learned that I had been taking the easy way out, running away from problems. I also learned that it is easier to do evil than it is to do good."

You can feel the maturity in his words. We can learn a lot from the old heads. Who do you want to be? How can you become the best you? Seek out ways to grow your potential and strengths.

Another great example of growth can be found in the life of Stanley "Tookie" Williams. In 1971, Williams and another teenager, Raymond Lee Washington, started the Crips street gang. Washington was killed by a rival gang member in 1979, and Tookie was eventually sent to California's death row for two robberies where four people were killed. It was on the Row where he began to grow into a man of wisdom and understanding.

During his time spent on the Row at San Quentin, Tookie began to write. He wrote an eight-book series aimed at preventing youth violence in 5 to 10-year-old students. That series, *Tookie Speaks Out Against Gang Violence,* co-authored with Barbara Cottman-Becnel, was a success and gained Tookie *recognition.* Because of his gang status, Tookie spent seven years in the hole. While in the whole he was only allowed 3 books at a time, but that didn't stop him from experiencing growth. He would *network* with his co-author by calling her collect and dictating to her what he had wrote. She would then type it into her computer and edit it. He completed another book, *Life In Prison,* which won two national book honors. Tookie formed his own educational website, *www.tookie.com* that has helped youth since 1997. He also conceived the Internet Project for Street Peace. Because of his crusade against youth violence and gangs, Tookie was nominated for the 2007 Nobel Peace Prize. Some of you may remember the made-for-TV movie, *Redemption,* starring Jamie Foxx as Tookie Williams. The state of California eventually executed Tookie, but that doesn't diminish his legacy, or his growth.

In June of 2000, lifer Kenneth E. Hartman founded the Honor Program in California State Prison— Los Angeles County. The Honor Program is based on the principles of positive behavior and accountability. Hartman was placed in administrative segregation after the release of the Honor

Program's handbook. But media pressure and outside support forced his release two weeks later. So far, the Honor Program has been a success.

In 2009, Hartman published *Mother California: A Story of Redemption Behind Bars*, in which he chronicles his growth. He continues to write and his 30 years of experience behind bars show up in his words. But in all of his work , the maturity of a Millionaire Prisoner shines through. For more information on the Honor Program, visit *www.prisonhonorprogram.org*.

Growth and maturity in prison are possible, but like Sinclair, Williams, and Hartman, you have to begin the process yourself. You either get busy living or you get busy dying. It's your choice. Those are the only two options. The fact that your life has been up to this point a waste, does not mean it has to stay that way. You can choose to move forward into growth. Because if you don't choose to control your life someone else will. As my friend, Big Trent, once said: "We are in prison because we were at war with who we were created to be." That is the whole key. When you embrace who you're supposed to be, you'll have success. Until then, your life will be in a constant state of flux.

Your growth may take time. Don't become discouraged if you don't change overnight. Your thoughts and ideas are the seed. Cultivate them. With a proper use of time they will grow. They will deliver you a harvest you never thought possible.

"True progress in any field is a relay race and not a single event."

—*Cavett Robert*

Resource
For more on growth, make sure you read this great book:
The 15 Invaluable Laws of Growth by John C. Maxwell

<u>Millionaire Prisoner Prosperity Keys</u>

- Stop defeating yourself and learn to grow.
- You can experience maturity in your life if you work on yourself.
- Don't stay on the road to destruction just because it's the easy way.
- Don't waste time, start right now.
- Write out your Millionaire prisoner Growth Plan.
- Get busy living or get busy dying. It's your choice.

HABIT

Habit is either the best of servants, or worst of masters.
—*Nathaniel Emmons*

It's been said that a man's fortune is delivered to him by his habits. Think about what you did every day before you came to prison. Were your habits fortune builders or prison deliverers? Some of you sold drugs? Some of you got high? Some of you drank too much? I robbed, stole, and cheated my way to money. No wonder I came to prison. My habits delivered me to the courthouse steps and the prison gates.

"What you do today will determine what you'll be and what you'll receive tomorrow."
—*Jesse Duplantis*

Now that you're in prison, most of you allow the same bad habits to control your lives. Some of you watch television all day, and neglect reading books. Some of you have bad health habits like smoking cigarettes, and drinking ten cups of coffee a day, which only feeds your addictive traits. Some of you eat junk food and don't exercise. Some of you don't write home, but get mad when you don't get any mail, or when your collect call is not accepted. Some of you spend all day talking about past crimes and old war wounds. Don't think I haven't been there, because I have. On my first bid, I did all of the above and more. Those habits set me up to violate parole and eventually got me life in prison. You must break these bad habits or you'll stay in a prison mentality, and you can't become a Millionaire Prisoner in that frame of mind.

What is Habit?

To paraphrase a great writer of the past let me say the following.

Unlike the shadow that departs when the sun is gone, your habits never leave. Habit can either be your greatest helper or your heaviest burden. When you were younger, you got into the habit of tying your shoes. If you didn't, you would trip and fall over your shoelaces. Habit will give you the needed push to achieve your *objectives*, or it will drag you down to the pits of failure. It's something that you control, that you do on your own. No one can make you form any habit, but you alone build the daily habit that create your life.

Habit is easily influenced, all you have to do is show it a couple of times how to do something, and then habit will do it automatically. Just like your subconscious mind, habit doesn't care if you're using it for profit or loss. It doesn't care if you're a success or a failure. But *it is* the foundation for all your successes or your failures. If you can learn to train your habits, they will place everything you desire at your feet. If you can't tame your bad habits, then you'll continue to get what you've got so far in life . . . And if you liked what you've got so far in life, then you wouldn't be reading this book right now. Bad habits are the unlocked doors to failure. After reading this chapter you'll have the tools needed to break your bad habits and form some new good ones.

Let's examine some of the habits that you've already learned, and some more that you'll read about in upcoming chapters.

One of the first habits that you read about is that of using self-suggestion to create a new positive *attitude*. As you change your thoughts and they become ingrained in your daily life, your subconscious will deliver plans to achieve your *objectives*.

In the chapter on *Baggage*, you learned to make it a habit to forget about the past. Instead you should think of the present and how to profit from temporary defeat.

You've also learned how to make wealth your slave, thereby building sufficient *capital* to secure financial independence . . . And that you must use *determination* to never, ever give up.

In the chapter on *education* you learned about the habit of reading non-fiction books and how to obtain free money for college, if that's what you need to accomplish your goals.

You've also learned the habit of placing yourself in a position to receive *favor* from those around you, and how to experience *growth* in your life.

Some of the habits that you'll learn in upcoming chapters are how to use your *imagination* to create useful ideas and see the possible where others think it's impossible; how to get the *justice* you deserve; and to have *knowledge* of all things.

You'll be taught how to use the power of *laughter* in the face of obstacles, and how to begin *marketing* your ideas and products, and building your *network*.

You'll learn how to set realistic goals, and the proper *preparation* to achieve those *objectives*.

You'll see the importance of producing *quality* work in all that you do and become familiar with the laws of *recognition, self-control*, and *tact*.

You'll understand that none of these ABCs are any good to you unless *utilized*, and that the missing ingredients behind your success is *valiancy* or courage.

You'll learn definite *ways and means* to become a Millionaire Prisoner and in the chapter of *Xerox*, you'll learn the secret habit of standing on the shoulders of giants, allowing you to leapfrog over everyone standing in line to ride the success rollercoaster.

Finally, in the last chapter you'll learn how to keep yourself charged up by using *zeal* as the fuel for your cause.

The power of habit can be an unstoppable force in your life if you use it to become a Millionaire Prisoner. When you finish this book you'll understand that you have all the ingredients for success and prosperity inside of you. These ABCs are the master recipe. Make them a habit, and we'll see each other in the penthouse at the top.

The First Good Habit

The whole purpose of this book is to help you develop certain habits that will take you from prison to prosperity. The first one that you need to acquire is the ability to use your time wisely. We've all heard the maxim: "Do the time, don't let it do you." Or "Don't serve time, make it serve you." There are many ways to say it, but the principle is still the same. The great prisoners like Malcolm, Mandela, Rubin "Hurricane" Carter and others all made time serve them. Using your time wisely has been a success principle that has been around for centuries.

"Know the true value of time, snatch, seize, and enjoy every moment of it. No idleness, no laziness, no procrastination. Never put off till tomorrow what you can do today."
—*Lord Chesterfield*

Nothing brilliant in the above quote, just common sense. And yet so many prisoners do exactly what Lord Chesterfield advises against. Allow me to give you an example.

Remember Mark from the chapter on *Capital*? The prisoner who ran up debt because of his coffee drinking habit. When Mark first returns to his cell, the first thing that he does is turn on his TV. Then he'll sit on his bunk sipping coffee, watching soap operas, music videos, and reruns of *Martin* until dinner. He just wastes away hours of his day. He's not *investing* his time. He'll never be able to get those hours back. His time isn't serving him, he's doing dead time.

After dinner, Mark goes to the gym and works out. That's good profitable exercise. He returns to the unit, takes a shower and goes back in his cell. What does he do? Once again, he turns on the TV, and wastes the rest of the night away in idle, lazy, unprofitable activity. How is he helping himself achieve his dreams in life? He isn't. Mark's TV habit will never allow him to achieve success and prosperity.

> *"Make use of time, let not advantage slip."*
> —William Shakespeare

Are You Doing Dead Time?

For Millionaire Prisoners dead time is the enemy. When I say "dead time," I mean *time that is wasted*. In the prison context, dead time is not yours. It's the BOP's or the state's. When you're doing dead time all you want to do is pass time as quickly as possible. You sleep all day, read fiction books or magazines, and watch TV with no purpose except to make the hours fly by. Other prisoners play cards all day. Or chess. On my first bid I went to prison as a 17-year-old. I came out no better off than when I went in. I lost 3 years of my life that I'll never get back. It's dead to me. Do not be like this. Respect time! True ownership comes with the ability to use your days for *education* and gaining *knowledge. It's the ability to take the time the judge gave you in prison and put it to work for you by honing your craft, working on your trade, or bettering yourself.* All of us prisoners have the option to either do dead time or turn our prison into a stepping-stone to success. A simple change in your daily habits can produce miraculous results in your future. Take control of your life by making time work *for* you.

Time Is Money!

To illustrate this principle allow me to share with you what Associate Professor of Economics, Emily Oster, teaches her students at the University of Chicago's Booth School of Business. Oster shows her pupils the basic economic principle of *opportunity cost.* It's really a simple question: What is the cost of my investment of time between two alternatives? For instance, I can spend two hours of my time washing clothes or I can pay another prisoner a couple bucks to do it. To figure out if I *should* outsource my laundry chore to Mr. Maytag Prisoner on the second tier, I need to decide if I can spend those two hours doing something profitable.

For me, it's a no brainer. I can easily use those two hours for studying the law, writing a chapter in my next book, sports handicapping, or writing a sales letter. All of the above will bring in more profits than the few crumbs it costs me to pay to get my laundry done. I only use laundry as an example. I also try to outsource my cooking, cell cleaning, and other trivial prison tasks that I hate doing. You might like doing laundry? Or cleaning? Or cooking? But this principle applies to all of your time. If you look at your time as an investment and use the opportunity cost comparison in deciding what you're going to do, you just might stop doing unprofitable things. Once again, it's all about building Millionaire Prisoner habits.

The Greatest Enemy

If you took a survey of the prisoners at your prison and asked them what is the most important item they own, 90% of them would say their television. A few religious prisoners' value their Bible or Koran over their TV. Some of us with kids value our photo albums more. But the majority of the prisoner's value their TV most. At the prison I'm in, we never had cable TV until a few years ago. On the cable contract that the administration signed, it says that they wanted us prisoners to have cable because it would help *pacify* us. Are you a baby? Do you need to be pacified? If you're going to become a Millionaire Prisoner you have to devalue your TV. Your mind holds more value inside of it than all of the television sets in the world combined. A collection of non-fiction books should be valued more than your TV. Stephen King calls TV the "glass teat." My grandfather called it "the idiot box." Watching television will not get you prosperity.

It will also not get you health. The *New York Times* recently reported that sitting for long periods of time in front of the TV can lead to weight gain, and increase the risk for heart disease and cancer. What does that say for the prisoner who lays in the bunk all day and watches TV? Watch yourself when it comes to sitting around all day doing nothing but watching TV.

> *"It is health that is real wealth and not pieces of gold and silver."*
> —Mahatma Gandhi

Let's go back to Mark. What can he do to change his bad TV watching habit? First, he must turn off the TV and do something in place of the time he'd normally spend watching TV. To get rid of a bad habit you must fill the void with a new good habit. Idleness is your greatest enemy in prison. Spend your time being productive.

My suggestion for Mark would be to spend those hours before dinner reading or writing, instead of watching TV. He needs to get in the habit of doing one specific thing every day at the same time. Things become easy with repetition. It's the foundation to building habits. Once you begin to do something over and over again, it will become natural. If it's profitable, you'll enjoy doing it . . . And that is the key: the new habit must be profitable or fill some need that you have.

Personally, I don't turn on my TV until at least five o'clock at night. My prison is much quieter during the day, and I get a lot of reading and writing done during this time. If something I'm working on isn't completed by 5:00 p.m., then my TV doesn't come on. This habit didn't come naturally. It took *self-control*, but it has delivered me numerous benefits. Now, don't get me wrong, I'm not against all TV. I like watching sports and movies just as much as the next prisoner. But daytime TV with its talk shows, soap operas, and reruns, is a major no-no for the success-minded prisoner. Get in the habit of doing more profitable things than watching TV. A great book on the downside of television is *Four Arguments for the Elimination of Television* by Jerry Mander.

Somewhere, in some prison, some prisoner is in their cell working on an idea, project, or task that will bring them prosperity. In true Millionaire Prisoner fashion they have no time to waste. Well, you don't have any time to waste either. You can't recover wasted minutes or hours. Those wasted minutes and hours add up to days, months, and years. You must spend your time wisely. Yes, you have been sentenced to prison time, but you can flip the script and make this time serve you. Invest your time now so that you can reap the benefits in your future.

A Daily Schedule

As you'll earn in the *objective* chapter, you need to plan your life. Part of this plan is your daily schedule. This schedule will help make things routine, and become your foundation. Make a list of your daily schedule and be specific. Here's an example of how it could look:

Josh's Daily Schedule

6:00 a.m.	Wake up; meditate; quiet thinking
7:00 a.m.	Breakfast
7:30 a.m.	Read; write
10:30 a.m.	Get ready for lunch
10:45 a.m.	Lunch
11:15 a.m.	Get ready for gym or yard
11:30 a.m.	Gym; yard; exercise
2:00 p.m.	Shower
2:30 p.m.	Read; write
4:15 p.m.	Get ready for dinner
4:30 p.m.	Dinner
5:00 p.m.	Answer all mail, TV if all tasks are completed
10:00 p.m.	Plan tomorrow's activities
10:30 p.m.	Meditate; quiet thinking
11:00 p.m.	Sleep

Your schedule may be different because of your prison's activities and programs. You may have gym or yard at different times. You may go to school, or have a job. Just be specific when writing out your daily routine and then follow it to make it habit. You'll start to feel better mentally and physically and get more things accomplished. Action breeds results but idleness breeds nothing. So get busy.

All successful people value their time and use it wisely. Doctors have appointment schedules. Lawyers bill by the hour. Businessmen and women keep calendars of upcoming meetings and events. Most of them use their Smartphones and apps to keep track of their schedule and itinerary. Of course, it's against the law for prisoners to possess cell-phones and PDAs in prison. But that should not stop you from doing it the old-fashioned way—*by hand*. Get a daily planner and keep track of your time. My mother found me a simple two-year daily planner at Walmart. Get one and plan your future. Then live it!

Your Greatest Asset

The one thing that you have available to you that is just as equal to those in the free-world is time. We all have a luxury of time. We all have 60 minutes in an hour, 24 hours in a day, and 365 days in a year. A rich person can't buy more time. A poor person can't lose time. But *the difference between the rich and the poor is how they spend their time*. Up to this point you've most likely spent your time foolishly. If you can spend your time wisely and invest it, you can break the back of poverty and become a Millionaire Prisoner.

"Nine-tenths of wisdom consists in being wise in time."
— *Theodore Roosevelt*

Malcolm X developed the habit of reading and studying in his cell. So did Nelson Mandela.

Don King developed the habit of reading Shakespeare and other classics in prison. Dan Manville developed the habit of studying the law while inside.

Rubin Carter swore off TV and spent his cell time reading and writing. Mumia Abu-Jamal has the habit of writing, and it has produced words of wisdom for the whole world to read.

All of the above prisoners developed habits that produced a better future. In the prisoner examples throughout these ABCs you'll find evidence of positive habits. Try and identify the good habits in each example and use them for your benefit. What daily habit are you developing that will create a miracle in your future?

> *"Even in prison your time is your own, if you use it for your own purposes."*
> —Robert Greene

How to Make the Most of Your Time

If *you are* watching a TV show or game, do tasks during the commercials. The ads are unimportant to us anyway. We're in prison and can't order a pizza, go to a restaurant, or buy a Mercedes. The commercials just make you daydream about what you're going to do when you get out. Instead, do pushups or sit-ups. Write down your thoughts or ideas. Read a few lines in your favorite book. Work on a crossword puzzle. Listen to an audio book. Do anything except pay attention to the commercials.

This single step will gain you about 20 minutes extra for each hour-long show. A typical 2½ hour basketball game would give you an extra 45 minutes, not including the time allowed for timeouts and other game stoppages. If you're disciplined enough, you may do your exercise during the game. Find your own routine that works best for you. Just remember that there is no law that says you have to sit still and watch TV.

Another way to gain time is in those moments when you're waiting. Take a pocketbook with you to the hospital. While you're waiting for the doctor or dentist to call you, read a chapter or two. Or take a pen and some paper and work on a poem or rough draft of a letter you've been meaning to write. There are so many moments in prison when you're just waiting. Learn how to turn these moments into profit by using them to your benefit. Take control of your time so it becomes your greatest asset. For more on time management read *168 Hours* by Laura Vanderkam.

> *"Things may come to those who wait, but only the things left by those who hustle."*
> —Abraham Lincoln

You must also watch out for time vultures. You know the type of prisoner I'm talking about. They ask you a question and they want to discuss or debate the answer with you for an hour. Or they want to tell you stories about their past. What you must do is politely excuse yourself and get back to work on you. Remember, it's your time, so value it. Time is money. If you can use your prison time wisely *you can turn your sentence into a benefit.*

> *"As every thread of gold is valuable, so is every moment of time."*
> —John Mason

Out With the Bad, In With the New

Now that you have your time under control, let's look at replacing your bad habits with some good habits. Most of you have great habits. You brush your teeth regularly. You shower daily. Some of you write letters. Some of you eat healthy and exercise. These are all great habits. But we need to discuss bad habits and how to get rid of them.

There is a system for getting rid of bad habits. It's not mine, but was passed down from Benjamin Franklin. In *The Autobiography of Benjamin Franklin*, he described the system that he used to get rid of bad habits. He called it his "project of arriving at moral perfection." Franklin wanted to live without committing "any fault at any time . . ." Pretty high goal? Well, he got pretty good at it, and this is how he did it.

Franklin decided that he wished to acquire thirteen virtues. He made a little book, into which he wrote down each of the thirteen virtues that he chose. He set the book up so that each virtue had one page a piece. Then he lined the page so that he had seven lines, one for each day of the week. Then he crossed those lines with 13 lines so that he could have one box or square for each of his virtues. In those boxes or squares, he would mark an "X" for every fault that contradicted his virtue. Franklin determined that he would spend one whole week on a virtue. If he kept that line clear he could move on to the next virtue in the following week. His idea was that he could complete all 13 virtues in 13 weeks, or go through the whole course four times a year.

Did Franklin complete his goal on the first try? Hardly so. He said that he had to get a new book because his first one had so many black spots and holes in it from rubbing out the "X's" due to his faults. It took him some time but he was eventually able to complete it in a year. Even after he completed his course, Franklin never went anywhere without his little book.

So how can you use this system in your own life? Simply by keeping score. For a start, make a list of the habits that you want to eradicate out of your life. Make your own little book with the days of the week on it. When you do the habit that you want to get rid of, mark an "X" on the square. Your goal is to go through the whole week without any "X's" in the squares. Only work on one habit at a time. Once you've completed a week without any marks then go on to the next habit.

It's a little game that you play with yourself. No one has to know that you're playing it either. If you want, give yourself a reward for completing a week without any marks. Soon, you will not even need your book anymore because you will free yourself from the bondage of bad habits.

To further assist you in getting rid of bad habits, I would like to share with you a page from my habit book. I learned it from W. Clement Stone who modeled it off Benjamin Franklin's little book. You'll see that I have an hourly box for each day. Use it as an example when you make your own.
Here it is:

Bad Habit: TV Watching Good Habit: Reading Nonfiction Imitate Malcolm X and Nelson Mandela							
Time	S	M	T	W	T	F	S
6-7 a.m.							
7-8 a.m.							X
8-9 a.m.							X
9-10 a.m.			X				
10-11 a.m.							
11-12 p.m.							
12-1 p.m.							
1-2 p.m.							
2-3 p.m.							

3-4 p.m.							
4-5 p.m.	X						
5-6 p.m.							X
6-7 p.m.							
7-8 pm.							
8-9 p.m.							
9-10 p.m.							

You will see at the top I listed the bad habit that I wanted to eradicate and the good habit I replaced it with. You must fill the void left by the bad habit with a new good habit. I also have a *Notes* section at the bottom of the paper. Sometimes you'll want to jot down a thought about the day so you can remember it for the future or next weeks' page.

Do you feel that this idea isn't something you want to do? I felt this way at first until I thought about Ben Franklin. He became a great person using this system. When we talk about "it's all about the Benjamins," we are speaking about the bills with his face on them. He's the only person on a U.S. currency paper bill that was never president. It wasn't too trivial for him, and who are we compared to him? Scoff at it if you want, but I dare you to try it. It works.

Frank Bettger, the famous salesman, and author of *How I Raised Myself from Failure to Success in Selling* said that he used 13 cards instead of a notebook. You may find that more convenient also. Or you can come up with your own system. But no matter what you choose, make sure you keep score somehow. Because if you don't keep score you won't know if you're winning or not.

Don't get upset if it takes a while to form new habits and get rid of old ones. A University College-London study fund that it takes an average of 66 days to form a habit. Other scientists say 30 days is the norm. You can't do it in one day so don't become discouraged. Keep working on it and you can form some new profitable habits.

"A habit cannot be tossed out the window; it must be coaxed down the stairs a step at a time."

—Mark Twain

Millionaire Prisoner Case Study

Stitch is a prisoner who I met many years ago. But Stich had a problem. He wanted to quit smoking, and knew he couldn't do it cold turkey. He decided that he would smoke one less cigarette a day. Every week he would lose another cigarette. The first week he smoked 16 cigarettes a day. The second week he smoked 15 cigarettes a day, and so on. He subtracted them weekly, so that his daily intake of nicotine was going down weekly. It got to the point where Stitch didn't even want cigarettes anymore. It took him a while, but he weaned himself off cigarettes.

That strategy will work for any habit. Wean yourself off your bad habits slowly. Use concentration, *determination*, and your will to break those bad habits. You can accomplish anything you want, and having good habits will assist you in any endeavor.

Resource

For more on habits, a great book to check out is:
Million Dollar Habits by Robert Ringer
If you received something from these pages on habit that helps you, then my goal for this chapter will be complete. One of

my newly acquired habits is the ability to have an open mind. It has given me the key to a better world which I thought was closed to me.

"Excellence, then, is not an act, but a habit."

—*Aristotle*

"Habit is a cable. Weave a thread of it every day, an at last we cannot break it."

—*Horace Mann*

Form some good daily habits and watch your desires be delivered to your cell door. Start with using your time wisely.

Millionaire Prisoner Prosperity Keys

- What you do daily will either create a miracle or tragedy in your future.
- The first habit you must acquire is the ability to use your time wisely.
- Idleness and watching TV are the greatest enemies keeping you from success.
- Set up a daily schedule where all your time is accounted for.
- Develop a system to get rid of bad habits and take it one step at a time.

IMAGINATION

Imagination is more important than knowledge.
Knowledge is limited.
Imagination encircles the world.

—*Albert Einstein*

This chapter will give you a few tips about how you can tap into your powers of creativity. It will aid you in becoming more resourceful and help you solve problems. Imagination will enable you to overcome the prison walls that confine you.

Christopher Columbus imagined another world and found it. Our founding fathers imagined a new nation and started it. Dr. Martin Luther King, Jr. imagined a nation without segregation and it's coming to fruition. Nelson Mandela imagined a South Africa without Apartheid and it has happened.

"What is now proved was once only imagined."

—*William Blake*

Napoleon Hill called imagination the workshop of the mind. Picasso said that everything you can imagine is real. Imagination will deliver ideas and thoughts that can enable you to become a Millionaire Prisoner. If you can't see it in your mind first, you'll never see it in your future. Your success first begins in the form of a thought or idea. An idea can be sold where a product can't. And creators of ideas set their own price. But you must put ideas to work if you're going to be able to achieve your *objectives*.

First, realize that all new ideas sound foolish in the beginning. Sometimes you have an idea and immediately think "that won't work." Or "nobody will like it." You have to learn to override those thoughts, and believe in your idea or dream. When I first came up with the idea for these ABCs, I didn't like it. It sounded too kindergarten-ish. I went even so far to change them. But after writing the rough draft, my original idea of chapters based on the ABCs made sense. Without that original idea, this book would not be in your hands today.

A Way To Capture Ideas

There are a few things that you can do to keep track of your ideas. One is to write them down. Bestselling author, Stephen King, gets a lot of his book and short story ideas from his own dreams. He writes them down immediately upon waking up so he doesn't forget them. This process allows King to review his notes, and search for new material when he needs ideas. The shoe company, Nike, got its name from an employee's dream. Stephenie Meyer dreamt about vampires, then turned those thoughts into the *Twilight* series. Mary Shelley's *Frankenstein* was a nightmare she turned into a book. Pay attention to your thoughts when you first awake in the morning. You might find something valuable.

All it takes is one good idea to cement your name in the halls of the successful. It would be a shame if you had that idea and then forgot it. Always remember the maxim: *a short pencil is better than a long memory.*

*"The presence of an idea is like that of a loved one.
We imagine that we shall never forget it and that the
beloved can never become indifferent to us; but out of
sight, out of mind! The finest thought runs the risk of
being irretrievably forgotten if it's not written down and
the beloved of being taken from us unless she has been
wedded."*

—Arthur Schopenhauer

Everyone is different. You may come up with your own way of keeping track of ideas, but you must secure them. When you're out of your cell, carry a pen or pencil and some paper with you at all times. When something comes to mind, whether an idea, thought, or quote, write it down so it won't be lost.

Of course, when you're in your cell, it will be much easier to capture ideas. Keep a pen or pencil and some paper next to your bed, or by your desk if you have one. This way it will be handy when you want to write something down. You must get in the *habit* of capturing your ideas. You never know which one will be profitable for you in the future.

*"A man would do well to carry a pencil in his pocket and write
down his thoughts of the moment. Those that come unsought are
commonly the most valuable and should be secured because they
seldom return."*

—Sir Francis Bacon

Keep your ideas, quotes, and thoughts in something. Whether it's a folder, box, or a bag, it doesn't matter as long as you're keeping them. Review them periodically, and you'll find unlimited power in these ideas and notes. You'll even be surprised at the many golden nuggets contained in your keepsake. Most of the words in this book started on scraps of

150

paper in my idea folder. As I worked on these ABCs I found a wealth of information and ideas in my notes. All I had to do was organize them and put them to work for me.

Take a look around your cell room. Everything you see was only once imagined by someone else. They decided to put their ideas to use. That is what you must do if you're going to be able to achieve success and prosperity. I believe that you possess at least one idea that could change the world. This idea could improve the way people do business, or it could improve on someone else's invention or idea. But all it takes is one good idea.

> *"One good idea can enable a man to live like a king the rest of his life."*
>
> — *Ross Perot*

A Goldmine Ready to be Seized

So what do you do if you're not the creative type? Or you don't come up with that many ideas? Go find gold! You can find it in the public domain. The public domain consists of works created by others that are not protected by copyright law and are free for all to use. These works include books, art, songs, movies, photos, plays, and more. Some of the more famous works that are in the public domain are:

Moby Dick by Herman Melville

Mona Lisa by Leonardo DaVinci

All of Shakespeare's plays

The Jungle Book by Rudyard Kipling

The Autobiography of Benjamin Franklin

Invictus, the poem by Henley at the front of this book

Anyone can use works that are in the public domain any way they wish. You can look in most book catalogs and find public domain works being republished and sold. These publishers don't own the original work, such as Shakespeare's *Hamlet*, only the new material they added to it. This means that if you find something in the public domain, you can do what you want with it. Just be careful that you don't use any new material that may be included in these other versions. For instance, I purchased an annotated version of *Alice In Wonderland*. The original was published in 1865, so it's in the public domain. The extra words in the annotated version are under copyright. If I wanted to use parts of *Alice In Wonderland*, I could only use the original version and not any of the new added words or explanations without first getting permission. So be careful when using someone else's material.

What all is in the public domain, and how do you find it? All works published in the U.S. before the year 1923 are in the public domain. This means that any newspaper, book, song, painting, magazine, photo, quotation, and letter that was created or published before 1923 is free to use in any way you wish. But the public domain doesn't stop there. All written works of the U.S. Government, whether published or unpublished, are in the public domain. All laws and court decisions are in the public domain. Also, any work donated to the public domain is available to use freely. Any database is in the public domain, and a list of addresses is a database. The only thing protected in a list of addresses is the order, arrangement, and selection of the addresses. The addresses themselves are not protected. Any fact, idea, or common property is in the public domain.

Another category of works that are in the public domain are works that were published between 1923 and 1963 that *did not* have their copyright renewed within 28 years. But these are a little more difficult to find. It has been said that 85% of all works in this category are in the public domain. If a book was published in 1962 and did not have its copyright renewed by 1990, the book is in the public domain. If you found such a book, you could use it any way you choose. So how do you find one of these gems?

The first place to start is the copyright page of the book? If it is copyrighted before 1923, then it's in the public domain and you do not have to do anymore research. You could use that book freely. Now if the book has a copyright date later than 1923, but before 1963, it had to have been renewed within 28 years, or you can use it freely. To check to see if a copyright was renewed you do a search at the U.S. Copyright office. Since you're a prisoner, you have to have someone do it for you. If you have the Copyright office do it, then you'll have to query them by mail, and there is an hourly fee for the search. $150 per hour is normal and a typical search lasts an hour. You also have to provide the copyright office with the title of the work, authors' name, copyright owner's name, year of publication, type of work, and the name or issue of the work. You should send the letter and money or check payable to the Register of Copyrights at:

Reference & Bibliography Section,

LM-451

Copyright Office

Library of Congress

Washington, DC 20559

Or you can hire a research firm to do the search for you. Some of these firms may be cheaper and faster than having the copyright office do it. You can find addresses to some of these firms in the appendix. If someone in your *network* has access to the internet, they can search online records for works published between 1950-63. The website is: *www.copyright.gov*. Searches for works published between 1923-63 can be done on Stanford University's Library website at:

http://collections.stanford.edu/copyrightrenewals/bin/page?forwar d=home.

There are other websites that allow you to search for public domain materials and some are provided in the appendix. But a word of caution is needed here. A lot of prisoners believe that anything on the internet is in the public domain. This is not true. The same copyright laws that apply to offline materials apply to online works as well. One thing is for sure, if the original work is in the public domain, then any copy of it on the internet is in the public domain. Just be careful that you don't use anything that is added to the original work such as a website URL or Hypertext link.

Another great place to find public domain materials is in non-fiction books. Any fact contained in such a book is in the public domain. You can't copyright a fact. You can only copyright how a fact is expressed. Because if someone were able to copyright a fact or idea, then no one would be able to create new works, and *knowledge* would not flow to others.

What are the price of works in he public domain? They are priceless. They are an untapped goldmine of riches waiting your excavation. The only limitation on their application and use is what you put on it. Allow your imagination to use public domain materials to supply you with the ideas you need to achieve success and prosperity.

> *"Good artists copy. Great artists steal."*
> —*Pablo Picasso*

How To Use Public Domain Works

To assist you, allow me to suggest a few avenues that a prisoner may use the public domain for:

Any tattoo artist could find a wealth of material that is in the public domain. This artwork could be used, adapted, and formatted to fit any tattoo pattern.

If you're designing a book, book cover, or a display ad and you want to enhance it with photographs, you could freely use any photo that's in the public domain.

A prisoner who writes urban novels could comb the case reporters in the law library for ideas. These case reporters supply true life urban crime histories. These stories are free for the taking. Use your imagination, change people's names, and spin these stories and case reports into a best-selling novel.

You could find a public domain book and adapt it into a screenplay, then sell it to a Hollywood movie studio. Or you could republish it through your own publishing company.

You could buy pen-pal lists and rearrange them according to where they live, or their likes and dislikes, and resell them. That's all these prisoner companies are doing. Let's look at them more in depth.

Pen-Pal Lists: Platinum or Fools' Gold?

As a prisoner who has bought, traded, and *sold* pen-pal lists, I think it's time to discuss if they are really worth the money. First, there are four kinds of lists that I'm talking about. They are:

Compiled Lists. These are lists of names and addresses that are taken from printed sources like telephone books, newspapers, magazine subscribers, and so on. My "*100 Chicagoland Women*" and "*100 Wealthy Women*" lists were examples of compiled lists. These types of lists have the least value because you don't know if these people will respond to your letters.

Pen-Pals. These are lists of names and addresses of people who requested pen-pals. A lot of companies comb the internet pen-pal websites and compile lists of women who did not say "no prisoners" in their ads, then sell these lists to prisoners. Yes, these are real people who want pen-pals, but you just don't know if they'll write a prisoner until you write them.

Pen-Pals Who'll write Prisoners. These are people who requested to write prisoners. This is the rarest list of all and the most valuable of all the lists. But I've only seen two such lists in the last five years, and the same list was being sold to many prisoners. That lowers its value.

Prison Pen-Pals. If you just want mail and can write prisoners, this list can be your platinum. In 2002, while in the county jail I purchased such a list and every prisoner but one responded. If you can't write prisoners, don't buy this kind of list.

Now that you know the different types of lists in the prison pen-pal game you must examine the problems with these lists . . . And the main problem with all of the above lists is that you can't know how old they are. It would be nice to write the company selling the lists and get answers to the following questions:

How did they compile the list?

Where did the names and addresses come from?

How old are the lists?

Do they replace "Return To Sender" letters (called nixies) with new names?

Do they sell the same list to different prisoners?

Most companies won't give you the answers, so you just won't know until you buy a list and start writing letters. I don't like those odds and neither should you.

My verdict is that pen-pal lists are more fool's gold than anything else. I've spent hundreds of dollars on such lists over the years and haven't had more than a few successes, except for the prison pen-pal list I ordered while in the county jail. There are better options available to get pen-pals, so save your money and don't buy pen-pal lists anymore. You've been forewarned.

Millionaire Prisoner Case Studies

Richard Vineski spent 24 years in the New York prison system. He spent his time working inside the law library and gathered addresses and resource lists that helped prison litigators. Upon his release he started selling a book compiled of those resources and addresses. He advertised his book in *Prison Legal News*, and sold it through the mail. Vineski profited from addresses that were in the public domain. You could do the same. Prisoners are one of the last markets in need of *quality* directories because we don't have access to the internet.

George Kayer is a prisoner on death row in Arizona and the now retired creator and editor of *Inmate Shopper*, a directory of companies that provide services and products to prisoners. Kayer reviews and rates these companies, and any prisoner who has time to do should own a copy of the latest edition of *Inmate Shopper*. More proof that there is still a market for *quality* databases and directories. Use your imagination and you may come up with one yourself.

What has been suggested is only the tip of the iceberg. Now you have no legitimate excuse for not having an idea. If you would like to know more about the public domain or copyright law, recommended books are: *The Public Domain: How To Find & Use Copyright-Free Writings, Music, Art and More,* and *The Copyright Handbook: What Every Writer Needs To Know,* both by attorney Stephen Fishman.

Imagine A New Combination

Most new ideas, inventions, and businesses are new combinations of old ideas, concepts and products. Ray Kroc didn't invent McDonald's. He just took what the McDonald brothers had going already and put his own spin on things. Howard Schultz didn't invent Starbucks. He took a coffee business and combined it with ideas he found in Italy and put coffee shops on every corner. Picasso was a master of combining old images into new combinations in his art. What can you combine?

Pay attention to everything you see or hear. Write down anything you feel is a good idea, thought, or plan. Try and form these notes into new ideas or combinations. Use your magazine and newspaper clippings to give your mind a spark. If you aren't paying attention by using your imagination you'll miss out.

One prisoner collects old newspapers and magazines. He then goes through them and cuts out images or pictures that he feels may be useful later. Some of his best drawings and paintings are really collages and images he put together in a never before grouping. His artwork commands hundreds of dollars. His imagination allows him to see new images where others only see old ones.

It was reported in the April 2008 *National Geographic Traveler* that historic jails are being turned into hotels. The Charles Street Jail once housed Malcolm X, and is now the Liberty Hotel. The Malmaison Oxford Hotel in England was once a prison and still bears the exterior from the past. At the Old Jail Bed and Breakfast in Taylor Falls, Minnesota, couples can stay in a suite in the 1884 town jail. Another prison's trash can become someone else's passion and profit center.

I read a recent *USA Today* article about 14-year Willow Tufano. She took discarded household belongings and trash, put them on *Craigslist*, and sold them for a profit. She made enough to buy a house which she rents out for $700 a month. She was able to see a potential profit source where others saw trash.

Look for the opportunities around you where you can either capitalize on someone else's trash or expand on their business. Sometimes being the first isn't always the best thing.
"Pioneers get slaughtered, settlers prosper."

—*Mark Cuban*

How To Solve Problems

Another department of imagination is called resourcefulness. This department aids you in looking at things with a fresh eye, and allows you to see things you couldn't see before. It's the ability to solve problems.

Here is a way to stimulate your imagination so that you can solve any problems that are blocking your path:

1. Get a blank piece of paper and write down your problem at the top of it.

2. On one side of the paper write the reasons why you should take action to solve the problem. On the other side of the paper write down the reasons why you should not. Sometimes an answer will come to you as you write.

3. If no answer comes, then put the paper away and allow your subconscious to deliver the answer. It may provide the answer a day later, or weeks later. But your subconscious will provide the answer. When it does, you must immediately act on it. Like any tool, your imagination and subconscious will get stronger with use.

4. When a considerable amount of time has went by and you still don't have an answer to your problem, then get out your paper again. Reread what you previously wrote, then turn the page over and write down every thought, tactic and/or strategy that comes to mind. Sometimes, this brainstorming will produce the answer.

5.If you still do not have an answer, then put the paper away again and allow your subconscious to act. Remember, as soon as you get the answer, act on it.

By concentrating on problems in this manner you'll be able to solve them as they come up. As you become more adept at this process it will be easier to come up with the solutions. You will also find that a majority of your problems are not problems at all. But the faster you solve problems, the faster you can achieve your goals.

"It's not about your resources, it's about your resourcefulness."
— *Tony Robbins*

The Art of Visualization

Your imagination also encompasses your ability to dream. Most prisoners have dreams of accomplishing great things. But for some reason, they don't allow imagination to lead them in achieving those dreams. Earlier in these ABCs the statement was made that you are being led by your experience instead of your imagination. Your experience is the failure of prison. That is why you can't achieve success. Your frame of mind is still about prison. But your dreams reside outside the walls of your confinement. *Allow your imagination to lead you over these walls.*

The poorest person in the world is not someone who doesn't have money, but the one who doesn't have a dream. Without a dream, that person will stay where he or she is at in life. For you, that means prison. Certainly, you do not want to stay in prison, do you?

If you dream it, you can do it. Using the same meditation process from the chapter on *Baggage*, you can learn to visualize your new life. Remember the process? Only now, after you drop all your worries and problems into the bottomless pit, turn around and visualize the life you want to live in your mind. Play out your dreams. See yourself accomplishing your *objectives*. Imagine yourself giving the speech, accepting the award, and living in the house by the lake. Pretend you're watching a movie about your life, and that everything goes right for you in that movie. Play this movie out in your mind every night before you go to sleep and watch your life begin to change. *Believe* that it can happen and you'll make it happen.

Dilma Roussef is a former Marxist guerrilla fighter who was imprisoned and tortured for resisting the military dictatorship in Brazil. She has also survived a battle with cancer. On October 31, 2010, Mrs. Rousseff was elected President of Brazil, becoming its first female leader. Not bad for a former prisoner.

Remember Dewey Bozella from the chapter on *determination*? He spent 26 years in prison for a crime he didn't commit. He said that he dreamed of achieving his goals at night in his cell. On October 15, 2011 he completed his dream at the age of 52 by winning his first and only professional fight. Never stop dreaming. These examples were given to show the truth behind the maxim: *what the mind can conceive and believe, man can achieve*.

"*The empires of the future are the empires of the mind.*"
—*Winston Churchill*

The Art of Thinking Big

Thinking big allows you to see over the gates and walls of your prison. It will allow you to see over and around the problems that arise on your quest. If you want to accomplish great things, you have to think on a higher plane.

This means leaving the comfy confines of your own little cell, and thinking as if the whole world is your playground. The world will be your playground if you're led by your imagination. Small minds accomplish small things. Those of you who can think big will become Millionaire Prisoners. In the chapter on *Objectives* I will show you how to take the steps to achieving your goals, but right now, think big about those goals. Dream big. Act as if there are no limits to what you can achieve. Because there are none!

I do understand that as a prisoner, you have higher hurdles that you have to jump to achieve success. But now you have something that will give you an advantage over others in achieving your dreams. Think big. Act big. But talk little. Be humble. Don't get a big head. The more success you have, the humbler you should become. Millionaire Prisoners don't brag arrogantly, but speak through our actions. That is the true sign of maturity. Let others talk big, while you think big and accomplish big things.

If you want to read more about the art of thinking big, some great books are Dr. Norman Vincent Peale's *The Power of Positive Thinking*, and Dr. David J. Schwartz's *The Magic of Thinking Big*. These books have influenced some of the greatest writers and speakers of our age. They are must-read classics.

"To me it's very simple; if you're going to be thinking anyway, you might as well think big. Most people think small, because people are afraid of success, afraid of making decisions, afraid of winning. And that gives people like me a great advantage."

—Donald Trump

An Unstoppable Weapon

It has been said that your mind is your only weapon. Contained in this mind is imagination. You've had it since birth. Think about children. They have the most vivid imagination of us all. Go back to your childhood and the roots of your imagination. Recapture that. Tap into this weapon of mind power. No matter how long its been, or how old you are, you can bring it back to life.

Seth Ferranti did 15 years in prison for a drug conviction. He used his time to write books like *Prison Stories*. Together, he and his wife ran Gorilla Convict Publications, which published his books. His imagination produced ideas that are benefitting him and his family. Some of the most famous writing in history has come from prisoners. John Bunyan was in prison when he wrote *The Pilgrim's Progress*. Dr. Martin Luther King, Jr. wrote his famous letter from the Birmingham jail. William Sidney Porter went to an Ohio prison for embezzlement. While in prison he committed himself to study and *preparation*. Upon his release he secured employment at $100 a week writing a weekly short story for the *New York World*. Fame and fortune soon found him under the pseudonym of O'Henry. These prisoners didn't allow their mind to be locked up. Neither should you. Free your mind by allowing your imagination to lead you.

Imagine this. Everything invented can be done better. The myth that nothing is left to be invented is completely false. Every day, someone thinks of something that would help millions of people. It's what they do with their idea that either turns them into a success or someone else into a success. Whatever you do, there is a way to do it better, bigger, and built with outstanding *quality*. Your life is filled with opportunities to serve better, build better, create more, imagine more, and to think bigger. By using the suggestions in this chapter, you can take advantage of these opportunities.

Another example of the power of imagination can be found in prisoner Omar Broadway. Locked up for a 1999 carjacking,

Broadway found himself in a New Jersey state prison. Using a smuggled video camera, he shot raw prison footage and then had his mom sell copies of the film for $5. Director Douglas Tirola then used it to make a documentary: *An Omar Broadway Film*. In 2008, the film was featured at the Tribeca Film Festival. It was picked up by HBO and aired in 2010. By using a little ingenuity, Broadway has taken a substantial step toward prosperity, and has found his profit center.

While reading the May 2013 issue of the *Conscious County Courier* I came across the ingenuity of Arizona death row prisoner Chad Lee. George Kayer (of *Inmate Shopper* fame) shared how Mr. Lee gets wooden dominoes and takes them to the recreation pen where he grinds off the paint. He then shapes them on the rough steel edges of the stool in his cell. I salute Chad's *determination* and imagination in crafting his cell-made jewelry. Here's his brochure so you can see for yourself:

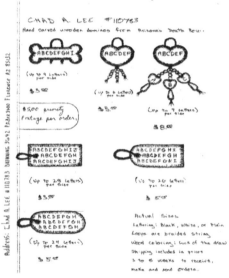

Once again, everyone is different. You may find different ways to build and strengthen your imagination. You may find that different people, places, and things stimulate your creative thinking patterns. When you find these things, use them in your life immediately. Always remember that the world of imagination is limitless.

> *"The world of reality has its bounds, the world of imagination is boundless."*
>
> —*Rousseau*

The difference between a prisoner who uses their imagination and one who doesn't, is simple. It can be found throughout these ABCs. Millionaire Prisoners are led by their imagination because to do the impossible you must imagine the invisible.

> *"Your imagination is your preview of life's coming attraction."*
> —*Albert Einstein*

Millionaire Prisoner Prosperity Keys

- Your imagination will give you a multitude of ideas that if you put to use will deliver success and prosperity.
- Find a way to capture thoughts and ideas as they come to you.
- Use the public domain as a source of ideas to build on.
- Your idea could be a new combination of old ideas and thoughts.
- Practice visualization. See yourself accomplishing your dream or implementing your idea.
- Don't think small, think big. Think outside the cell.
- Allow your imagination to lead you on your journey.

JUSTICE

Wrong none by doing injuries, or omitting the benefits that are your duty.

—*Benjamin Franklin*

Most of these ABCs are based on character traits that if you acquire, will lead you to prosperity. This chapter contains one of the most important virtues you can hope to acquire. As Arthur Schopenhauer stated many years ago, "Justice is, therefore, the first and fundamentally essential cardinal virtue." If that is so, and I believe it is, then what is justice?

The Definition of Justice

Simply defined, justice is fairness and equality. Think for a minute about the statue of Lady Justice. You can find replicas of her in most courtrooms. She has a blindfold over her eyes. This represents the ability not to take sides in a dispute. The scales she holds are balanced equally. They are not tipped one way or the other. This represents being fair and weighing both sides. The sword she carries represents punishment for violators of this virtue. Some of you may think of Lady Justice and laugh. You've been through the court system and think, where was the fairness? But that feeling of injustice should cause you to want to be fair in all that you do.

Of course, if you've begun to develop a different *attitude* you can easily see that justice is best meted out fairly. If you've been wrongfully convicted, it should make you want to correct wrongs, not do wrong. You can't become a Millionaire Prisoner when you are busy plotting the downfall of those who've harmed you. Throw away that old mentality and begin to live in the present and not the past.

"Revenge is the delight of a mean spirit and petty mind."
—Juvenal

Petty Injustice

I once had a cellmate named John who would stand at the cell door and grab the food trays when they were placed in the food slot. He would then hold them in his hands and weigh each tray to see which one felt heavier. He was trying to keep the one that had more food. Sometimes he would go as far as to open the trays up and see which one had bigger portions of food contained in it. Was he being fair and just? No, he was being petty, and acting like the fool he was. The right thing to do is grab the trays and ask your cellmate which one he wants. As it has been said, fairness is cutting an apple in half, and letting the other person choose which half they want.

But was this petty act by John really that big of a deal? It ended up being one. John was in the cell with Steve after me. Steve is a good jailhouse lawyer and a quiet guy who minds his own business. John kept up his petty tray thing with Steve. Steve noticed it, but didn't say anything. A couple of months later, John received a letter from the court stating that he had ten days to file a memorandum of law about why his post-conviction petition should not be thrown out of court. He asked Steve to help him, but Steve politely refused. The court deadline passed and John's petition was thrown out. He couldn't understand that his petty, unfair act with the food trays caused him to miss his deadline. Now he may possibly spend the rest of his life in prison because of his petty ways. Remember, every cause has an effect, every action a reaction.

This above scenario about John was an isolated incident. But it could happen and probably has happened to many others. I'm not saying Steve was right in his actions either. He should have assisted John with his petition because that is the *right* thing to do. But I understand why he didn't. The Muslim prisoners say that one hour in the execution of justice is worth seventy years of prayer. Justice can go a long way, either for or against you.

The Law of Consequences

One of the Universal Laws of the Cosmos is Karma, or the law of consequences. Karma is a Sanskrit word that means "comeback." What goes around *does* come back around. No relationship, business, enterprise, or endeavor can last unless it's built on justice. If it isn't, Karma will repay it in stride. This can be evidenced by the recent scandals in the Illinois government. From the "liscense to bribe" and "pay to play" investigations that lead to the conviction and imprisonment of Former Illinois governor George Ryan, to the impeachment, conviction, and imprisonment of former governor Rod Blagoevich. You also have the conviction of Lt. Jon Burge, a former police detective in Chicago who lied about torturing suspects and making them confess to crimes they didn't do. These Illinois officials experienced temporary success only to have their houses of cards crumbled by Lady Justice. Time has dealt them a blow they may never recover from.

Corruption and criminal acts by government officials and police is not limited to Illinois alone. Mike Carona was the sheriff of Orange County in California. He was sentenced to 5 and a half years in prison because he took bribes and used his office to enrich himself. Another former sheriff, Daniel Presgraves, of Page County, Virginia, was sentenced to 19 months in prison for corruption charges.

The former Commissioner of Corrections for the state of New York, Bernard Kerik was sentenced to four years in federal prison after he pled guilty to charges of tax fraud and lying to federal agents. He lied to IRS agents about profits from his autobiography: *The Lost Son: A Life In Pursuit Of Justice*. We can say: he lost, son; justice pursued him.

More space is needed than allotted here to chronicle the list of officials who have been brought down by the sword of Lady Justice. There are many more who feel that they may never get caught, but they'll eventually be destroyed. Someone is always watching. No matter what side of the fence you're on, justice will prevail. This principle has no reversal. The scales will eventually balance out. What goes around comes around. To become a Millionaire Prisoner you must put yourself on the right side of Karma.

One prisoner who did just that was Wilder "Kendric" Berry. Mr. Berry was wrongfully convicted and spent more than eight years in the Illinois Department of Corrections. He is now a senior paralegal at the high-powered Chicago law firm of Winston & Strawn, LLP., where he protects the justice that others deserve.

Justice Frees The Innocent

For the prisoner reading this who has been wrongfully convicted and believes that justice may escape your grasp, I offer the following examples to give you hope. Don't ever give up.

An Oklahoma man, Alvin McGee, Jr. was held in prison for 14 years for a rape he didn't commit. DNA eventually freed him and he settled his wrongful imprisonment claim for $12 million. In Indiana, a federal jury awarded $9 million to Larry Mayes for 19 years in prison for a rape he didn't commit.

Ray Krone spent over 10 years in prison for a murder he didn't commit. The main evidence at his trial were bite marks on his victim, which were erroneously linked to Krone. Because of those bite marks, he became known as the "snaggletooth killer." He was eventually freed and made famous on the television show *Extreme Makeover*, when he was given a winning smile. Krone was awarded $4.4 million for his bogus conviction and imprisonment.

In my home state of Illinois, a state replete with wrongful convictions, a federal jury awarded Alejandro Dominguez over $9 million for four years in prison for a bogus rape conviction. He was 16 years old when he was arrested and had to endure the stigma that comes with having to register as a sex offender.

Kevin Fox was arrested in 2004 for the sexual assault and murder of his 3-year-old daughter, Riley. He was eventually exonerated and an Illinois jury awarded him over $15 million for the violation of his civil rights.

In a malicious prosecution case, a $100 million dollar verdict was secured on behalf of four men who were framed by FBI agents Dennis Condon and H. Paul Rico. Of the four men framed, two died in prison. The other two men were released after serving 29, and 33 years, respectively. In a true showing that Karma and the principle of justice balance things out, Rico was arrested for the murder of an Oklahoma businessman. He died in prison awaiting trial on those charges.

Rubin "The Hurricane" Carter, a world-class prizefighter, was framed for a triple homicide in New Jersey. He spent the next two decades fighting for his release. Justice eventually did prevail, and in 1993, he was awarded the world Championship for his fight outside the ring, the only person to ever be able to make that claim. You may be aware of his story from the movie, *"The Hurricane"*, starring Denzel Washington, that was based on his struggle. Carter is another example showing that you must continue to fight for your justice. Use *determination* and go after your freedom.

The Most Rehabilitated Prisoner in America

As a 19-year-old eighth grade dropout, Wilbert Rideau was arrested in 1961 of murder and robbery at a bank in downtown Lake Charles, Louisiana. He was convicted and sentenced to die, and spent the next 13 years on death row. Rideau's conviction would be overturned four separate times. Upon entering prison, he could barely read and write, but on his own *will* he became a prolific writer. He began a small bimonthly magazine called *Lifer*, that serviced the prisoners serving life sentences at Angola. He wrote a column about prison called *The Jungle* for a chain of African-American newspapers in the South. Because of these successes he was appointed as editor of *The Angolite*, Angola's prison newspaper. His article in the September-October 1978 edition of *The Angolite*, "Conversations With The Dead," won the 1979 ABA Silver Gavel Award, the first time a prisoner ever won it. His 1980 article, *The Sexual Jungle*, won the 1980 George Polk Award. Rideau also published an article about incarcerated veterans in *Penthouse*.

Under his guidance, along with co-editor, Billy Wayne Sinclair (see *Growth* chapter), *The Angolite* was a seven-time finalist for the National Magazine Award. Because of his work, Rideau had appearances on *Larry King Live*, ABC's *20/20*, and traveled to Washington, D.C. to attend the annual American Society of Newspaper Editors. He also directed the Oscar nominated film, *The Farm*, which recounts life at Angola. Rideau became known as the "most rehabilitated prisoner in America." He was eventually released from prison after 44 years. Although it took a while, justice did come. If you would like to read more about Rideau's story, see his book: *In The Place of Justice: A Story of Punishment and Deliverance.*

Millionaire Prisoner Case Study

Kerry Max Cook was born and raised on a military base by an Army father. After his father left the military, his family moved to a small town in Texas. Cook started getting into trouble with the law for stealing cars. He was sent to Ferguson Farm in the Texas Department of Corrections in the 1970's. Released at the age of 18, he went back to his small town. But as most of us know, once you're in the system you become a target. Cook certainly became one. He was put on probation, and spent time in a mental hospital. But major trouble was looming on the horizon.

In 1977, at the age of 20, Cook was arrested and falsely accused of the rape and murder of Linda Jo Edwards. Thrown in jail, and denied bail, he was harassed and questioned without his lawyers being present. The district attorney was an overzealous prosecutor who was trying to win re-election. Police beat him, and set him up to be beaten by other prisoners. When he was placed in solitary confinement, he wasn't given a shower for days. Cook's subsequent trial was a gross injustice in itself. The presiding judge overruled all of his attorney's objections at trial and denied most of the major pretrial motions. The police Lt. who testified about fingerprint evidence got his accreditation from a 6-month correspondence course. The blood found at the crime scene was never sent to the lab for comparison. The prosecution put on bogus jailhouse snitch testimony. The jury found Cook guilty and his lawyers presented no evidence on his behalf in the penalty phase of his trial. The judge sentenced Cook to die.

Upon his arrival on Texas' death row, Cook became a target because of his case, his youth, and his looks. He was raped in the exercise yard by a shank wielding prisoner. After returning back to his cell he tried to kill himself with a razor. The despair he felt pushed him to start reading law books to try and find the key to getting out of prison. The jailhouse snitch who testified at his trial recanted, and a new lawyer filed an appeal for him. It took the appellate court 8 years to rule on it. Like so many other court decisions, they admitted that there were errors in his trial, but that these errors were harmless. His conviction and sentence were upheld.

While in prison, Cook's brother, Doyle Hayne, was shot and killed outside of a bar over a pair of sunglasses. He became determined to get out of prison. He started to go through his trial transcripts and find what he thought were errors. He typed them up on an old Royal typewriter that he bought from another prisoner. Cook couldn't afford typewriter ribbons, so he recycled old ones by using mineral oil, and rubbing carbon paper over the ribbon. He then sent his notes to the *Dallas Morning News* editor, who showed him *favor* and assigned a reporter to investigate the case. In 1988, the *News* ran a front-page article declaring that Cook had been railroaded at his trial. He was able to obtain new attorneys, who secured affidavits from expert witnesses that contradicted the state's witnesses at trial. The Texas Court of Criminal Appeals once again affirmed his conviction and depression set in on Cook.

Eventually the Texas appeals court did reverse his conviction in 1992. Cook was sent back to the same county jail as before, and once again thrown into solitary confinement. With the help of Centurion Ministries and Jim McCloskey, his second trial ended in a hung jury. During the deliberations, the jury opened an evidence bag and found a stocking inside a pair of the victim's pants. The stocking was alleged by the prosecutor at the first trial to have been taken by the killer. In 1994, at a third trial, he was again convicted and sentenced to die.

Back on death row things were a little different this time. Cook received an average of 10 letters a day in support from people on the outside. Once again, TCCA reversed his conviction in 1996. After 20 years in prison, Centurion Ministries helped bond him out of jail for $100,000 after receiving donations for his support. He was shown more *favor* when given a job assisting a criminal defense attorney. When his used car was broadsided, this attorney helped get him a new car. In 1999, the murder victim's panties were sent to the lab and semen was found. DNA would eventually prove that he was not the person who left the semen on the panties. On the day of jury selection, the State allowed him to plead no contest and maintain his innocence. He was finally officially free.

Cook's story would be one of several told in *The Exonerated*, a play based on injustices in the court system. In 2005, Court TV aired a made-for-television movie based on the play. Cook went on a tour speaking about the errors of the court system. In 2000, on *Live with Geraldo Rivera*, he was on a panel that debated the death penalty. Cook would go on to write his own book, *Chasing Justice: My story of Freeing Myself After Two Decades on Death Row for a Crime I Didn't Commit*. After being released from prison, Cook and his partner, Sandra, had a son. His name—Kerry Justice. Justice had been delivered.

It's written in the U.S. Constitution that someone accused of a crime has the right to a fair and impartial trial. While Nancy Grace and the "murder media" feel this isn't so, it's the law. The moral to the Kerry Max Cook story, and the other exonerated prisoner stories, is that if they would've been given a fair trial in the first place, they would've never been convicted. The moral to this chapter is that if we give everyone a fair and impartial deal, we'll experience true prosperity.

The above examples were given to demonstrate that like the Universal Law of Karma, the principle of justice will in the end, balance out. There are many more examples of prisoners being freed across America because of wrongful convictions. It would take a book unto itself to give those prisoners their proper justice and *recognition*. If you're interested in reading more about wrongful convictions, there are numerous books available. Check out John Grisham's *The Innocent Man*, or *Actual Innocence* by Barry Scheck, Peter Neufeld, and Jim Dyer. Never lose faith or give up hope in your case. Should you find yourself becoming discouraged about your appeal or case, come back to this chapter and reread the examples given. Use them for hope and inspiration. Don't ever give up.

From Prison To Law Man

Shon Hopwood was sentenced to 12 years in prison at the age of 23 for five bank robberies in rural Nebraska. Instead of participating in the usual prison folly, Hopwood spent most of his time in the prison law library getting an *education* and helping other prisoners. One case he worked on made it all the way to the U.S. Supreme Court where the court not only accepted the *pro se* brief he filed for prisoner John Fellers, but sided with his argument. Upon his release from prison, Hopwood was shown *favor* by the Bill and Melinda Gates Foundation and given a scholarship to law school at Washington University. You can read more about his story in the book, *Law Man: My Story of Robbing Banks, Winning Supreme Court Cases, and Finding Redemption*. Or more on his website; *www.shonhopwood.com*.

Maybe you've heard about Jerry "the Jew" Rosenberg. He was incarcerated and given a life sentence for the murder of a police officer. A lot of people believe that Rosenberg was innocent. While in prison he became the first prisoner in New York to earn a law degree and represent a client in a jury trial. You can read about him in Stephen Bello's book: *Doing Life: The Extraordinary Saga of America's Greatest Jailhouse Lawyer*.

These two prisoners turned their *knowledge* of the law into something great. They invested their time and were able to help their fellow prisoners. They are Millionaire Prisoner's in their own right and so are you. All you have to do is put your time to good use and go after your dreams.

Resource Box: Some of you will need to write your own legal briefs during your journey. I recommend you get copies of the following books and study them:

Writing To Win: The Effective Legal Writer by Stephen D. Stark;

The Winning Brief by Bryan A. Garner;

Self Help Post-Conviction Handbook by Joe Allan Bounds;

Legal Research: How To Find and Understand the Law by Stephen Elias and Susan Levinkind.

Don't forget to study what books your law library has available. You can find a few gems around, but you have to look.

The Fallacies of Illicit Prosperity

Because you are trying to become a Millionaire Prisoner, you need prosperity that will last. To paraphrase Theodore Roosevelt, only prosperity that is based on justice can last. A lot of us were illegal entrepreneurs in the free-world. Think about the money you made through your criminal acts? Do you have any of it left? Or are you dependent on friends and family members for money for commissary? Because your money was not based on justice it didn't last.

A perfect example of prosperity gained by illicit means that did *not* last can be found in a group of female prisoners housed in Pennsylvania. These imaginative cons decided to scam thirsty males in the free-world out of money by using pen-pal websites to post profiles on with promises of companionship, sex, and marriage. While the scam netted over $200,000 for those women, it was a pyrrhic victory. Government officials seized their assets and the prisoners were given additional years in prison for fraud.

Other prisoners have defrauded the U.S. government out of thousands of tax refund dollars only to receive years in prison tacked on to their sentences after losing the money they received. Remember, there is no such thing as something for nothing. I've talked to plenty of prisoners who had similar get-rich-quick schemes and advised them not to pursue them. You can't build lasting prosperity on the foundation of an illegal scheme. Your house will eventually crumble down on itself.

Count Victor Lustig, the famous con-man who once swindled Al Capone, and who sold the Eiffel Tower twice, died in a prison hospital, broke. Crime doesn't pay.

These examples illustrate two principles that I hope you make part of your *knowledge*. One, only a prosperity built on justice will last. Two, someone is always watching. With these principles in mind, it's best to practice being honest and fair with all. Pretend that someone is always watching you, because someone always is—*especially in prison*.

> *"Justice is the gift of the most compassionate and wise."*
> —*Gerry Spence*

Sowing Justice to Reap Justice

Being fair when you deal with people in everyday life will cause them to want to deal with you in the future. Every day you are faced with opportunities to bless others in your interactions. If you do them right, they will do you right. It's Karma all over again. Build a reputation for being fair. This will cause others to seek you out. That in turn will enable you to recognize opportunities to prosper. But we have to practice being fair to all, because Karma is not selective. Neither should we be.

"Justice is indiscriminately due to all, without regard to numbers, wealth, or rank."

— John Jay

How many of us can say we treat everyone with impartiality? Most of us can't say that truthfully. I know that I'm no saint in this regard. But this is a character flaw that has formed in our mind. For different reasons of race, crime, status, and posture, we discriminate on those we deal with. Prison has its pecking order. While you may believe this is a good thing, I believe differently.

In prison you form the daily *habits* that will determine your actions once you're released. These are the habits that make up who you are, and what you are. If you are being partial in your everyday actions in prison, how do you expect to act once you're released? Most of you will continue to practice these same prejudices that have formed in your mind over the course of your incarceration. I did this when being released from prison last time. The way to stop this from happening is to begin practicing being fair right now. That way, you can make it a habit, and it will become natural for you.

Of course if you deal with someone and they lie, cheat, or steal from you, then you have a valid reason to cut them off. If you know someone who is always scheming, lying, or stealing, then don't make any deals with that person. If you do, you'll be forever trying to clean up your mess. It isn't worth the lost sleep, lost time, and lost merch that you'll end up paying in the long run. Millionaire Prisoners deal with the just, and are just in all their deals. Make it your foundation.

> *"You can't make a good deal with a bad person."*
> —*Warren Buffett*

When you get a reputation for being fair and just, and of doing the right things, people will trust you with positions of great power and responsibility. They will do this because they'll trust that you won't abuse these positions. Not only do things right, but do the right things. Stand out by being fair. Don't allow anyone to leave your table feeling like they lost. Practice a "win-win" philosophy in life. Great deals are ones in which all parties benefit. If you can produce these deals for yourself and others you will achieve true prosperity.

> *"I engage in no transaction, intentionally, that does not benefit all whom it affects."*
> —*Napoleon Hill*

If you do this one deal at a time, you'll become a Millionaire Prisoner.

Millionaire Prisoner Prosperity Keys

- Acquire the *habit* of being fair and just in all that you do.

• Practice being impartial to all those you deal with.

• Do the right things at the right time, thereby sowing seeds of justice.

• Don't allow someone to leave the table without feeling that they've won.

KNOWLEDGE

The knowledge of all things is possible.

—Leonardo DaVinci

To know is to be. To know one's self is the greatest knowledge. There are many areas in your life where you can become more knowledgeable. This will greatly aid you on your journey. In this chapter you will learn how to become knowledgeable of yourself and others.

While it may be impossible to completely know someone else, you can learn your strengths and weaknesses. The great military strategist, Sun-Tzu, wrote in *The Art of War* that if you know yourself and the enemy you will never be at risk. Do you really know yourself and your enemies? Understand that your greatest enemy is yourself and the way you thought that brought you to prison. Knowing this is half the battle. The other half is doing something about it.

How To Become More Knowledgeable

One of the best ways is to ask questions. Go back to that simple school of *Who? What? Where? Why?* and *When?* Also add *How?* Asking the right questions will enable you to solve problems that arise. Continue to learn and keep your intellect in use by asking questions. If you don't have the right answers you haven't asked the right question.

> *"Always the beautiful answer who asks a more beautiful question."*
>
> —E.E. Cummings

Just as the doctor gives you a physical for your health, you need to give yourself a physical for your mental health. This examination will consist of a series of questions that are designed to reveal weaknesses, cancers, and viruses that hold you back. You will also learn about your strengths, talents, and dreams. When you answer the below questions be ruthless with yourself. The knowledge acquired from the *truthful* answers can be worth more to you than all the gold in the world. The reason is because if you had all the gold, but didn't know these answers you would surely lose all that gold to a more knowledgeable person.

The keys to becoming a Millionaire Prisoner can be found in your honest answers to the following questions.

<u>Self Knowledge 101</u>

1. *Who are the people who would like to see me fail most? Your answer will reveal the people that you should stay away from.*
2. *Who are the people I would like at my beside if I was dying? Your answer will reveal the people who you care about the most. Don't wait for your looming death to say or do what you should say or do today.*
3. *What person's life and accomplishments most excites me? Your answer will possibly reveal your calling in life. It could also reveal a possible mentor or someone you should study.*

4. *Who are the people I would not want to know my weaknesses? Your answer will reveal those people who are untrustworthy because they talk too much. These people could want you to succeed, but because they are a blabbermouth, may tell other people your weaknesses and plans, and therefore jeopardize your quest. Be careful.*

5. *Who are the people I would share my weaknesses with? Your answer will reveal the people you can trust. These are your true friends. Cherish them.*

6. *Where do I want to be in five years and how will I get there? Your answer should be explicit and detailed. As you achieve this goal your answer will change.*

7. *Where do I want to be in ten years and how will I get there? Same principle as number six, just more long term.*

8. *Where do I want to be in 30 years and how will I get there? The answers to questions six and seven may be steps you take to get to this answer. Set the bar high and go after your dreams.*

9. *What do I want to most improve in my life this week, and how will I do it? Find the easy step to making your life better, then do it.*

10. *What do I want to most improve in my life this month and how will I do it? Number 9 could assist you in accomplishing this answer?*

11. *What do I want to improve most in my life this year and how will I do it? Same principle as questions nine and ten, except you can't accomplish this answer in a week or month.*

12. *Who do I need to forgive for a past wrong or deed? Holding on to anger, or to grudges, will only hold you back. If at all possible forgive these people openly and in person. If not, do it yourself and move on.*

13. *What upsets me most in someone else? Don't ask yourself this so you can go around pointing this trait or quirk out to people.*

You find this answer so that you can work on yourself and your reaction to these people.

14. *What most excites me in someone else? Your answer will reveal the kind of people you like to be around, are compatible with, and the kind of environment you would thrive in.*

15. *What do I want most, which I will never get? Don't chase after false dreams and illusions. A blind man may never see. While miracles do happen, to wait on one is insanity. Things you can never get should be ignored.*

16. *In what conditions and at what time am I most receptive to learning and completing a task? Your answer reveals the optimal time to conduct the studies that you've laid out. This time is what Dr. Oz of the Doctor Oz Show calls your chronotype. Find the time of day when your energy and creativity are at their peak.*

17. *What most distracts me from learning and completing a task? Not only can people distract you, but certain noises, environments, and times of day can hinder you. Some of us prisoners have ADD and other mental illnesses and knowing what distracts us can greatly aid us in our quest. When you find the answers to this question, avoid them at all cost.*

18. *What personal character flaw do I need to conquer? We all have flaws but they are only flaws because we haven't corrected them. Find the answer, then correct it.*

19. *What personal character trait attracts others to me? Find this answer then learn how to emphasize this trait to make it better and brighter.*

20. *What are my mental strengths and how can I use them? Find this answer, then, put your strengths to work to assist you on your journey.*

21. *What are my mental and physical weaknesses and how can I improve them? This answer could be the same as the one in*

question 18, but it could be different because it's just an area you are weak in.

22. *What is my worst habit and how can I break it? This is probably something you do daily and causes you harm. Use the system in the chapter on Habit to get rid of it.*

23. *Which good habit would I most like to acquire and how will I do it? Fill the void left from the bad habit that you eradicated with this one.*

24. *Am I using my time wisely, and how can I improve my usage of time? As a prisoner, you have an abundance of free time. But this time is only beneficial if you're using it wisely. Use the steps in the chapters on Habit and Objective to make time your ally.*

25. *Am I working harder than my competition? If not, how come if you have a business, or sell products, you have competition. Find the answer to this question and you can become the market leader in your chosen field.*

The next 73 questions are not annotated like the first 25, but I believe you now get the agenda behind these questions. You have before you the example of what to examine in each answer. Do the same when you answer the next 73 questions.

26. *Do I put things off that could be dome today? If so, why?*
27. *Do I offend people easily? If so, how?*
28. *Do I watch daytime television like soap operas? If so, why?*
29. *Do I constantly compare myself to others? If so, why?*
30. *Do I constantly think about the past? If so, why?*
31. *Do I think big and make bold plans? If not, why?*
32. *Do I think life is hopeless, or I'll never get out of prison? If so, why?*
33. *Do I think of failure more than of success? If so, why?*
34. *Do I learn from my mistakes? If not, why?*

35. *Do I have an alcohol, drug, or other addiction? If so, why?*
36. *Do I accept correction easily? If not, why?*
37. *Do I worry about what others will say before I make decisions? If so, why?*
38. *Do I allow others to influence my decisions? If so, why?*
39. *Do I practice good spending habits and save money? If not, why?*
40. *Do I associate with the wrong people? If so, why?*
41. *Do I get angry easily? If yes, why?*
42. *Do I deliver my best in all that I do? If not, why?*
43. *Do I deliver more than I'm paid for? If not, why?*
44. *Do I still fantasize about a life of crime? If yes, why?*
45. *Do I ask my mentor all the questions I need answered? If not, why?*
46. *Do I show my mentor that I appreciate their time? If not, why?*
47. *Do I listen to my mentor's counsel by using their advice in my own life? If not, why?*
48. *Does my mentor correct my weaknesses? If not, why?*
49. *Is my mentor interested in my success? If not, why?*
50. *Does my mentor have the power to get leaders to listen to me? If not, who does?*
51. *Does my mentor give me the keys to prosperity? If not, why?*
52. *What do I constantly visualize about in my life? Does it help me?*
53. *What am I willing to ask help from others on? Can I ask for more?*
54. *What am I willing to wait patiently for? Am I ready for it?*
55. *What am I willing to prepare for, even if it takes years?*
56. *Are my objectives realistic or just pipe dreams? How can I correct it?*
57. *Who hates me for my desire to achieve? Are they close to me?*

58. *Who feeds my weaknesses instead of my strengths? Why am I with them?*

59. *Who wants to discuss my past instead of my future? Why do I still have discussions with them?*

60. *Who is unhappy and blames everything on being unlucky? Do I stay away from them?*

61. *Who does not want to learn and gain wisdom? Do I hang around them?*

62. *Have I tried to create opportunities where there were none? If not, why?*

63. *Do I close the door on opportunity? If so, why?*

64. *Do I keep my word and meet deadlines? If not, why?*

65. *Do I believe that I can accomplish all that my mind can conceive? If not, why?*

66. *Do I utilize my strengths to maximum benefit? If not, why?*

67. *Do I play the poor hands I'm dealt in life well? If not, why?*

68. *What prisoner around me still believes in get-rich-quick-schemes? Is he or she in my circle? If so, why?*

69. *What prisoner waits for things to happen instead of making things happen? Can I stay away from them?*

70. *What prisoner spends more money than they have and doesn't pay their debts? Do I make deals with them? If so, why?*

71. *What group of people could I solve a problem for? How can I capitalize on it?*

72. *Where can I go that will allow me to be noticed? Am I there? If not, why?*

73. *Is what I'm doing with my life what I desire most? If not, why?*

The Most Important Selection You Can Make

In *Think and Grow Rich*, Napoleon Hill Wrote that the most common cause of failure is the wrong selection of a mate in marriage. Be careful in selecting your partner, especially if you're considering marrying someone while you're in prison. The next 28 questions deal with you and your partner. These questions and how you answer them should reveal to you if your significant other is the right one or not.

74. *Am I willing to give my partner time devoted solely to them?*
75. *Are they willing to give me their time?*
76. *Is what I love to do also what he or she loves to do?*
77. *Do I impress my significant other?*
78. *Does he or she ask me questions about my plans or goals?*
79. *Do we continue to bond and become closer?*
80. *Does he or she learn from their mistakes?*
81. *Does he or she keep company with the wrong people?*
82. *Do they accuse me before hearing my side of things?*
83. *Has he or she had a string of bad relationships?*
84. *Does my significant other's parents look at me favorably?*
85. *Does he or she overreact to small problems?*
86. *Does he or she have a job, or going to school for a profession?*
87. *Is he or she a self-motivator?*
88. *Does he or she have an inferiority complex?*
89. *Would I like to have children with them?*
90. *Would I be willing to spend the rest of my life with them if they never changed?*
91. *Have I introduced them to my loved ones?*
92. *Are they respectful to my parents?*
93. *Are they grateful when receiving a gift?*
94. *Do they respect where I've been?*
95. *Do I find it hard to talk to him or her?*

96. *Do we discuss things together before we make major decisions?*
97. *Can I trust them with my money?*
98. *Can we trust each other with our secrets?*
99. *Can we trust each other with our most painful memories?*
100. *Can we trust each other around our friends when we're not there?*
101. *Can we trust each other when we're not together?*

"A husband or wife is the greatest environmental influence for any man or woman."
— W. Clement Stone

Get in the *habit* of asking yourself these questions. Set aside a specific time once a week and go over these questions and your answers. Write your answers down. This will allow you to check your progress. Your answers will be different as you experience *growth* in your life and knowledge. Make sure that you are alone when conducting your self-examination. Do not allow others to get hold of this information. The above 101 questions are timeless and you can use them for the rest of your life.

"The quality of our lives is determined by the quality of the questions we ask ourselves."
— Anthony Robbins

Instruction From History

Some of the greatest minds in history have discussed the tactic of self-examination. The great philosopher Plotinus said: "Withdraw into yourself and look, and if you do not find yourself beautiful yet, act as does the creator of a statue that is to be made beautiful, he cuts away here, he smooths there, and he make this line lighter, this other purer, until a lovely face has grown upon his work . So you do also; cut away all that is excessive, straighten all that is crooked, bring to light all that is overcast, labor to make all one glow of beauty, and never cease from chiseling your statue until there shines out from you the God-like splendor of virtue, until you see the perfect goodness in the stainless shrine."

After Nelson Mandela's wife, Minnie, was sentenced to jail time, he wrote her a letter giving her advice that all prisoners could use: "You may find that the cell is an ideal place to learn to know yourself, to search realistically and regularly the process of your own mind and feelings . . . Regular meditation, say of about 15 minutes a day before you turn in, can be very fruitful in this regard. You may find it difficult at first to pinpoint the negative factors in your life, but the tenth attempt may reap rich rewards. Never forget that a saint is a sinner that keeps on trying."

In your self-examination, and the answers to the questions you ask yourself, can be found the way to success. But sometimes you need other people to point out your faults before you become aware of them.

The person who read me the riot act was the mother of my twin daughters. Of course, at the time she was no longer interested in having a relationship with a long-term prisoner. She had become my foe and wrote me a vicious *"Dear John"* letter. In my case, *"Dear Josh."* In this letter she proceeded to tell me everything that was wrong with me and why she couldn't stand me anymore. She was writing on emotion and anger, but did reveal weaknesses in my nature, and some bad habits that I had acquired. Some of these destructive qualities I ignored before her letter, and yet some, I wasn't even aware of. I still have her letter and reread it periodically. It's the fuel for my fire to change, and allows me to check my progress in correcting my weaknesses.

Pay attention to what your enemies say about you. Pay attention to what people say about you in anger. Pay particular attention to what ex-lovers and jilted friends say. Sometimes a few truths will come out. In their words you can find knowledge of yourself that you may never know otherwise.

"By my foes, sir, I profit in the knowledge of myself."
— *William Shakespeare*

How To Become Knowledgeable of Others

We've dealt with learning about our Self. Now we must examine ways to learn about others and the world. Kids learn by being curious about everything, and they are the best learners. They are eager to learn. As we grow older, we seem to lose that curiosity we had when we were little. We need to get that back. Approach life with the curiosity that you had when you were a child. Ask questions, examine objects, do research. Be eager to learn.

I've discussed keeping an "idea folder" in the *imagination* chapter. Write down what you learn in your folder. Da Vinci kept a journal where he recorded his drawings, sketches, answers, and notes. He was curious about everything and recorded everything. Great minds ask great questions. Become curious again. Seek, and you shall find.

"A sense of curiosity is nature's original school of education."
— *Dr. Smiley Blanton*

Another thing you can do to become more knowledgeable is to doubt. Doubt what you see. Doubt what you hear. Doubt what you read. People make mistakes. Everyone doesn't know everything. If you aren't sure about something, check it out on your own. Never assume the other person is right. If they are wrong, keep it to yourself. It isn't worth your time to teach them. You have to work on yourself. Always doubt, especially if it comes off the TV, or from one of your prisoner peers.

You can also make your friends and acquaintances your teachers. Everyone brings their own life experiences to a conversation. In that experience is knowledge. Ask them questions. Where did they buy something? Where did they learn something? Where did they meet that person? Where did they read it? How did they do it? There are a million questions that you can ask that will enable you to learn valuable information.

After the conversation or meeting, ask yourself: Did I listen? Did I achieve what I wanted? Did I learn anything new? Did I make any progress? Do I need to set up another meeting? Do I need to cultivate this person as a friend? Every conversation is an opportunity to learn if you ask the right questions.

When you read, try out what the authors say. See if it works. Don't take their word for it. This goes for me too. Try out what I say in these ABCs. By demonstration, you will find what works best for you. If you find something that works, use it. If something doesn't work for you, then discard it and move on.

> *"Learn from others what to pursue, and what to avoid, and let your teachers be the lives of others."*
>
> — *Cato*

True Power

There is the oft repeated "knowledge is power" maxim. But that is only half true. There are some words missing.

"Organized knowledge that is put to use is power."
— *Napoleon Hill*

Think about this statement for a minute. Now think about your prison library. If the library just had books, but no order, or any system or way to identify books, it would be useless. But the library is arranged by subject and genre. A library that is arranged well, with easily identifiable research tools, has unlimited power.

Think about what you learn. Then organize it. Organize the facts into relevant categories. Facts are either relevant or irrelevant. The only ones that matter are the ones that will aid you, or hinder you, on your quest. Everything else is irrelevant. Your mind should be like a file system, ready to retrieve facts at will. Organize them correctly and you can experience true power. One caution on facts: they can become obsolete. What you learned in school may no longer be true because technology improves and science advances things. For more about this, check out *The Half-Life of Facts: Why Everything We Know Has an Expiration Date* by Samuel Arbesman.

In your use of curiosity and quest for knowledge, do not become like my fellow prisoner—Eisenberg. Mr. Eisenberg is very book smart. He doesn't own a television and spends all day reading. He's very good at trivia questions and *Jeopardy*. A guard comes every day to Eisenberg's cell and they will discuss questions on the *Trivial Pursuit* game. They went so far as to give themselves 'the moniker': "gurus of useless knowledge." All the book smarts is a waste because it's unorganized. Your goal is not to become a guru of useless knowledge. Your goal is to become a Millionaire Prisoner. Learn about yourself, those around you, and your chosen *objectives*. The rest is irrelevant. Organized knowledge put to use is true power.

How To Become An Expert On Any Topic

You don't have to ever do anything to become a so-called "expert." An expert is just someone who knows more than you about a topic. Think about all the talking heads on TV who are recognized experts on a topic, yet they've never got any results in that field. You can do it with this system. This system works, as I've used it over the years to learn. As you'll see, each step can easily be accomplished by a prisoner.

1. Pick a topic. Then read over anything you have available about this topic. Utilize the steps contained in the *Education* chapter on "The Art of Reading Non-Fiction."

2. Read more basic texts and periodicals on the subject. The prison library should have these materials available. Or request them from the Books to Prisoner projects included in the Appendix. *The Complete Idiot's Guide To* and *For Dummies* series of books are great to start with. Don't let the names fool you. These books are packed with the information you need. As you read these books, write down any books or periodicals mentioned in the text. Pay attention to other works listed in the bibliography. Also, write down the names of the experts who keep being quoted in the books you read.

3. Go back over your original books, records, and notes. Your examination should now be heightened because of your other reading.

4. Consult your mentor, or write the experts that you wrote down with any questions that you have. Ask them what other materials you can study. To get the best response, try to ask questions that the expert can answer off the top of their

head. No matter what your topic is, there's an expert on it. Here's a way to find experts on your topic:

A. Have someone you know do a search on your topic at *findarticles.com*. They can enter your search term and select "free articles only," and they would get all the available free magazine articles on your topic.

B. Get them to print out the articles on your topic and send them to you.

C. Read the articles to get the names of experts and authors of the articles. They should list their website and/or book at the end of the article. Write this down.

D. Do an online search through Google or another search engine, and get the expert's contact information. If you can't use the above steps, then I've listed a couple of companies in the Appendix who may help you. You can also search for experts on *www.guru.com* and *www.elance.com*.

5. Follow through on anything your mentor or expert suggests. Do not neglect this step.

6. Study any opposing views or texts. Now is the time to read the books that you wrote down from your earlier study.

Write different experts and ask them questions. Sometimes authors list ways to contact them. Do so. Never assume, always ask.

Incorporate what you learn into your life by acting on it, trying it out, and testing it. Get some results and experience.

Keep consulting with your mentors and experts. Keep studying your materials until you've mastered the subject or topic.

Always keep up-to-date with new technologies and ideas that pertain to your subject or topic.

"If you are an expert in something, you will never go hungry."
— *Paul Sarnoff*

The Bon-a-Fide Prison Expert

Most of us prisoners have heard of Robert "the Birdman of Alcatraz" Stroud. He became interested in birds while incarcerated at Leavenworth prison in Kansas. Stroud became an expert on canaries and authored a number of books and magazine articles about them. He was able to do this from segregation and extreme isolation. The Birdman is just another example of a prisoner finding his niche and becoming successful. You can do it too!

Always remember that no one has the final knowledge on anyone point. Life is a constant learning process. Do your own research, and gain your own knowledge. If it's relevant to reaching your *objectives* in life, you need to acquire the facts on how to do it. You can do this by using the steps above. Don't waste time on frivolous topics. Become knowledgeable of your line of work, that's it. Become master in that line and you can become a Millionaire Prisoner.

"I believe the true road to pre-eminent success in any line is to make yourself master in that line."
— *Andrew Carnegie*

As you learn, teach it to others. You will reinforce your own knowledge at the same time. Be patient with any student you acquire. Sow seeds of knowledge to reap harvests of it.

One final thought. Knowledge is knowing the right facts. But *wisdom* is being able to use that knowledge to achieve your goals in life. Do not become a guru of useless knowledge. Become a Millionaire Prisoner.

"We're all born ignorant, but one must work hard to remain stupid."

—Benjamin Franklin

Millionaire Prisoner Prosperity Keys

• Examine yourself by asking questions to find your weaknesses and your strengths. Then use your strengths to correct your weaknesses.

• Spend regular time in your cell going over yourself and recreating what you don't like about your life.

• Pay attention to others and learn from them. Ask questions, be curious, and doubt what you read, see, or hear.

• Do not become a guru of useless knowledge.

• Become an expert on any topic that is relevant to obtaining your objectives.

• Teach what you know to others, thereby reinforcing your own knowledge.

LAUGHTER

Against the assault of laughter nothing can stand.

—*Mark Twain*

It's said that happiness is the wine that sharpens the taste of the meal. Our meal is success and prosperity, and unless we can enjoy it, it will be useless to us and our loved ones. In the chapter on *Justice* we discussed the strategy of building your foundation on fairness. That will enable your prosperity to last. Laughter will enable *you* to last. What good will prosperity do if you're not around to experience it? This chapter will give you five easy steps on how to be happy in life.

The First Step

The first thing to do is laugh at the world. Everything will pass, so enjoy life while you can. Too many prisoners worry about things they can't control or change. Instead, they would be better off enjoying the good things in their life. Laugh at the things in life that bug you. Most of them are trivial and not worth your time.

In this classic book, *How To Stop Worrying and Start Living*, Dale Carnegie expressed the perfect idea: "About 90 percent of the things in our lives are right, and about 10 percent are wrong. If we want to be happy, all we have to do is concentrate on the

90 percent that are right, and ignore the 10 percent that are wrong." What are you worrying about that can be classified as belonging in that 10 percent? Pay attention to the 90 percent that is right in your life. Stop worrying and start living. Become happy and learn to laugh at the world.

In *Million Dollar Habits*, Robert Ringer calls this *"The Perspective Habit."* It's the ability to say "so what?" when problems arise. Of course, this way of thinking doesn't come natural to us humans, especially not prisoners. But it's one you should acquire that will help you on your journey. Why? Because the truth is: none of your problems really matter in the big picture of things. I certainly have learned this the hard way.

When I first started O'Barnett Publishing with my mother, I acted as if every little problem that came up was life threatening. If we missed a deadline my stress level went through the roof. When the prison administration confiscated our personal typewriters I acted like the world was going to end. My overreaction to these minor problems didn't help the situation, and in fact, contributed to my mother becoming ill because I was pushing her too hard. In the end none of these problems were worth getting upset over. I should've laughed at them and looked to the positive lessons contained in them. But I didn't, and I experienced a lot of unnecessary headaches.

When you learn to perceive problems as just the minor inconveniences that they are, you can laugh at them. They are not the end of the world, and you aren't going to die. Learn to say "So what?" Your prison went on lockdown? Laugh at that and say, so what? You didn't get honey buns at the commissary? Laugh at it and say, so what? You didn't get your phone call to go through? Laugh at it and say so what? You see, you'll always come off lockdown, get to go to another commissary, and make another phone call. But you only get one life to live, so why worry about trivial matters on your journey. Learn to laugh at the world and the problems that arise in your daily walk. If you can do this you'll be far ahead of everyone else on the road to success.

The Second Step

The second step is to control your anger. How many friends have you lost because of your anger? How many jobs or opportunities have you lost because of anger? I quit a job in anger over someone else's bad attitude. That decision was one in a series of bad choices that led me back to prison. Sometimes it's one inconsequential act or word that makes us blow up. But this anger is problematic. People don't respect the person who can't control their temper. Become a Millionaire Prisoner by controlling your anger and your reactions to what life brings your way.

"Our anger and annoyance are more detrimental to us than things themselves which anger or annoy us."
—Marcus Aurelius

No one can make you angry. No one can put thoughts in your head. It's your choice if you're angry or not. Anger messes up your day, gives you the feeling of being unhappy, and clouds your mind to the opportunities around you. Have you ever tried to accomplish something when you were mad? It doesn't turn out that well. This will cost you time and money in the long run. Try and keep a level head.

"If any man be unhappy, let him remember that he is unhappy by reason of himself alone."
—Epictetus

There will be times when your anger is justified. Do not allow people to see it. This will give the impression that you have everything under control. A person who seems to have things under control will be given many opportunities. These opportunities will lead to prosperity if you can capitalize on them. Don't allow people to see you sweat.

The Third Step

The third step is to practice compassion. In the prison complex, there are many who are less fortunate than you. Compassion allows you to understand the other person and assist them in their time of need. Because you want others to assist you, you should assist others. It's the Golden Rule and it works.

> "If you want others to be happy, practice compassion. If you want to be happy, practice compassion."
> —Dalai Lama

The funny thing that happens is when you make others happy you can't help but feel better. Have you ever brought a smile to someone's face? It's contagious. Seeing someone smile makes us want to smile. Happiness is the same way. If you help others become happy, you'll become happy.

> "Happiness is a perfume you cannot pour on others without getting a few drops on yourself."
> —Emerson

Some of the happiest people in the world are those that work with disabled children. It never ceases to amaze me how happy these people are. Their compassion towards these precious kids has brought them untold happiness.

Some of you may be worried that if you spend your time helping others you won't achieve your goals? That you may not achieve your own prosperity? You don't have to help everyone that you see, even though that would be the right thing to do. Instead, help the truly needy. Allow me to give you an example.

At my prison there was a prisoner named Murphy. He was born with Cerebral Palsy. Because of this affliction, Murphy has the use of his left hand only. His right hand is curled up, and can only be used for balance. He also talks funny because of his handicap. Most of the prisoners shunned him, called him names, and expressed other ill-truths about him. Why did they do this? Because they ignorantly prejudged him based on his looks and the way he talked. Instead of getting to know Murphy and find out that he has cerebral palsy, they judged him incorrectly.

Maybe it's because one of my daughters is in a wheelchair? Or maybe because of my studies I've learned to be more compassionate than my fellow prisoners? Whatever the case may be, I spoke to Murphy. Within minutes, he had me smiling, and revealed a creative mind, who was in the process of developing a comic book. By practicing compassion, and allowing Murphy to be happy in knowing that he had a friend, my day became better.

"Helping someone up won 't pull you down."
—*Harvey Mackay*

The Fourth Step

The fourth step is to rediscover life again. Basically, the way to rediscover life is to slow down and enjoy everything that life has to offer.

How many of you have lost your love of life? Do you allow the prison gates and walls to confine you not only in body, but in mind and soul also? By discovering all there is to love about life again, you can escape prison. But how do you rediscover this love of life again? Slow down, turn off the TV, and listen. Listen to music. Go out to the yard and listen to the bird singing its song. Listen to the wind rustle through the trees if you have some around you. Don't listen to the daily grind of the American prison complex. Listen to a child's laughter. Watch little children and their happiness as they discover all the new things in life. See nature and her beauty. See the beautiful inside people. Feel the air on your skin. Feel the caress of your loved one. Try to experience life and the world as you've never experienced it.

Learn to love life again. Learn to see all the beautiful things that the world beholds. Slow down and enjoy your friendships. Enjoy your children and your family members. Discover the romance of life again and you'll be happy.

"Nothing gives such complete and profound happiness as the perpetually fresh wonder and mystery of exciting life."
—Dr. Norman Vincent Peale

The Fifth Step

The fifth thing to do is love what you do. Most self-help and business books express that to become successful you must love what you do. That's common sense. Someone who is miserable in their job will not advance up the ladder of success. Someone who does not love what they do, will not look forward to getting up in the morning. They won't look for ways to improve what they do, make more money doing it, or share it with others. If you don't love what you're doing, others will see it on your face and will not want to help you on your journey.

An example of someone who loves what he does can be found in Ronaldinho. If you don't know him, Ronaldinho plays soccer for a living. He hails from Brazil, which has produced some of the world's greatest soccer players. But a cellmate of mine had me watch Ronaldinho play one time and I became hooked. Why? Because he is always smiling and laughing. When he is on the pitch, he is happy. Ronaldinho doesn't run, he floats. He doesn't kick, he strikes. When he makes a mistake, he laughs it off. When he does something spectacular, he laughs it off as if to say he got lucky. His joy and laughter brings joy and laughter to all those who watch him play. Laughter is truly the best medicine.

Live life like you love it. Make your life sing. Enjoy what you have. Enjoy what you do. *If you don't like doing it, and it's not imperative that you do it, then don't do it.* Do what you love. Fill your cell with laughter. Watch a great comedy. Enjoy a great joke. Not only is this good for your spirit, it's good for your health. It's been reported that a good laugh can boost your immune system's defenses for up to three days. So smile. Make laughter and happiness a tool in your arsenal on your way to becoming a Millionaire Prisoner.

Millionaire Prisoner Case Study

Julius Caesar is one of the most famous leaders in history. He was a politician and a military genius. At the age of 19, he won the *Corona Civica*, Rome's highest award for service in battle. But in all his great achievements, there's a little discussed episode in Caesar's early life that is perfect for our discussion on laughter.

At the age of 25, Caesar was on his way to Rhodes to study under the great teacher, Apollonius. During his trip, Caesar's ship was captured by pirates, and he was taken to an island. The pirates demanded 20 talents for his release. Caesar laughed at the sum, and told the pirates that he was worth more and they should ask for 50 talents. He then sent off his traveling companions to get the money.

Plutarch, the historian, says that during the 58 days Caesar was held captive by the pirates, he acted like he was their leader. When he went to sleep, he ordered the pirates to stop talking. Caesar participated in their sports and exercises with the pirates. He wrote speeches and poems, which he read to the pirates. Some of these works were not well received by the pirates. Caesar's reply to their scorn was to laughingly threaten them with crucifixion. Because of his humor and boldness the pirates accepted him. Caesar's friends put together the ransom and he was released. He immediately gathered a crew and warships. Then he went straight back to the island where the pirates were and seized them, their booty, and the 50 talents paid for him. Caesar had the pirates put in prison, then went to see the governor of Asia. He requested that the pirates be executed, but this request was denied. Caesar went back to the prison, and ordered the pirates executed by crucifixion. He had kept his word.

Become like Caesar, and learn to laugh in the face of obstacles. The whole time he was laughing in their face, Caesar was planning the pirate's execution in his mind. That is how you must be. Laugh in the face of the mountains in front of you, but plot their destruction in your mind. Keep this strategy in mind the next time you are faced with an obstacle.

Laugh at the little problems that bug you in life. Forget the *baggage* of the past and the worries of tomorrow. Laugh at the world. Have fun on life's journey. Love life and all it has to offer. If you walk around looking sorrowful and mad, you'll find yourself in a sorry state of affairs. By utilizing laughter in your daily life, you can become a Millionaire Prisoner.

The Pursuit of Happiness

Our forefathers wrote in the Constitution that we all have the right to pursue happiness. Yes, we prisoners have a *right* to be happy. This does not mean that we have a right to have things done our way. Life just doesn't work that way. Prison doesn't work that way. How we choose to react to what prison throws at us determines if we are happy or not. Here are some tips to help you improve your mood about life.

6. Don't chase happiness. If you do, you'll never get it. Follow these ABCs and you'll experience joy, peace, and happiness in your life.

Have a major *objective* in life that helps others. The motto for our publishing company is "Changing lives one prisoner at a time." When you have a purpose to add value to others you will find that life is fun.

Be grateful and give thanks. A lot of experts say you should keep a gratitude journal where you write down what you're thankful for daily. Consider it.

Master your emotions, especially anger. Keep a level head about you, and don't worry about the little stuff.

Concentrate on solutions, not problems. A simple change in your outlook can produce grand results in your life.

Strengthen your social connections. Don't go for quantity, but *quality*. Get to know your people and develop true friendships.

Act as if you're happy. Smile. Laugh. Pretend to feel good. If you do these things, you will feel good.

Prison is an environment that breeds depression and sorrow. But that doesn't mean you have to be like everyone else. Learn to be content with your life and find the little joys that come every day.

Resources

For more about happiness, check out *Stumbling on Happiness* by Daniel Gilbert, Ph.D.; *Happiness: Unlocking the Mysteries of Psychological Wealth* by Ed Diener, Ph.D.; and *The How of Happiness* by Sonja Lyubomirsky, M. D.

"Happiness is the meaning and purpose of life, the whole aim and end of human existence."

—Aristotle

The Destination

Many prisoners have heard the story of Tim Allen. He went to prison for cocaine charges. But a lot of you don't know that it was in prison where he found the power of laughter. Allen used to crack jokes and make the other prisoners laugh to survive. He performed in prison talent shows and created his character "Tim the Tool Man" while inside. After his release he became a star on television with the *Home Improvement* sitcom. He has a new sitcom on ABC in *Last Man Standing,* and continues to do what he loves, make people laugh.

As the earlier example of Ronaldinho, and this one of Tim Allen show, the goal is to achieve success so that you can do what you love. If you can get paid for doing what you love, you'll be much happier. Should you have to toil away in an occupation that is not what you truly love, don't allow it to become your final destination. Many people say they want money, but that is not what they really want. What they really want is what money allows them to do. They forget this. Do not ever forget this on your journey. The *objective* is to find success by doing what you love. Something you love to do, you would do for free. Whatever this may be for you, it's your destination. Find it, and you can find true happiness. A good book to read is *The Master Plan* by Robert DeRopp. By doing what you love you'll have something to strive for. It will give you meaning and purpose.

> *"The man who regards his life as meaningless is not merely unhappy but hardly fit for life."*
>
> —*Albert Einstein*

Be happy and have fun and we'll see each other at the top.

Millionaire Prisoner Prosperity Keys

- Remember to laugh at the world. It's never as bad as it seems.
- Learn to control your anger.
- Be compassionate to others. Everyday, try to make someone's day.
- Rediscover your love of life again.
- Do what you love and love what you do.
- Laugh in the face of obstacles as you plot their destruction.

MARKETING

The only factor that determines success or failure is the way in which a product or service is marketed.

—Jay Conrad Levinson

To become a Millionaire Prisoner you'll have to market your ideas, products and services to others. Even though you're in prison, you should never stop marketing. This chapter is divided into three parts. The first explains briefly what marketing is. The second part shows how to successfully market yourself. The third gives you avenues and strategies to market your products and services. After reading this chapter you should have the basic knowledge of how to successfully market anything you have to offer. At a minimum, you'll have enough information to conduct your own research into marketing and becoming a prosperous prisoner by selling your products or services.

What is Marketing?

Dictionaries define marketing as the way a product or service is priced, promoted and distributed. Marketing has evolved over the years, but can trace its roots to after World War II. Before the war, you had companies that were the only line to produce that kind of product. So it didn't matter if they marketed or not, because if you wanted that product there was only one company that produced it. After the war, competition spread because many different companies brought products to market. These companies realized that they had to successfully market their products and services or they would lose customers to their competitors. It's easy to see if you're the only company to produce that product. But if you have competitors, your marketing efforts are how you get your products and/or services in the minds of your customers. Successful marketing not only gets your stuff on your customer's minds, but induces them to buy what you're selling.

Read any marketing book and you'll hear about the four basic principles called the *four P's*. They are:

1. Product
2. Price
3. Placement
4. Promotion

These four P's are the foundation behind telling people about what you have to offer and why they should buy it. In essence, marketing is the ability to create demand for your product or service. If you can create this demand and then supply that demand, then you can achieve prosperity.

The Law of Supply and Demand

To understand this law you need to understand why people buy things. People purchase products or services either because they *need* to, or because they *want* to. People *need* clothes, food, adequate shelter to the climate, and medical care. People *want* 60-inch plasma TVs, alligator shoes, Gucci handbags, and luxury sports cars. Products of need are those that you *need* to live. Products of want you can live without, but *don't* because you *choose* not to. Understanding this allows you to have the right product, set the right price, place it in the right spot, and promote it effectively. To get rich, sell people what they want!

Why must you market your ideas, products, and services? The short and simple answer is because your competition does ... And if you don't, you'll lose your customers to the competition. If you aren't selling, people aren't buying. If people aren't buying then you're not making money. An old convict once told me, "The game is played for bread and meat, if I don't win, I don't eat." Well, marketing is how you make money so you can win the game.

There are many factors as to why and how you must begin to market your ideas, products, and services. Here are a few:

People need to notice what you have to offer. If they don't know about you, they can't buy what you're selling.

You have to stay in your customer's minds. *Out of sight, out of mind* is still a fact. But you have to be consistently in your audience's mind because they have short attention spans.

You have to help your target audience decide what's best for them. Your marketing plan should assist them in this process.

You must overcome the preconceived perceptions that people bring unconsciously into their decision-making process.

Your marketing plan should be set up based on why people buy things and services and tailored to these reasons.

The truth is, we all must have a marketing strategy if we plan on getting ahead. The prisoner who wants to get the prison industry job should develop a marketing plan to obtain that position. The prisoner who is writing a new pen-pal is marketing him or herself to the prospective pen-pal. Based on the marketing ploy used, the pen-pal decided to buy what you're selling or not. Every day of the week you're selling and buying. Marketing is selling on a grand scale. With these thoughts in mind, I will now begin to show you ways to market what you're selling.

The Doable Marketing Plan

A lot of marketing books speak of the need to have a marketing plan. And I believe you should have one also. But because I'm not trying to overcomplicate life, I like to find simple and easy strategies that can be used to accomplish my *objectives*. I found one in *The Art of Self-Promotion* by Ilise Benun. In "The Doable Marketing Plan" chapter she gives the steps to a one-page marketing plan. Since she wrote about it better than I can, here's an excerpt from her book.

* * * * * * * * * *

Marketing Plan = Freedom

Since you design your own plan, you have the freedom to choose only those things you want to do and to change the steps according to the evolution of your priorities. Your marketing plan is not a weapon; it's designed to help you, not hurt you. It is as unique and individual as you are and can be as flexible as you need it to be. It can save you time, energy, and money—if you let it.

How To Create Your One Page Marketing Plan

1. *Determine What You Want*

Ideally, you'll have more than one marketing plan and each one will be designed to achieve a specific objectives. Here are some examples of objectives: to get 3 new projects, to get an article in the paper, to get one monthly retainer client. For the purpose of this exercise, let's say you are a copywriter and your objective is to introduce yourself to a new market and to get one new project in one month.

2. *Choose Your Market and Find a List*

Market: direct mail agencies, ad agencies and design studies. List source: trade publications and local association directories.

3. *List the Marketing Tools You Will Use*

Tools: research phone calls, introductory letter/packet, follow up phone calls, networking meetings, promotional follow up postcard.

4. _Determine How Much Time and Money Are Available to You_

Time: 3 hours per week. Money: $1,000.

5. _Break Down Your Plan Into Logical, Manageable (i.e. small steps)_

Determine which tools you will use and in what order.

Week 1: Gather the information to create a list of 20 prospects.

Week 2: Write an introductory letter. Have someone proofread it.

Week 3: Call first 10 companies for contact name.

Week 4: Send first batch of letters.

Week 5: Follow up calls to the first batch.

Week 6: Call second 10 companies for contact name.

Week 7: Send second batch of 10 letters.

Week 8: Follow up calls to second batch.

Week 9: Evaluate plan so far and make any necessary changes.

Your One Page Marketing Plan

Step 1: Objective

Step 2: Target market and list source.

Step 3: Marketing tools

Step 4: Time and money budgets

Step 5: Timetable for tasks

    Week 1

    Week 2

    Week 3

    Week 4

    Week 5

    Week 6

    Week 7

    Week 8

* * * * * * * * * *

There you have it, an easy one-page marketing plan that can be easily adapted for any objective. Use it on your way to becoming a Millionaire Prisoner.

How To Successfully Market Yourself

Everything begins with you. Whatever you're offering comes from you. *You* are a product that the world buys or sells. The only way you can become a Millionaire Prisoner is if people believe in what you're selling. The first step is to garner attention. If no one knows you exist, then how can you succeed? You can't sit in your cell and do nothing and expect people to take notice. No, you have to get your name out there. But in putting your name out there, *you must believe that you are your best product*. Use the principles in the *Attitude* chapter to develop the best you that is possible. If you don't believe that you are the world's number one product, then no one else will.

Have faith in yourself. No one can do what you do. If they could, they would have already done it. You are unique and special. The world needs you, but you have to believe it also.

But it's not enough for you to believe in yourself, you also have to get others to believe in you as well. You do this by standing out and producing results. Think of the TV commercials during the Super Bowl. The best ones are the ones that stand out. Those are the ones people remember. By standing out you can be remembered.

How To Stand Out

First, think of the package you present to others. You are a total package. The rest of this book is about what is on the inside of your package—*your inner worth*. This part deals with the outside of your package—*your appearance*.

Your appearance is what everyone sees first, and you must make a good first impression if you want to be successful. In the chapter on *Attitude* you learned how to be positive and think positive thoughts. But you also have to put up an appearance of positivity as well. You can't be positive if your clothes are dirty, sloppy, and wrinkled. If you can look the part you may start feeling the part. If you can feel the part you may start thinking the part. And if you can think the part you can *make* the part. It's all about getting the right success *attitude*. Here are some tips about appearance that Millionaire Prisoners use to develop *habits* of standing out:

1. *Shower Daily*. If you can't shower daily, take bird baths. Body odor is offensive, and being clean is good for your health. Because of the enclosed environment, prisons are breeding grounds for diseases and other afflictions like MSRA. So be clean.
2. *Take Care of Your Hair*. Shampoo it regularly. Keep it styled in an up-to-date manner. Different prisons sell different products, so do your best with what you've got. Dirty, unkempt hair states that you don't care about yourself. If you don't care, why should anyone else?
3. *Shave Often*. As much as you have to. Being unshaven is the norm in prison, but it's not a good marketing strategy unless you're selling to cavemen or bums. Some of you can't shave your beard for religious reasons. If so, then trim it and wash it regularly. People look at your face first, so present something nice.

4. *Women Prisoners and Makeup.* Do not put it on so that you look like a raccoon. Less is more. It should only be used as an accent. Also, keep your nails done and polished. Let them be another accent. There is no such thing as an ugly woman, only a lazy woman.
1. *Men should also keep their nails neat and trimmed.* For some reason, some male prisoners keep their nails long? Then they go out and play basketball and scratch up their fellow prisoners. Not only does this cause fights, but is a health risk. Trim your nails.
2. *Cologne and perfume.* A little is best. Don't put it on with a spray can. It should be subtle. It should not announce your presence and it should not linger when you're gone.
3. *Smokers.* There are still some prison systems who let you smoke. If you smoke, don't allow your fingers to become stained from cigarettes. It looks bad.
4. *Brush and floss your teeth regularly.* Have your teeth cleaned by a dentist as much as possible. When you smile people see your teeth. A great smile says a lot. I understand that most dental programs in prison are severely inadequate, but do the best that you can until you get out. Remember to floss.
5. *Keep fit.* Lose those extra pounds. This will give you more energy. Plus you'll feel better about yourself. Start small and work your way up to more advanced workouts. If you have health problems, consult your doctor before starting any exercise program.
6. *Eyeglasses.* As a prisoner who wears eyeglasses, I'm all too familiar with the problems prisoners face in getting good glasses. If you are able to order glasses, then check out some of the vendors in the appendix. Make sure your lenses fit, and the frames are the right width. Keep your lenses clean and your glasses tightened regularly. If you have to wear the gigantic frames that prisons give out, then smile a lot. That way, your smile will override those frames. Besides, big frames are back in style.

7. *Never Slouch.* Stand up, stand tall and stand erect. Head up, shoulders back. *You are number one,* so act like it. Millionaire Prisoners never slouch.

8. *Clothes.* Keep them clean, neat, and if you can, pressed. Wear sizes that fit. Don't wear undersized or oversized clothes. *And don't sag.*

9. *Shoes.* Buy the best you can afford. All white shoes are great because they go with everything, but you must keep them clean. If you wear boots, keep them clean and shined. Keep the paper that comes inside your shoes so that you can put it back in your shoes when you're done wearing them. That allows your shoes to keep their shape longer. Wear new, clean socks. If you have foot odor, invest in some foot powder. Take care of your feet, because without your feet, you can't take the steps needed to complete your journey.

These above steps will help you develop great *habits* that will enable you to successfully market yourself in the near future. These tips should allow you to get your foot in the door. Once you get your foot in the door you can begin to sell what you have to offer. In the next part, you'll find tips, tactics, and strategies that will help you market your ideas, products, and services. These steps can be used to sell anything to anybody.

All of the above being said, your status as a Millionaire Prisoner is not dependent on your clothes. As I write this book I sit on my bunk in my cell-office, wearing grey gym shorts and a white t-shirt. Strapped to my face are big, black, gaudy, DOC eyeglasses. Guess what? No one cares about this because I'm here to help my fellow prisoners achieve their goals. Understand: standing out is easily done when you make others feel great about themselves and about doing business with you.

How to Successfully Market Your Products and Services

Most books tell you to develop a product or service, then identify a market for it. This market is called your *target audience*. But I want to suggest something different. I want you to identify your target audience first, then develop products or services that help them solve the problems they have. For instance, my target audience is prisoners. Prisoners are a school of starving hungry fish. There will always be prisons and prisoners because the system is a never-ending cycle. So, if I can service these hungry fish with *quality* products that they want, I'll do pretty well.

When evaluating your potential target audience, you need to ask some specific questions to determine if you can make money from these people.

Does this target audience have problems or needs that I could solve?

Is this target audience big enough and growing so that I can continue to sell them products and/or services over and over?

Can I easily identify my target audience?

Can I easily reach this target audience?

Lastly, can I easily reach my target audience on a continuing basis?

As you ask yourself these questions you must be realistic in your answers. I can't solve problems for senior citizens, nor do I want to. But I can solve prisoner problems. I know how to reach them, and I can reach them over and over again. Because you'll have limited resources when starting out, your goal should always be to spend the least amount of money to reach as many people as you can. But the only way you can do this effectively is to identify your target audience.

Here are a couple of examples to get you thinking about what I mean. One prisoner came to me with the idea of a children's book. It was a good idea, but he had no clue about who his real target audience was. It wasn't the 5-8-year old's he was writing for because they don't have the know-how or the money to purchase his book. So who was his real target audience? Parents and family members of the children might buy the book. Elementary schools, libraries, teachers, and churches might buy the book. But he had no idea whatsoever how to reach this target audience with his children's book. He will not be selling any books soon because he will not put in the effort to locate his target audience and find out how to reach them.

Now let's examine a better case study of identifying your target audience. George Kayer is the now retired editor and creator of the *Inmate Shopper*, a directory of companies and services for prisoners. Who is his target audience? If you said prisoners, you'd be wrong. "Prisoners" is too broad of a word. There are 2.3 million prisoners in the U.S. alone, not including the rest of the world. You have to break "prisoners" down to find Kayer's target audience. Because his *Inmate Shopper* directory has many different users, I have targeted three readily identified people. Here they are:

1. Prisoners in the U.S. looking for services and products and the low-down on the companies that provide these products/services;
2. Prisoners who have stuff to sell (like me);
3. Businesses that service prisoners.

These are 3 *different and unique* target audiences. They can be easily reached over and over, and they're growing. They are good target audiences. So here's the lesson: Don't get caught up trying to market to everyone. If you try and please everybody, you'll wind up pleasing no one. Besides, you don't have the kind of money it takes to market to everyone. Find your niche, then fill it and get rich.

> *"If you want to get rich, target a niche. If you want to go broke, market to all the folks."*
> —Stephen Pierce

Do You Have a USP?

Once you find your target audience you must determine how you're going to position your product or service to stand out.

Rosser Reeves is an advertising agency chairman and the originator of the marketing term, *Unique Selling Proposition (USP)*. In his 1961 classic, *Reality in Advertising*, Reeves delivered 3 factors in a successful USP:

1. It must make a proposition;
2. It must be unique, i.e., offer something the competition cannot or doesn't offer;
3. It must pull new customers.

I especially like the acronym that marketing experts and best-selling author, Robert Allen uses for *USP*: *U*ltimate Advantage, *S*ensational Offer, and *P*owerful Promise.

When you develop your products or services, always keep in mind their USP! The first product that I developed was my *How To Get FREE Pen-Pals* booklet. The title alone delivers my proposition. It was unique because no other prisoner company at the time was selling something that teaches you how to get FREE pen-pals. It also pulled new customers because every prisoner whoever bought a pen-pal list or paid for an online ad would rather keep their money and get pen-pals for free. Your USP is what makes you different from the competition. (A great book to read about difference is *Differentiate or Die* by Jack Trout).

You should try to incorporate your *USP* into the name of your product or title of your service. Then put this in bold letters on all your marketing materials. The key to a great *USP* is the benefits it solves for your target audience. Always remember this:

> *Your customers only care about the benefits they'll get from using your products and/or services!*

You didn't buy this book because it took me two years to write or the fact that it has 26 chapters. No, you purchased it because of the major benefits it promises—success and money from your cell! The same is for your customers. Sell them on the benefits of your products or services and you'll make plenty of money.

In the November 2012 issue of *Prison Legal News* there was a full-page ad for a book called *Facing the U.S. Prison Problem, 2.3 Million Strong: An Ex-con's View of the Mistakes and the Solutions*. It was selling for $24.95. Does this title move you to act? It didn't make me want to buy the book. Neither did the display ad. While it *may* be a good book, the title and the ad did nothing to make me want to cough up $24.95 to order it. And therein lays the problem. You are trying to get people to give you something—*their money*— for something you have—*a solution to their problem*. Give them the benefits of why they should do so. Lead with these benefits in all your marketing materials. Put your most powerful benefit at the top of your ads. Highlight it with bold print, capital letters, italics, and punctuation to make sure it's seen, and seen loudly. Do this for all your products and services.

Resource

By far, the best book ever written on writing marketing materials (my belief at least) is *Cash Copy: How To Offer Your Products and Services So Your Prospects Buy Them . . . Now!* by Dr. Jeffrey Lant. Get it, study it, and master writing cash copy.

Placement and Promotion

Once you've identified your target audience, developed your product and/or service for that target audience, and have your *USP*, then you need to place your product where your target audience can see it. . . And you have to place it so that your target audience sees it consistently.

The goal is to place your product where your target audience can see it consistently. . . and do it in a way that costs you the lowest amount of money. What do I mean by see it consistently? Mail-order expert Tyler Hicks says he sends four follow-up responses over a six-month period. Marketing expert Dr. Jeffrey Lant says you should contact your prospects *at least* seven times in 18 months. As you see this means more than once. Consistency is the key. How you get them to see your product depends on your target audience. Once again, ask yourself some questions:

What magazines do my target audience read?

Are there any social networks just for my target audience?

What websites do they visit?

What blogs do they read?

Are there Associations that they belong to?

Are there newsletters (print or online) that they read?

If you find the answers to some of the above questions then you can get your product in front of your target audience so they can see it.

For my product (this book) I had to find where I could place it so prisoners would see it. . . and cost me the least. I came up with *Prison Legal News, Inmate Shopper,* and *The Best Resource Directory for Prisoners.* Once you know where you can place your product so that it can be seen, then you need to promote it.

There are several factors you can use to effectively market and promote your product or service. One of the best ways to promote is to give something away for free. It can be a newsletter, article, blog, e-book, CD or some other gift. But whatever you choose to give away, make sure it *adds value* to your customer's life. They don't want a gimmick toy or something trivial. *They want value!*

I wrote newsletter articles that I donated to *Corcoran Sun,* placed a free ad in the *Inmate Shopper* mall, and placed an ad in *Prison Legal News.*

Prisoner Tim Twitty created the *Secrets to Instant Wealth* book for prisoners, and promoted it by giving away free newsletters. The newsletters were easily put together and copied, but they did one thing—they added value. In his newsletters Twitty offered free *knowledge,* free pen-pal addresses, and free celebrity addresses. At the back of his newsletter he offered an order form that a prisoner could use to purchase his book and/or other services that his company offered. You can do the same with your product or service. Here's how:

1. Place a small ad in the classified section of a publication that your target audience reads so they'll see it. Say you're offering a "FREE" (*newsletter, CD-Rom, etc.*), and give your address. Here's how the first ad for my *How To Get Free Pen-Pals* booklet looked in *Prison Legal News*:

How To Get FREE Pen-Pals!
for more info send SASE to:
O'Barnett Publishing
P.O. Box 473
Catlin, IL 61817-0473

---

2. When the prospective customer sends for your "free" product, include a sales brochure or letter to whatever it is that you're really trying to sell. Remember: anything you send is free.

3. Set up your sales literature so that it says something like this: "If you like _____, you should check out our new. . ." Then tell them about your real product.

Selling this way is called "baiting" of the hook. You're "fishing" for leads or prospective customers, and your free product is the bait used to get them on the hook. This is a great, low-cost way of marketing. Some companies even make the prospective customer send in a fee to cover the postage, like I did with my requesting a "SASE." If you use a bait plan like the one above, your only cost is the cost of the ad and how much it costs you to produce your free product and marketing materials. It's a simple way to market and build a mailing list. But you're not done once they send for your "free" item. The next step is why

MIKE ENEMIGO & JOSHUA KRUGER

you must capture the names and addresses (or e-mail addresses) of your leads or prospects.

Follow Up is King!

You must follow up with the people who inquire about your products or services. It never ceases to amaze me how few prisoner companies send me follow up information after I write for their initial brochure or application. If all they're going to do is let me know about their service one time, then I'm not going to be doing business with them. Matter of fact, I probably forgot about them: *out of sight, out of mind*. Yes, I read every piece of mail I get, but maybe their offer wasn't good, their marketing material didn't move me, or I forgot about it. I'm busy writing.

Most companies don't follow up on their leads. That's where you can get ahead of your competition. Every time you develop something new (you are creating new stuff right?), send it to the people on your mailing list. Let them know the *benefits* of why they need it and give them a deadline of when the offer is up. Do this over and over again. Here's one tip: People keep catalogs around longer than sales material. Edward R. Hamilton knows this well. That's why they send new catalogs periodically to people who have bought books from them in the past. If you want to become a Millionaire Prisoner you must follow-up with your customers and prospects.

Learn From My Mistakes!

The above classified ad that I used was a mistake. Here's why. The rule when placing ads that you're paying for is: *spend the least amount of money that you have to so you get your prospect to act!* Prison *Legal News* has a three-line, 96 character classified ad that costs $60 for 2 months. Using the above rule, my classified ad should've been this:

> How To Get FREE Pen-Pals! Send
> SASE to: O'Barnett Publishing
> P.O. Box 473 Catlin, IL 61817

Not only would that have produced the same results, but would've saved me $10 (or $60 over the whole year). *PLNs* classifieds are by lines and characters, whereas most magazines and newsletters go by word count. But the rule is the same: Use as few words as possible, thereby costing you the least amount of money. Remember: Money saved is money earned!

Another rule: Stay away from "Bargain Ads." You'll see these advertised in lots of mail-order publications. Ads like: "Your ad to 250,000 for $2!". . . And "We publish your ad in 50 publications, over 1 million readers." It's not true. In my ignorant days I fell victim to such a scheme. For $50, my 2-inch ad was supposed to go into 50 different mail-order ad sheets with a reach to 250,000 people. Guess what? No one bought anything because these ad-sheets were poorly printed and probably weren't even mailed. So the lesson is that you should stick to real newsletters and magazines. Stay away from bargain ads in crappy mail-order leaflets and ad-sheets. You've been warned!

A Few Words About Space Ads (Big and Small)

Some people just won't buy your product until it's in a display/space ad. Why? Because they feel you aren't a "real" company unless you advertise. Nonsense. You should do what makes you the most money and costs you the least amount of money. I was successful using the classified ad and sending my mini-sales catalog as follow-up to the prospects who responded to make sales. Of course, there are advantages to having a space ad designed and placed. Here are a few:

You can sell directly from a space ad, whereas you shouldn't sell from a classified ad.

You can use your ad over and over again in every piece of mail you send out, or marketing document you produce.

You will get more leads and make sales faster with a space ad than a classified ad.

Those are some of the advantages, but the main disadvantage is that space ads are more costly than a classified. Look at some numbers: A 5-line classified ad in *Prison Legal News* costs $70 for two months. But a 1/12 page (the smallest space ad) costs $175 for two months in *PLN*. A full-page ad in *PLN* will set you back $6,835 for the year. As you can see it's costly to run space ads, and this doesn't count the cost of designing the ad if you can't do it yourself. My advice is for you to stick to making money using classified ads until you have the money to do space ads right.

In case you have the budget now, here's some Millionaire Prisoner rules you need to know about space ads:

Only use ads in publications that your target audience reads! If you don't know which ones they are, you haven't done your research. Don't guess, find out!

If you're using one or more magazines or newsletters for different ads, make sure you code your ads so you know which periodicals are profitable and which ones aren't.

Because you have to pay more for color, only use color in your space ads if it's absolutely imperative that your prospects see your product in color.

You can tell (i.e. sell) a lot more in a full-page ad and these ads can be used for years to come in your own catalog.

Your goal should be to make 2 to 3 times your cost. So, if it costs $2,500 for a full-page in a magazine, your goal is to bring in $5,000, hopefully $7,500 in sales.

You should have a hard sell and a soft sell in your space ad. A "hard sell" is asking for the order outright, a "soft sell" is asking the prospect to send for more information.

Pay attention to your competition's ads. What size ad are they using? Are they repeating the same ad for more than

6 months? What is their USP? How can you differentiate your product or service?

Remember the headline! It's the most important part of the ad. It should scream prospect benefits.

Lastly, your space ad should stop your prospect from turning the page, compel them to read your copy (words), and convince them to act. If it doesn't do these things it's weak and you'll lose money on it.

Why use space ads? Not so your company looks good. There's only one reason to place ads: TO MAKE MONEY! So, say it with me, *if it doesn't make dollars it don't make sense*. Keep good records and you'll know soon enough if your space ads are making money or not.

For more about using space ads and making them work for you, get a copy of: *Breakthrough Advertising: How To Write Ads That Shatter Traditions And Sales Records* by Eugene M. Schwartz.

Different Types of Marketing

As a prisoner you have a limited budget to spend on promoting your product and services. But I would like to offer you some other ways that you can promote your stuff. These descriptions will be brief, and I've included them here to stimulate your mind and get you thinking about other ways to market your stuff. If you see something that you think might help, do some research on it for cost and effectiveness.

Traditional Marketing

Some of these are advertising on TV, radio, and in print. Billboard ads, and direct mail pieces are also traditional ways of marketing. Prisoner Jamie Snow put up a billboard for a little under $2,000 to get the word out about his wrongful conviction. Analyze your product or service and decide if your target audience would see your ad on one of these venues. If not, don't bother. Save your money for more reliable marketing ploys.

Influence Marketing

One of the best ways to promote is to get someone else to do it for you. In *The Tipping Point*, Malcolm Gladwell explains the *Law of the Few*. This theory is that 10 percent of your target audience influences what the other 90 percent buys. Gladwell called these people *influencers*. Another way to influence people is through celebrity endorsements. These endorsements are based on one word: *leverage*. Find the influencers that can help promote your products to your target audience. You want to find the people who can influence the largest amount of people so you save time and money.

Buzz Marketing

Buzz marketing is also called word-of-mouth marketing. A perfect example of this is when a prisoner gets a few hits on their pen-pal site and tells everyone about it. The news spreads like wildfire throughout the prison. It's great for the pen-pal business. Word-of-mouth marketing of this kind is much more credible than if the company tried to sell to each prisoner. The ways to get people to talk about your stuff is to be unique, and add your own spin. Be careful after you put out your products to pay attention to any negative buzz about them. Bad news always spreads faster than good news. For more, check out: *Building Buzz: How To Reach and Impress Your Target Audience* by Marisa D'vari; and *Word-Of-Mouth Marketing* by Jerry Wilson.

Telephone Marketing

Telemarketing is big business. Many companies set up call centers and have a staff that spends all day on the phone cold calling prospects. But cold calling and telemarketing aren't for the faint of heart. Because a prisoner most likely will not be able to participate in telemarketing, I will not go into much detail about cold calling. If you want to read more about the art of selling by phone, then I suggest reading *Telephone Marketing:*

How To Build Your Business by Telephone by Murray Roman; and *Selling On the Phone: A Self-Teaching Guide* by James Porterfield.

Stunt Marketing

Men like P.T. Barnum and Harry Houdini used stunt marketing many years ago to promote themselves and their acts. It works best when used to develop hype. It could be used for a grand opening, or the launch of a new line of your product. Beware of any consequences to any stunt you may choose to use. If you do decide to use stunt marketing, make your target audience see it. Also, make sure it's appropriate for your audience.

Experimental Marketing

Magazine publishers do this when they offer a free trial subscription. Supermarkets do it when they offer samples of food products they sell. If your product is new to the market and you have a *quality* product, consider this form of marketing. If your customer likes it they will do a little buzz marketing about your product to others. Sometimes you have to give to get.

Ambient Marketing

This form of marketing is also called "place-based" marketing. It's all about location. Your goal in this plan is to get your message or ad to your target audience as they go about their daily activities. Some forms of this type are posters at bus stops, in rest rooms, banners on airplanes flying over a beach, and ads at sports arenas. Some less expensive ways are around colleges and apartment complexes. It comes down to who your target audience is and how to reach them.

Viral Marketing

Viral marketing is where your message goes from person to person without your direct involvement. The difference between viral marketing and buzz marketing is that in the viral type you use technology to assist you in spreading the word. Make sure the message is simple, catchy, and funny. Some of the most common forms of this are being used in pass-along emails, on YouTube, and using website links. You can also start a Wikipedia page for your company. For more about viral marketing checkout *Unleashing the Ideal Virus* and *Permission Marketing*, both by Seth Godin.

Social Marketing

This is using social media websites to spread your message or influence your target audience. I will discuss social networking more in depth in the next chapter, but this is a great way to get the word out about your product and/or services. The great thing about social marketing is that it can be done for *free*. You can promote your stuff for free on a blog, on your Facebook page, and other free websites. Don't be fooled by companies that charge prisoners large sums of money to set up a Facebook page, or provide other services. They get these services for free. For more, check out: *Social Media Marketing For Dummies* by Shiv Singh; *Social Media 101* by Chris Brogran; and *The Zen of Social Media Marketing* by Shama Kabani.

Mobile Marketing

This is the new rage in business. Getting people to notice your stuff by advertising on their cell phones and other handheld devices. This form of marketing is particularly effective in reaching teenagers and college students. Because the costs of this type of marketing may be out of range for a prisoner to set up, wait till your sales take off. Then consider this type of marketing.

E-mail Marketing

E-mail communication has become the norm. Even some prisons now afford you access to e-mail. Some companies offer free E-newsletters through e-mail. But it's illegal to spam people using e-mail. As long as you give your full name and address, are honest, and provide what you promise, you should be okay. In the 2011 Direct Marketing Association's Statistical Fact Book, it was said that 34 characters or less on an e-mail produces the best click-through rate. So keep your e-mail ploys short and simple.

Affiliate Marketing

Affiliate marketing offers you the opportunity to make money in two ways. One, other people or companies promote your products and get a commission off each sale or referral. Two, you make money by referring people to websites or companies and get a percentage off each sale or every time someone clicks through to the website. Because these are referrals, they are more valuable than someone they marketed to.

One of the largest online affiliate programs is Amazon Associates. Others are *ClickBank.com* and Commission Junction (*cj.com*). I suggest that the proper way to take advantage of affiliate marketing is to ask someone else if they will let you promote their stuff first. You must *give* to get. Then after you've made them some sales you could come back and ask them to promote your stuff. But make sure that the companies or products that you choose align with your products or services. For instance, if I wanted to get into affiliate marketing on my website, *www.millionaireprisoner.com*, I would only recommend websites or companies that help prisoners and their families. Or those that provide services to prisoners.

But you don't even need a website to be an affiliate. One of my first business ideas was to help my mail-order mentor sell his books and products to prisoners. This was a market he was not yet selling to, and I had the mailing list and know-how to market to prisoners. We split each sale 50/50, and both made a nice profit. In the Appendix you'll find a sample letter that you can use to ask for permission to promote someone else's products or services. In case you decide to partner up with some other business, here are a few things that I learned along the way:

1. Always ask for references and check out testimonials from customers. You don't want to promote a bogus service.
2. Never give out your list of names or mailing list of buyers. This is your most valuable asset. Create it, keep building it, and guard it with your life.
3. Have all orders come to you first, take out your cut, and then send the rest on to your partner for processing and delivery.

You can get rich with affiliate programs online. If interested, I suggest you read *Make A Fortune Promoting Other People's Stuff Online: How Affiliate Marketing Can Make You Rich* by Rosalind Gardner.

These are some of the most used forms of marketing. Use the ones that you can afford. Remember to constantly seek out *knowledge* about your subject. One of the most important areas you should stay up-to-date on is social media marketing. It's cheap and effective. Unless you are marketing to prisoners or senior citizens, then your target audience most likely is on the internet. Get your products online and you can become successful. Because in today's world the internet is king. We must discuss setting up your own website.

The Platform—Your Website

Setting up a website is even easier now than it's ever been. The cost for such services has lowered dramatically, and some are even free. You can design and publish your own website for free with Google Page Creator, Facebook, and Google+. There are also cheap host services. *Weebly.com* is a low-cost website design company and will host your site for free. For those of you who have never been on the internet or seen a website, I will briefly describe what they consist of.

Most websites have an address or Universal Resource Locator (URL). The URL for Facebook is *www.Facebook.com*. The URL for this book is *www.millionaireprisoner.com*. A website consists of different pages. These pages can be accessed by people logging on to the web and clicking on to hyperlinks. If you log on to the site for this book you would get the home page. But if you added */authors.bio* to the end of the URL, you would go straight to the page with my bio on it. A website can have animation, sound effects, audio and video streams, free downloadable material, e-mail blogs, and podcasts. If you plan on selling books, artwork, or craft items from a website then you'll need to add a shopping cart. This allows people to purchase products or services using a credit card or online shopping account like Pay Pal.

I recommend that you become familiar with setting up a website. You could have your own personal website. My friend Snow has his own site that he uses to get the word out about his wrongful conviction. Have someone check it out at: *www.freejamiesnow.com*. The barrier to getting your own site is very low. You would have to:

- purchase a domain name (no more than $9 a year)
- find a host site (anywhere from free to $7 a month)

So for under $100 a year you could have your own website. Of course if you wanted it designed professionally you'll have to pay the web designer to build it. That could cost anywhere from $300 to $10,000 depending on what you need your website to do. In this day and age, if you have products to sell, then you need a website to allow people to buy online. There are over 240 million internet users in the U.S. alone, and there's no other way available to reach that many people for under $100 a year.

For now, I want to give you some tips to remember if, and when, you set up your own website:

1. Put your website address (URL) on everything you send out. Snow puts his URL (*www.freejamiesnow.com*) on the envelopes he sends out, and his family and friends write it on the money they spend. Have your family and friends put it on

their bumper stickers on their cars. Have them participate in chat rooms and casually mention your site. Put your URL in your e-mail signature and on your Facebook page if you have one. You must drive people to your site. If you build it they will come, *if they know about it.* Being online is all about traffic. You must get traffic to come to your online store.

2. When you have your site designed, make sure you:

Have a clean, uncluttered home page with text showing your offers;

Have a bio page about you and your company;

Offer a free sample of your product or service;

Have a link or button that the customer can click to purchase your product or service;

Have a way to catch names and e-mail addresses. For instance, an "opt-in mailing list."

Offer an e-mail newsletter, or "E-Zine";

Offer contests and suggestion boxes. Get people to participate;

Have a media page listing all your achievements and/or the times when you or your products were mentioned in the press;

Have a way for users to send/forward your website pages to others via e-mail;

Offer your blog, or online journal;

Have your page's search engine optimized (SEO);

Offer a Links page where you share other relevant websites that your customers might be interested in. In The Art of Self-Promotion, Ilise Benun has a whole chapter, "All About Linking," on the proper way to do your links page, and link your website with other sites. Or check out the book Ultimate Guide to Link Building by Eric Ward and Garrett French.

Simplify everything. Use bullet points (short separate lists). You want your site to be easy to read and easy to use, especially by people using your site on a mobile phone.

Get a copy of the latest edition of *Building A Website For Dummies* by David A. Crowder. If you are serious about making money on the internet, then get a copy of *Get Rich Click!* by Marc Ostrofsky and *Multiple Streams of Internet Income* by Robert G. Allen. Read them, study them, and master them.

CAUTION: Don't set up a website just to be online. Since you're going to be paying a small fee, have an *objective*. Make it an investment. As Brendon Burchard explained in *The Millionaire Messenger*, your website must *add value, capture leads, and make money*. If you're just looking for pen-pals, then follow the tips in the next chapter to get them. If you have something to sell, then set up a website and get paid. Find the internet-savvy person in your *network* and get them to help you. Then find another one. Use them for different reasons. There is no excuse for not being on the web anymore if you have something to sell. Lack of effort is not an option.

Building Buzz Through Blogging

A web log, or "blog" is one way to generate buzz about yourself, your products, and/or your services. You can set up a blog for free using Blogger, Vox, and Yahoo!360. You can also blog by posting on Myspace, Facebook, and Google+. Or you can blog on your own website using a free service like *wordpress.org*. It doesn't take but a few minutes to set up a blog. Here's how to do it using Blogger. I'm using Blogger as an example because it's free and is owned by Google. Google is great because it's the largest search engine in the world, and that in itself gives you hidden advantages. In three simple steps, here's how to set up your blog on Blogger:

1. Go to *blogger.com* and create a free account. You can either use your name, or come up with a different name that you want to be displayed on your blog posts.
2. Name your blog and give it an address. My blog is "The Millionaire Prisoner," and the address is *millionaireprisoner.blogspot.com*.
3. Choose one of the templates that Blogger offers to layout your blog.

That's it. Simple and easy. Now you're ready to publish on your blog by posting what you write. To publish on your blog all you do is click on "New Post." Then title your blog entry and write that day's blog. After your blog entry has been proofread, all you have to do is click on "Publish Post" and you're a published blogger.

Since most of us prisoners don't have access to a computer, we need someone else to post our entries for us. In the next chapter I'll show you how to find this person and cultivate them for your *network*. Because you should be actively blogging you should consider sending this person seven different blogs at a time, and have them publish an entry once a day for the week. Or you could do it over the phone, but that would be more expensive, so the snail mail route is probably a more viable option for you, albeit a slower one.

Here are some Millionaire Prisoner blog tips to remember when writing your blogs:

1. Write about what interests you and don't worry about what others may think.
2. Don't try to be the voice on everything, instead carve out your own niche.
3. Limit your blog to one central idea or theme per blog post.
4. Use photographs to enhance your blog posts if you can.
5. Always give credit to your sources.
6. Make sure what you write adds value to your readers' life.

7. Have something for people to look forward to. For instance: "Tuesday's Tips" or "Wednesday's Wacky News" and "Friday's Forecast."

8. Have a way for people to comment on your blog or suggest ideas to you. Always list your mailing address on your blog.

9. Keep your posts under 750 words in length.

10. Ask questions so you encourage your readers to comment on your posts and share them with others.

11. List your blog on the blog listing directories using key words.

12. Set it up so that your blog posts are automatically fed to your social networking pages, or website if you have one.

According to *Technorati.com*, a blog research site, 346 million users on the internet read blogs. This offers you many different ways you can make money through your blog by the power of leverage. Using Blogger, you can add a "visitor counter" to your blog. This allows you to know how many people are actually visiting your blog. Once you get a sufficient following, you can use the steps below to generate income.

1. Use Google AdSense. Google pays you when someone clicks on the ad. It costs you nothing. Because you want readers to click on the ads, make sure the ads are relevant to your blog.

2. Donations. Have a link so that people can donate to your "blog fund." Prisoners should write a blog explaining the reason for the donations and how the money is spent.

3. Affiliate products. Allow others to place ads on your blog where you get paid a commission off each sale.

4. Selling your own products and services. You should actively promote your stuff, but just don't overdo it.

Some prisoner companies charge you $5 per blog post. It only takes a few minutes to type 750 words into a computer and click "Publish." Don't pay for a service like that unless you absolutely have to. Use the tips in the next chapter to get someone to do this for free. Blogging is just another way to market your ideas and generate multiple streams of income. It's a tool to use in becoming a Millionaire Prisoner. Don't forget its value on your climb up the ladder.

How To Build Your Brand

The American Marketing Association defines a brand as a name, term, sign, symbol of design or a group of sellers that differentiates them from those of other sellers. A brand is the visual, emotional, rational or cultural image that one associates with a product. McDonald's, Starbucks, and Taco Bell are all brands. Robert Kiyosaki created his own brand in the *Rich Dad, Poor Dad* (www.richdad.com) series of books. Donald Trump has branded his name. Karrine Steffens, of *Confessions of a Video Vixen* fame, branded the "Superhead" moniker and turned it into a clothing line and more. To create a brand you form an image that stays on the minds of your prospects and customers. Branding makes selling easier because people want to buy from companies they know, like, and trust.

You might think that all the well-known brands have a stranglehold on the marketplace, but there is room for the little guy. The world has many different niches, and if you find your target niche you can build your brand by following these simple tips:

1. Don't try to be everything to everybody. Find your target audience. Spend time with them and help solve their problems.
2. Always use words that link back to your products or services.
3. Stay connected with your customers through social media and respond to all inquiries. Always use *tact* and talk to them about them.
4. Don't use your company logo, but a photo of yourself when building your brand. My brand is *The Millionaire Prisoner*,™ and I call myself that. But people see a photo of me, not my book.

5. Come up with a catchy tagline for your brand and place it everywhere. Think of Nike's "Just Do It."
6. Be honest and trustworthy. If you can't do something, let your customers know it. If you screw up, let them know that too.
7. Don't be fake. Don't promote stuff that your customers will know you don't like, use, or have any connections to. Live your brand!
8. Claim your brand on *Yelp.com*, Wikipedia, and any other handle out there. Try and get all your online addresses to match your brand. For instance, my e-mail is *millionairepriosner@gmail.com*, my blog is *millionaireprisoner.blogspot.com*, and my website is *www.millionaireprisoner.com*.

Always remember that your brand is your culture and your service. If you concentrate on those two areas you can easily build a successful brand. If you would like to learn more about building a brand, check out *The Business of Brands* by Jon Miller and David Muir; and *The 22 Immutable Laws of Branding: How To Build A Product or Service Into A World-Class Brand* by Al and Laura Ries.

The Hidden Ingredient

Before I close this chapter I would like to discuss something that a lot of marketers seem to forget. You must create demand. People have to see that others want you, your products and/or services. Most people do what others do. If others are buying them there must be a reason why. So create conditions where people convince themselves to buy products. How can you do this? By using testimonials and getting referrals from others. Here's how to get testimonials:

If you're new in business, send samples of your product to select prospects of your target audience with a questionnaire asking for their explicit opinion of your product or services.

If you're already in business then send your stuff to known names in your field. Hint: If you're a prisoner-service company, you need to send such to me or Mike Enemigo of The Best Resource Directory for Prisoners. We'll tell you the truth!

Don't forget the Joes and Janes in your target audience either. Solicit your customer's opinions. Always invite them to contact you. Once they do, send them a testimonial letter request. (See Appendix for sample).

What do you do with these testimonials once you get them? Put them in all your marketing materials. Many companies don't even use testimonials. I guess they're lazy or have enough sales? (FYI: you can't have enough sales!) Don't be this way. Get and use testimonials.

But even the big dogs forget the power of testimonials every once in a while. Nowhere in any of *Inmate Shopper's* ads or brochures are there any testimonials. But on the inside of the catalog you'll find plenty. Here's three taken from the March 2013 *Inmate Shopper* that should be used in all their marketing materials including display ads:

> *"Solid reviews and ratings of businesses. Informs prisoners of knowledge not available from any other source."*
> —*Kate in N.Y.*

> *"I truly appreciate Inmate Shopper. Your content is priceless for us inmates."*
> —*Ryan in PA*

> *"Inmate Shopper is our most requested title."*
> —*Inmate Book Services*

Why are these so powerful? Because we know an ad is trying to sell us, but these are real people telling us *Inmate Shopper* is legit and in demand. These testimonials should be on every marketing piece *Inmate Shopper* puts out. Sadly, they're wasted on the inside of each issue. (FYI: I correspond with George Kayer, retired editor of *Inmate Shopper*, and he knows I'm not ragging his product. It's the best product of its kind for prisoners.)

There's a reason expert marketers use testimonials . . . because they sell! My mentor, Dr. Jeffrey Lant, says you need two testimonials for every page of your marketing materials. It may be hard to get that many when you're first starting out, but you can get them if you ask. Whatever you do, don't neglect testimonials in your marketing!

A Few Final Words On Marketing

Lastly, whatever you do, make sure you add value and create *quality* products and services. You want long-term customers that will keep buying your products or services as you come up with them. Create the demand. Make yourself the object of desire and others will seek you. When they do, you'll have more opportunities to market yourself. First, create the demand, then sell yourself and your product.

Remember: You *are* number one. The rest of these ABC's contain principles that will enable you to sell yourself more successfully. You must live these ABC's and they must become a part of your everyday life.

Do one thing each day to market yourself and your products and services. Even if it's only writing a letter, do it. Spend at least 15 minutes a day building your brand. Your brand is you! If you do this it will become *habit* and you'll market your product or service the best way possible. Become a salesman and promote yourself and your products to others. If you can do it well, you'll be on your way to becoming a Millionaire Prisoner.

Resources

Because you need to continue to learn how to market your products or services better, I'm recommending the following books.

The Best of Guerrilla Marketing—The Remix by Jay Conrad Levinson and Jeannie Levinson;

Money Making Marketing: Finding The People Who Need What You're Selling and Making Sure They Buy It by Dr. Jeffrey Lant.

The New Rules of Marketing & PR by David Meerman Scott;

The 22 Immutable Laws of Marketing: Violate Them At Your Own Risk by Al Ries and Jack Trout.

Millionaire Prisoner Prosperity Keys

- Believe that you are number one!
- Learn to package yourself in the most optimal way.
- Find your target audience.
- Develop a plan to market your products or services to others.
- Do not neglect the power of the World Wide Web.
- Create demand so that people sell your stuff themselves.
- Do at least one thing a day to promote yourself.
- Promote by giving something of value to your prospective customers.
- Remember: If you're not selling, you're repelling.

CONCLUSION

On the human chessboard, all moves are possible.

—Miriam Schiff

Congratulations!

You've arrived at the end of Part 1 of these ABCs, but the real beginning of your journey is just starting. Thoreau said: "For every thousand hacking as the leaves of evil there is one striking at the root." This book is my attempt to strike at that root. The root is the American prison system. I have no political power and I don't have millions of dollars. I can't influence from the outside in. But that would only be superficial change. Real change comes from within. That was, and is, my quest and vision. We need to change the prison system. But we can only change it from the inside out. Those of us on the inside can influence those on the outside. We can begin by getting out *attitude* in order, and use these ABCs to lead a productive life. Then others on the outside will take notice and maybe give prisoners better opportunities and aid upon coming home.

But we shouldn't wait on that. It's our battle that we're fighting and it begins with us. Don't be naive and think the prison system cares about you. It only cares about how many dollars are involved in your incarceration. You care about yourself and your fellow prisoners care about you. Together we can become

243

Millionaire Prisoners. That will allow us to change the system legally. Change starts in the heart, and prisoners are the heart of the system. Only we can change things. We need to stop procrastinating about what we're going to do and start doing it. It's a bold move to declare yourself going legit, no longer a criminal. You know, become a "square" in the eyes of you prisoner peers. But trust me, you won't regret it.

> *"Success for the most part attends those who act boldly, not those who weigh everything, and are slow to venture."*
>
> -Xerxes

My books are gifts from me to you -- my fellow prisoners. You are my people. I understand you and your needs. I chose prison when I was living under my alias J-Roc. Now I choose to give back. Some of you will leave these gulags and accomplish great things in life. Maybe one or two of your will pass on your new found prosperity? That's my hope and desire, my vision. That will be winning the war.

What is your life about? What is your life for? These are only questioning you can answer. I do know that prison is not your destiny in life, but only a detour. There's a sleeping giant inside you. You have to awaken it, and go after your dreams. Of course, there will be times when doubt springs up in your mind. In those times you can think of the olive tree. The ancients considered it one of the greatest trees because it takes 100 years for an olive tree to reach maturity. But when it does, it's magnificent. Or think about the oak tree. It comes from within a tiny acorn. It takes many years to grow and mature. It doesn't just spring up-overnight. Becoming a Millionaire Prisoner takes time. In the end, it will be worth the wait.

"No matter how great the talent or effort, some things just take time: you can't produce a baby in one month by getting nine women pregnant."

--Warren Buffett

You have half the TMP philosophy and all you'll need to accomplish in life. You know how to develop a positive attitude, and get rid of baggage in your life. You have the means to start getting sufficient capital to achieve your dreams. You know you need to strive with determination, constantly educating yourself, and accepting all favor bestowed upon you. Doing this will allow you to experience growth, develop good habits, and use your imagination to see a better life for yourself. On your way, remember to practice justice, become knowledgeable, and laugh at the world. At the same time, you must keep marketing your products, services, and ideas. This is how you'll make yourself great and become a Millionaire Prisoner.

A Scenario of Success

In these ABCs you have seen other prisoners use these principles to achieve success. I've tried to give you enough examples to illustrate how these principles can work for prisoners. But you have to take hold of these ABCs and make them work in your life. To help you do this, I'll share another story now. Maybe you have heard of Gregory David Roberts or read his book, *Shantaram*. If you haven't, you should. The book is a fantastic, epic, 900+ page novel. But as all books, it has a semi-autobiographical slant to it. His story is that of a Millionaire Prisoner for sure.

Gregory David Roberts became addicted to heroin after going through a divorce and losing custody of his daughter. He started committing armed robberies to support his habit.

Eventually caught and convicted, he was sentenced to 19 years in a maximum-security prison in Australia. He escaped and spent 10 years on the run, most of that in India. It was his time on the lam where he got most of the material for *Shantaram*. While on the run he set up a medical clinic in a slum and worked as a gunrunner and money launderer for the Bombay Mafia. It took him 13 years to write his book because the first two drafts (six years' worth of work), were destroyed in prison. Even when his finger became frostbitten by the cruel winters in the punishment camp of his prison, he had the *determination* to keep writing. As I quoted earlier in this book: "Masterpieces take time." After he was recaptured and released again, Roberts established a successful multimedia company.

I've shared Mr. Roberts' story here to once again illustrate that it's possible for you to achieve your dreams. He is just one more of the many prisoners to throw off the cloak of prison *baggage* and become successful. And he's still more proof of the ability to make the past dance. Can you still deny the truth evident in the real-life prisoner examples I've chosen to include in these ABCs? Use them as motivation to begin your journey. The time for you in now. You can't get to the tomorrow of your dreams without going through today. So, plant the seed today that will bear fruit in your tomorrow.

The Time is Now

Now that we've come to the end of our journey you have a choice to make. You can choose to be a prodigy or a peon. You can stay a jailbird or become a genius. You can choose to be called moron or the master. Will they remember you for being the wizard or the weasel? It's your choice.

Understand that you don't have a thousand years to live. Time slays all. In the game of life, those who are slow to act are the losers. Now is the time to begin. Now is the time to become a Millionaire Prisoner. Keep this book with you and use it to remind yourself that you can achieve your dreams. Share these ABCs with others who do not know them. By doing so, you will reap a harvest you never thought possible.

Just because this is the end of *The Millionaire Prisoner: Part 1* doesn't mean that our journey should end. You should consider getting a copy of *The Millionaire Prisoner: Part 2*. In that book you'll find the second half of *The Millionaire Prisoner* philosophy. Briefly, I'll share what you'll find in *Part 2:*

Because success is a team sport, you'll need to get assistance from others along your way. That's Why ' I've included a *Network* chapter. You'll learn the greatest gift you can give; how to get FREE pen-pals; how to successfully use prison pen-pal sites; the 6 things you need to know to build a lifetime of contacts; and the ability to use the power of correspondence.

It goes without saying that you need to know where you're going in life; and in the *Objective* chapter you'll learn how to properly set goals; the secret to the successful; how to swap a losing strategy for a winning one; how to put together a Millionaire Prisoner Prosperity Scrapbook; and 5 steps to becoming a grand master in life.

None of this will do you any good unless you are ready for your day. In the *Preparation* chapter you'll learn how to become ready to win; the right way to prepare; and how to get the edge.

Next, you'll learn how to set yourself apart by using the power of *Quality*. In that chapter you'll learn the law of compensation; that little things count just as much as big things; the Millionaire Prisoner motto; and how to deliver your best every time.

So many prisoners wish they were somewhere else, but in the *Recognition* chapter, you'll learn how to find your own acres of diamonds right where you stand; how your life can instantly change; and 24 facts of life that you should know and utilize.

In the *Self-Control* chapter you'll learn the highest hurdle you have to climb and how to get over it; the art of sacrifice; how to find self; and a great analogy about a race car.

The following chapter on *Tact*, will give you the most important ingredient of success; the art of listening; the easiest way to get people to like you; how to deal with annoying people; 10 tips to dealing with confrontation; and how to persuade others to get what you want.

Without putting action behind these principles you'll never achieve your goals. That's why you need to read the *Utilization* chapter, where you'll find the biggest complaint prisoners make and how you can get over it; your greatest tool; how to use your tools properly; and the power of your hidden room and how you can go there.

To put your ideas into practice you'll need courage, and you'll learn how to get some in the *Valiancy* chapter. You'll also learn how to conquer fear; dare to win the game of life; and have no fear.

You didn't get this book to learn abstract principles, did you? No, I'm sure you want to be able to do something right now from your cell to start generating income right? Well, you'll learn two easy ways to do just that in the *Ways & Means* chapter. These avenues will allow you to create multiple streams of income.

We all need role models and people to copy. That's why there is a *Xerox* chapter. Inside you'll find the secret to standing on the shoulders of giants; how to learn from the Prince; where you should build your second home; and where the school for fools is and how you can stay away from it.

There will come a time when you need to give back. You'll learn how in the *Yield* chapter. You'll be taught how to plant seeds and expect a harvest; the power of the Lance Armstrong Effect; and a powerful story of two seas.

Finally, in the *Zeal* chapter, you'll learn the easiest way to become a Millionaire Prisoner; how to stop surviving and start thriving; and how to make it necessary to succeed.

Be sure to get your copy of *The Millionaire Prisoner: Part 2* today. May you be blessed in all your future endeavors. May you succeed against all the odds. May you find true prosperity. Remember: All moves are possible on the human chessboard of life!

"Make opportunities present themselves and never give up. Even from prison a prisoner can accomplish much more than those in the outside world."

-Christopher Zoukis

THE CELL BLOCK

BOOK SUMMARIES

MIKE ENEMIGO is the new prison/street art sensation who has written and published several books. He is inspired by emotion; hope; pain; dreams and nightmares. He physically lives somewhere in a California prison cell where he works relentlessly creating his next piece. His mind and soul are elsewhere; seeing, studying, learning, and drawing inspiration to tear down suppressive walls and inspire the culture by pushing artistic boundaries.

THE CELL BLOCK is an independent multimedia company with the objective of accurately conveying the prison/street experience with the credibility and honesty that only one who has lived it can deliver, through literature and other arts, and to entertain and enlighten while doing so. Everything published by The Cell Block has been created by a prisoner, while in a prison cell.

THE BEST RESOURCE DIRECTORY FOR PRISONERS, $17.95 & $5.00 S/H: This book has over 1,450 resources for prisoners! Includes: Pen-Pal Companies! Non-Nude Photo Sellers! Free Books and Other Publications! Legal Assistance! Prisoner Advocates! Prisoner Assistants! Correspondence Education! Money-Making Opportunities! Resources for Prison Writers, Poets, Artists! And much, much more! Anything you can think of doing from your prison cell, this book contains the resources to do it!

A GUIDE TO RELAPSE PREVENTION FOR PRISONERS, $15.00 & $5.00 S/H: This book provides the information and guidance that can make a real difference in the preparation of a comprehensive relapse prevention plan. Discover how to meet the parole board's expectation using these proven and practical principles. Included is a blank template and sample relapse prevention plan to assist in your preparation.

CONSPIRACY THEORY, $12.00 & $4.00 S/H: Kokain is an upcoming rapper trying to make a name for himself in the Sacramento, CA underground scene, and Nicki is his girlfriend. One night, in October, Nicki's brother, along with her brother's best friend, go to rob a house of its $100,000 marijuana crop. It goes wrong; shots are fired and a man is killed. Later, as investigators begin closing in on Nicki's brother and his friend, they, along with the help of a few others, create a way to make Kokain take the fall .... The conspiracy begins.

THEE ENEMY OF THE STATE (SPECIAL EDITION), $9.99 & $4.00 S/H: Experience the inspirational journey of a kid who was introduced to the art of rapping in 1993, struggled between his dream of becoming a professional rapper and the reality of the streets, and was finally offered a recording deal in 1999, only to be arrested minutes later and eventually sentenced to life in prison for murder... However, despite his harsh reality, he dedicated himself to hip-hop once again, and with resilience and determination, he sets out to prove he may just be one of the dopest rhyme writers/spitters ever .... At this point, it becomes deeper than rap .... Welcome to a preview of the greatest story you never heard.

LOST ANGELS: $15.00 & $5.00: David Rodrigo was a child who belonged to no world; rejected for his mixed heritage by most of his family and raised by an outcast uncle in the mean streets of East L.A. Chance cast him into a far darker and more devious pit of intrigue that stretched from the barest gutters to the halls of power in the great city. Now, to survive the clash of lethal forces arrayed about him, and to protect those he loves, he has only two allies; his quick wits, and the flashing blade that earned young David the street name, Viper.

LOYALTY AND BETRAYAL DELUXE EDITION, $19.99 & $7.00 S/H: Chunky was an associate of and soldier for the notorious Mexican Mafia – La Eme. That is, of course, until he was betrayed by those, he was most loyal to. Then he vowed to become their worst enemy. And though they've attempted to kill him numerous times, he still to this day is running around making a mockery of their organization .... This is the story of how it all began.

MONEY IZ THE MOTIVE: SPECIAL 2-IN-1 EDITION, $19.99 & $7.00 S/H: Like most kids growing up in the hood, Kano has a dream of going from rags to riches. But when his plan to get fast money by robbing the local "mom and pop" shop goes wrong, he quickly finds himself sentenced to serious prison time. Follow   Kano as he is schooled to the ways of the game by some of the most respected OGs whoever did it; then is set free and given the resources to put his schooling into action and build the ultimate hood empire...

DEVILS & DEMONS: PART 1, $15.00 & $5.00 S/H: When Talton leaves the West Coast to set up shop in Florida he meets the female version of himself: A drug dealing murderess with psychological issues. A whirlwind of sex, money and murder inevitably ensues and Talton finds himself on the run from the law with nowhere to turn to. When his team from home finds out he's in trouble, they get on a plane heading south...

DEVILS & DEMONS: PART 2, $15.00 & $5.00 S/H: The Game is bitter-sweet for Talton, aka Gangsta. The same West Coast Clique who came to his aid ended up putting bullets into the chest of the woman he had fallen in love with. After leaving his ride or die in a puddle of her own blood, Talton finds himself on a flight back to Oak Park, the neighborhood where it all started...

DEVILS & DEMONS: PART 3, $15.00 & $5.00 S/H: Talton is on the road to retribution for the murder of the love of his life. Dante and his crew of killers are on a path of no return. This urban classic is based on real-life West Coast underworld politics. See what happens when a group of YG's find themselves in the midst of real underworld demons...

DEVILS & DEMONS: PART 4, $15.00 & $5.00 S/H: After waking up from a coma, Alize has locked herself away from the rest of the world. When her sister Brittany and their friend finally take her on a girl's night out, she meets Luck – a drug dealing womanizer.

FREAKY TALES, $15.00 & $5.00 S/H: Freaky Tales is the first book in a brand-new erotic series. King Guru, author of the Devils & Demons books, has put together a collection of sexy short stories and memoirs. In true TCB fashion, all of the erotic tales included in this book have been loosely based on true accounts told to, or experienced by the author.

THE ART & POWER OF LETTER WRITING FOR PRISONERS: DELUXE EDITION $19.99 & $7.00 S/H: When locked inside a prison cell, being able to write well is the most powerful skill you can have! Learn how to increase your power by writing high-quality personal and formal letters! Includes letter templates, pen-pal website strategies, punctuation guide and more!

THE PRISON MANUAL: $24.99 & $7.00 S/H: The Prison Manual is your all-in-one book on how to not only survive the rough terrain of the American prison system, but use it to your advantage so you can THRIVE from it! How to Use Your Prison Time to YOUR Advantage; How to Write Letters that Will Give You Maximum Effectiveness; Workout and Physical Health Secrets that Will Keep You as FIT as Possible; The Psychological impact of incarceration and How to Maintain Your MAXIMUM Level of Mental Health; Prison Art

Techniques; Fulfilling Food Recipes; Parole Preparation Strategies and much, MUCH more!

GET OUT, STAY OUT!, $16.95 & $5.00 S/H: This book should be in the hands of everyone in a prison cell. It reveals a challenging but clear course for overcoming the obstacles that stand between prisoners and their freedom. For those behind bars, one goal outshines all others: GETTING OUT! After being released, that goal then shifts to STAYING OUT! This book will help prisoners do both. It has been masterfully constructed into five parts that will help prisoners maximize focus while they strive to accomplish whichever goal is at hand.

MOB$TAR MONEY, $12.00 & $4.00 S/H: After Trey's mother is sent to prison for 75 years to life, he and his little brother are moved from their home in Sacramento, California, to his grandmother's house in Stockton, California where he is forced to find his way in life and become a man on his own in the city's grimy streets. One day, on his way home from the local corner store, Trey has a rough encounter with the neighborhood bully. Luckily, that's when Tyson, a member of the MOBTAR, a local "get money" gang comes to his aid. The two kids quickly become friends, and it doesn't take long before Trey is embraced into the notorious MOB$TAR money gang, which opens the door to an adventure full of sex, money, murder and mayhem that will change his life forever... You will never guess how this story ends!

BLOCK MONEY, $12.00 & $4.00 S/H: Beast, a young thug from the grimy streets of central Stockton, California lives The Block; breathes The Block; and has committed himself to bleed The Block for all it's worth until his very last breath. Then, one day, he meets Nadia; a stripper at the local club who piques his curiosity with her beauty, quick-witted intellect and rider qualities. The problem? She has a man – Esco – a local kingpin with money and power. It doesn't take long, however, before a devious plot is hatched to pull off a heist worth an indeterminable amount of money. Following the acts of treachery, deception and betrayal are twists and turns and a bloody war that will leave you speechless!

HOW TO HUSTLE AND WIN: SEX, MONEY, MURDER EDITION $15.00 & $5.00 S/H: How To Hu$tle and Win: Sex, Money, Murder edition is the grittiest, underground self-help manual for the 21st century street entrepreneur in print. Never has there been such a book written for today's gangsters, goons and go-getters. This self-help handbook is an absolute must-have for anyone who is actively connected to the streets.

RAW LAW: YOUR RIGHTS, & HOW TO SUE WHEN THEY ARE VIOLATED! $15.00 & $5.00 S/H: Raw Law For Prisoners is a clear and concise guide for prisoners and their advocates to understanding civil rights laws guaranteed to prisoners under the US Constitution, and how to successfully file a lawsuit when those rights have been violated! From initial complaint to trial, this book will take you through the entire process, step by step, in simple, easy-to-understand terms. Also included are several examples where prisoners have sued prison officials successfully, resulting in changes of unjust rules and regulations and recourse for rights violations, oftentimes resulting in rewards of thousands, even millions of dollars in damages! If you feel your rights have been violated, don't lash out at guards, which is usually ineffective and only makes matters worse. Instead, defend yourself successfully by using the legal system, and getting the power of the courts on your side!

HOW TO WRITE URBAN BOOKS FOR MONEY & FAME: $16.95 & $5.00 S/H: Inside this book you will learn the true story of how Mike Enemigo and King Guru have received money and fame from inside their prison cells by writing urban books; the secrets to writing hood classics so you, too, can be caked up and famous; proper punctuation using hood examples; and resources you can use to achieve your money motivated ambitions! If you're a prisoner who want to write urban novels for money and fame, this must-have manual will give you all the game!

PRETTY GIRLS LOVE BAD BOYS: AN INMATE'S GUIDE TO GETTING GIRLS: $15.00 & $5.00 S/H: Tired of the same, boring, cliché pen pal books that don't tell you what you really need to know? If so, this book is for you! Anything you need to know on the art of long and short distance seduction is included within these pages! Not only does it give you the science of attracting pen pals from websites, it also includes psychological profiles and instructions on how to seduce any woman you set your sights on! Includes interviews of women who have fallen in love with prisoners, bios for pen pal ads, pre-written love letters, romantic poems, love-song lyrics, jokes and much, much more! This book is the ultimate guide – a must-have for any prisoner who refuses to let prison walls affect their MAC'n.

THE LADIES WHO LOVE PRISONERS, $15.00 & $5.00 S/H: New Special Report reveals the secrets of real women who have fallen in love with prisoners, regardless of crime, sentence, or location. This info will give you a HUGE advantage in getting girls from prison.

THE MILLIONAIRE PRISONER: PART 1, $16.95 & $5.00 S/H

THE MILLIONAIRE PRISONER: PART 2, $16.95 & $5.00 S/H

THE MILLIONAIRE PRISONER: SPECIAL 2-IN-1 EDITION, $24.99 & $7.00 S/H: Why wait until you get out of prison to achieve your dreams? Here's a blueprint that you can use to become successful! *The Millionaire Prisoner* is your complete reference to overcoming any obstacle in prison. You won't be able to put it down! With this book you will discover the secrets to: Making money from your cell! Obtain FREE money for correspondence courses! Become an expert on any topic! Develop the habits of the rich! Network with celebrities! Set up your own website! Market your products, ideas and services! Successfully use prison pen pal websites! All of this and much, much more! This book has enabled thousands of prisoners to succeed and it will show you the way also!

THE MILLIONAIRE PRISONER 3: SUCCESS UNIVERSITY, $16.95 & $5 S/H: Why wait until you get out of prison to achieve your dreams? Here's a new-look blueprint that you can use to be successful! *The Millionaire Prisoner 3* contains advanced strategies to overcoming any obstacle in prison. You won't be able to put it down!

GET OUT, GET RICH: HOW TO GET PAID LEGALLY WHEN YOU GET OUT OF PRISON!, $16.95 & $5.00 S/H: Many of you are incarcerated for a money-motivated crime. But w/ today's tech & opportunities, not only is the crime-for-money risk/reward ratio not strategically wise, it's not even necessary. You can earn much more money by partaking in anyone of the easy, legal hustles explained in this book, regardless of your record. Help yourself earn an honest income so you can not only make a lot of money, but say good-bye to penitentiary chances and prison forever! (Note: Many things in this book can even he done from inside prison.) (ALSO PUBLISHED AS *HOOD MILLIONAIRE: HOW TO HUSTLE AND WIN LEGALLY!*)

THE CEO MANUAL: HOW TO START A BUSINESS WHEN YOU GET OUT OF PRISON, $16.95 & $5.00 S/H: $16.95 & $5 S/H: This new book will teach you the simplest way to start your own business when you get out of prison. Includes: Start-up Steps! The Secrets to Pulling Money from Investors! How to Manage People Effectively! How To Legally Protect Your Assets from "them"! Hundreds of resources to get you started, including a list of "loan friendly" banks! (ALSO PUBLISHED AS *CEO MANUAL: START A BUSINESS, BE A BOSS!*)

THE MONEY MANUAL: UNDERGROUND CASH SECRETS EXPOSED! 16.95 & $5.00 S/H: Becoming a millionaire is equal parts what you make, and what you don't spend – AKA save. All Millionaires and Billionaires have mastered the art of not only making money, but keeping the money they make (remember Donald Trump's tax maneuvers?), as well as establishing credit so that they are loaned money by banks and trusted with money from investors: AKA OPM – other people's money. And did you know there are millionaires and billionaires just waiting to GIVE money away? It's true! These are all very-little known secrets "they" don't want YOU to know about, but that I'm exposing in my new book!

HOOD MILLIONAIRE; HOW TO HUSTLE & WIN LEGALLY, $16.95 & $5.00 S/H: Hustlin' is a way of life in the hood. We all have money motivated ambitions, not only because we gotta eat, but because status is oftentimes determined by one's own salary. To achieve what we consider financial success, we often invest our efforts into illicit activities – we take penitentiary chances. This leads to a life in and out of prison, sometimes death – both of which are counterproductive to gettin' money. But there's a solution to this, and I have it...

CEO MANUAL: START A BUSINESS BE A BOSS, $16.95 & $5.00 S/H: After the success of the urban-entrepreneur classic *Hood Millionaire: How To Hustle & Win Legally!*, self-made millionaires Mike Enemigo and Sav Hustle team back up to bring you the latest edition of the Hood Millionaire series – CEO Manual: Start A Business, Be A Boss! In this latest collection of game laying down the art of "hoodpreneurship", you will learn such things as: 5 Core Steps to Starting Your Own Business! 5 Common Launch Errors You Must Avoid! How To Write a Business Plan! How To Legally Protect Your Assets From "Them"! How To Make Your Business Fundable, Where to Get Money for Your Start-up Business, and even How to Start a Business With No Money! You will learn How to Drive

Customers to Your Website, How to Maximize Marketing Dollars, Contract Secrets for the savvy boss, and much, much more! And as an added bonus, we have included over 200 Business Resources, from government agencies and small business development centers, to a secret list of small-business friendly banks that will help you get started!

PAID IN FULL: WELCOME TO DA GAME, $15.00 & $5.00 S/H. In 1983, the movie Scarface inspired many kids growing up in America's inner cities to turn their rags into riches by becoming cocaine kingpins. Harlem's Azie Faison was one of them. Faison would ultimately connect with Harlem's Rich Porter and Alpo Martinez, and the trio would go on to become certified street legends of the '80s and early '90s. Years later, Dame Dash and Roc-A-Fella Films would tell their story in the based-on-actual-events movie, Paid in Full. But now, we are telling the story our way – The Cell Block way – where you will get a perspective of the story that the movie did not show, ultimately learning an outcome that you did not expect. Book one of our series, *Paid in Full: Welcome to da Game*, will give you an inside look at a key player in this story, one that is not often talked about – Lulu, the Columbian cocaine kingpin with direct ties to Pablo Escobar, who plugged Azie in with an unlimited amount of top-tier cocaine at dirt-cheap prices that helped boost the trio to neighborhood superstars and certified kingpin status... until greed, betrayal, and murder destroyed everything....

OJ'S LIFE BEHIND BARS, $15.00 & $5 S/H: In 1994, Heisman Trophy winner and NFL superstar OJ Simpson was arrested for the brutal murder of his ex-wife Nicole Brown-Simpson and her friend Ron Goldman. In 1995, after the "trial of the century," he was acquitted of both murders, though most of the world believes he did it. In 2007 OJ was again arrested, but this time in Las Vegas, for armed robbery and kidnapping. On October 3, 2008 he was found guilty sentenced to 33 years and was sent to Lovelock Correctional Facility, in Lovelock, Nevada. There he met inmate-author Vernon Nelson. Vernon was granted a true, insider's perspective into the mind and life of one of the country's most notorious men; one that has never provided...until now.

BMF, $18.99 & $5 S/H: The Black Mafia Family was a drug organization headed by brothers Demetrius "Big Meech" Flenory and Terry "Southwest T" Flenory. Rising up from the shadows of Detroit's underbelly, they created a cross-country cocaine network, becoming two of the wealthiest, most dangerously sophisticated drug traffickers the United States has ever seen.

BLACK DYNASTY, $15.00 & $5 S/H: After their parents are murdered in cold blood, the Black siblings are left to fend for themselves in the unforgiving streets. But when the oldest brother, Lorenzo, is introduced to his deceased father's drug connection, he is given the opportunity of a lifetime to put his family back on top.

THE MOB, $16.99 & $5 S/H. PaperBoy is a Bay Area boss who has invested blood, sweat, and years into building The Mob – a network of Bay Area Street legends, block bleeders, and underground rappers who collaborate nationwide in the interest of pushing a multi-million-dollar criminal enterprise of sex, drugs, and murder.

AOB, $15.00 & $5 S/H. Growing up in the Bay Area, Manny Fresh the Best had a front-row seat to some of the coldest players to ever do it. And you already know, A.O.B. is the name of the Game! So, When Manny Fresh slides through Stockton one day and sees Rosa, a stupid-bad Mexican chick with a whole lotta 'talent' behind her walking down the street tryna get some money, he knew immediately what he had to do: Put it In My Pocket!

AOB 2, $15.00 & $5 S/H.

PIMPOLOGY: THE 7 ISMS OF THE GAME, $15.00 & $5 S/H: It's been said that if you knew better, you'd do better. So, in the spirit of dropping jewels upon the rare few who truly want to know how to win, this collection of exclusive Game has been compiled. And though a lot of so-called players claim to know how the Pimp Game is supposed to go, none have revealed the real. . . Until now!

JAILHOUSE PUBLISHING FOR MONEY, POWER & FAME: $24.99 & $7 S/H: In 2010, after flirting with the idea for two years, Mike Enemigo started writing his first book. In 2014, he officially launched his publishing company, The Cell Block, with the release of five books. Of course, with no mentor(s), how-to guides, or any real resources, he was met with failure after failure as he tried to navigate the treacherous goal of publishing books from his prison cell. However, he was determined to make it. He was determined to figure it out and he refused to quit. In Mike's new book, Jailhouse Publishing for Money, Power, and Fame, he breaks down all his jailhouse publishing secrets and strategies, so you can do all he's done, but without the trials and tribulations he's had to go through...

KITTY KAT, ADULT ENTERTAINMENT RESOURCE BOOK, $24.99 & $7.00 S/H: This book is jam packed with hundreds of sexy non nude photos including photo spreads. The book contains the complete info on sexy photo sellers, hot magazines, page turning bookstore, sections on strip clubs, porn stars, alluring models, thought provoking stories and must-see movies.

PRISON LEGAL GUIDE, $24.99 & $7.00 S/H: The laws of the U.S. Judicial system are complex, complicated, and always growing and changing. Many prisoners spend days on end digging through its intricacies. Pile on top of the legal code the rules and regulations of a correctional facility, and you can see how high the deck is being stacked against you. Correct legal information is the key to your survival when you have run afoul of the system (or it is running afoul of you). Whether you are an accomplished jailhouse lawyer helping newbies learn the ropes, an old head fighting bare-knuckle for your rights in the courts, or a hustler just looking to beat the latest write-up – this book has something for you!

PRISON HEALTH HANDBOOK, $19.99 & $7.00 S/H: The Prison Health Handbook is your one-stop go-to source for information on how to maintain your best health while inside the American prison system. Filled with information, tips, and secrets from doctors, gurus, and other experts, this book will educate you on such things as proper workout and exercise regimens; yoga benefits for prisoners; how to meditate effectively; pain management tips; sensible dieting solutions; nutritional knowledge; an understanding of various cancers, diabetes, hepatitis, and other diseases all too common in prison; how to effectively deal with mental health issues such as stress, PTSD, anxiety, and depression; a list of things your doctors DON'T want YOU to know; and much, much more!

All books are available on thecellblock.net website. You can also order by sending a money order or institutional check to: The Cell Block; PO Box 1025; Rancho Cordova, CA 95741

PRISON PROFILE ALERT!

We have a new profile feature on our website, thecellblock.net. The profiles are $30.00 a year for unlimited text and photos, but you must have your friends or family upload them for you. We do not provide the uploading service. We only provide the platform.

What makes our profile platform unique is that it is on our main website, not a separate one. We spend thousands of dollars a year advertising our website, and it's linked to by all our friends who also have websites. Because of this, we have people coming to our website to buy books, read our free magazine, and more. So now you can capitalize on this, by uploading a profile of your own, be it to seek pen-pals, promote your book, post your art, etc., you feel me? We gonna do it big. We one big movement! Have your people go to thecellblock.net today and download you the application so you know what info to provide them, such as where you're from, how much time you got, what you're interested in, etc. Tap in ASAP 'cause this price will be goin' up!

PS: Have your people order you $100.00 or more of books on our website, get the Prisoner Profile FREE!

PRISON RIOT RADIO

Industry reps want to hear you!

Are you a rapper? We will upload your freestyles to our website, prisonriotradio.com, FREE for top industry execs to hear!

Pick up the phone and become a star!

We will record you on the phone! All raw freestyles will be recorded FREE. If you need a recording and a beat, the prices are below...

$25 Per Recording

$150 For 8 Recordings

$30 Per Beat

$10 For Cover Art

We accept songs, spoken word, podcasts and interviews! Learn the game and how to get your money!

For more information, to send material, or to set up a phone recording session, email prisonriotradio@gmail.com or jayrene@prisonriotradio@gmail.com.

Made in the USA
Middletown, DE
10 September 2024

60600446R00159